D0947422

THE THREAD

GOD'S APPOINTMENTS WITH HISTORY

RONALD L. DART

Wasteland Press
Shelbyville, KY USA
www.wastelandpress.net

The Thread: God's Appointments With History
By Ronald L. Dart

Copyright © 2006 Ronald L. Dart
ALL RIGHTS RESERVED

Second Printing – January 2007
ISBN13: 978-1-60047-029-5
ISBN10: 1-60047-029-7

NO PART OF THIS BOOK MAY BE REPRODUCED IN ANY FORM, BY
PHOTOCOPYING OR BY ANY ELECTRONIC OR MECHANICAL MEANS,
INCLUDING INFORMATION STORAGE OR RETRIEVAL SYSTEMS,
WITHOUT PERMISSION IN WRITING FROM THE COPYRIGHT
OWNER/AUTHOR.

All scripture quotations, unless otherwise indicated, are taken from the New King
James Version®. Copyright © 1982 by Thomas Nelson, Inc. Used by permission.
All rights reserved.

Printed in the U.S.A.

*To Allie, the love of my life,
my unfailing support, without whom
this book might never have been written.*

Table Of Contents

Acknowledgements

My profound thanks to Mickie Ranaldo for bearing up under so many readings, and to Faye Brown, Linda Benton, Teeka Glasgow and my wife, Allie, for helping me present a clean manuscript.

Prologue

*Let not the wise man boast of his wisdom
or the strong man boast of his strength
or the rich man boast of his riches,
but let him who boasts boast about this:
that he understands and knows me, that I am the LORD,
who exercises kindness, justice and righteousness on earth,
for in these I delight, declares the LORD (Jeremiah 9:23-24 NIV).*

The Bible is a marvelously compact work, considering its scope. The essential things are plainly stated. There is nothing obscure about the Ten Commandments, for example, and the Gospel of the New Testament is easily understood. There is, however, much more to be known about God and what he is doing than can be made plain in the 66 short books that make up the Bible. The Apostle John, when finishing up the 21 chapters of his Gospel, underlined the problem: "Jesus did many other things as well. If every one of them were written down, I suppose that even the whole world would not have room for the books that would be written." [i]

And that provides a neat summary of why we have to work so hard if we want to push beyond the margins of what is plainly stated. The Bible is a rewarding book for the serious student. There is so much more to be found if we care to look for it and if we are willing to follow ideas wherever they lead.

There are any number of reasons why we might not understand what is before us. One is the cost of obedience. Jesus warned his disciples to count the cost before embarking on this spiritual journey. [ii] More than one person has faced the cost of discipleship and flinched. There are things in the Bible that a person, consciously or unconsciously, may choose not to understand because it will cost him more than he is willing to pay.

Sometimes, God seems to be deliberately obscure, which is, of course, his privilege: "It is the glory of God to conceal a thing: but the honour of kings is to search out a matter." [iii] I sometimes wonder if God just doesn't want it to be too easy. After all, it is only human to appreciate more the things we have to work for.

A few years ago, I produced a series of radio programs which systematically explored what the Bible calls, "the feasts of the Lord." I did the series more out of a sense of duty than for audience response. To my surprise, the response to the programs surpassed that of any series I had done on the air. I had been aware that increasing numbers of biblical teachers and evangelists had been talking about the holydays, but the depth of interest from the public was unexpected.

I hadn't thought about writing books back then, but with the advent of print on demand publishing, I was left without an excuse. This book, then, grows out of a series of radio programs titled, "Christian Holidays." Because each program had to stand alone, there is inevitably some repetition. And the style is more oral than written.

The biblical festivals all lie along the same thread, a thread we will follow back in time and far into the future to see if we can apprehend in greater depth what God is doing. In the process, we will look at the practice of the first Christian churches which later generations lost.

The book is not intended as a polemic, but as a pursuit of a mystery. There are a number of technical issues that will not interest some readers, and will be covered in endnotes or appendices, so the reader can stay in the flow of the book. All quotations are from the King James Version or the New King James Version, unless otherwise indicated.

Abbreviations:
KJV Authorized King James Version.
RSV Revised Standard Version.
NASB New American Standard Version.
ISBE International Standard Bible Encyclopedia.

NIV New International Version.
NRSV New Revised Standard Version.
NKJV New King James Version.

---

i. John 21:25 NIV.
ii. Luke 14:26 ff.
iii. Proverbs 25:2.

1

Picking Up the Thread

Take now thy son, thine only son Isaac,
whom thou lovest, and get thee into the land of Moriah;
and offer him there for a burnt offering
upon one of the mountains which I will tell thee of. [i]

Everyone knows that the two most important holidays throughout the Christian world are Easter and Christmas. They have been called "the bookends of Christianity."[ii] But there is something odd about that. Neither of these days is found *observed* anywhere in the Bible. And if they were as important to the early church as they are today, you would think someone would have said something. Luke might have recorded somewhere in the book of Acts, "We stayed over at Troas through Christmas and then sailed across to Philippi." Or maybe: "We hastened in order to be in Jerusalem for Easter." But no, nothing like that is found in the Bible.

What we do find may be mildly surprising. We find holidays in the Bible, quite prominently, and in both Testaments. Not only that, but they are found observed by the church in the New Testament. Luke wrote, for example, "And we sailed away from Philippi after the days of unleavened bread, and came unto them to Troas in five days; where we abode seven days" (Acts 20:6 KJV). Later, "For Paul had determined to sail by Ephesus, because he would not spend the time in Asia: for he hasted, if it were possible for him, to be *at Jerusalem the day of Pentecost*" (Acts 20:16). Before that he had told the Ephesians, "Farewell, I must by all means keep this feast that cometh in Jerusalem: but I will return again unto you, if God will" (Acts 18:21).[iii]

Nowadays, these holidays are usually dismissed as being merely Jewish; but then we are left to wonder why the earliest Christians followed on in their observance. The days clearly have Jewish/historical roots and yet they were still observed faithfully in *Christian* churches known to be primarily Gentile. There has to be a reason for that.

But first, let me point out some minor issues that are commonly overlooked relative to the holidays of the Bible. For example, the days are not merely "Jewish holidays." Consider this short passage from the law:

> Speak to the people of Israel and say to them: These are the appointed festivals of the LORD that you shall proclaim as holy convocations, my appointed festivals (Leviticus 23:2 NRSV).

Note well, these are the *Lord's* festivals, not "Jewish holidays." Not only are these the Lord's feasts, they are so designated by his *name*. They are "The appointed festivals of *Jehovah.*"[iv]

Then there is the Hebrew word that is here rendered "appointed festivals." The word in Hebrew is *moed,* and it means literally "appointed times." The NRSV is correct in rendering it "appointed festivals," because *moed* is repeatedly used for festive occasions.

Apparently, these "appointments" were there right from the beginning. In the creation account God said: "Let there be lights in the dome of the sky to separate the day from the night; and let them be for signs and for seasons [*moed*] and for days and years" (Genesis 1:14 NRSV). This could just as easily (and more consistently) have been rendered, "Let them be for signs, and for *appointed times.*"

What this suggests to me is that there were divine appointments, holy days, if you will, right from the beginning. And really, there is no reason to think there were not. If God had a plan, then it should not be surprising that he would have special times marked for special events right from the start.

Here is another example which has been somewhat obscured by the translations. Later in Genesis, God visits Abraham on what appears to be one of these appointed times. These encounters with God were rare and they may have occurred at a festival season. On this occasion, God startled Abraham and Sarah by promising them a son in their old age. Mind you, Abraham is 99 and Sarah nearly as old. Sarah couldn't help herself, she laughed. When Sarah laughed, God replied:

> Is anything too hard for the LORD? At the appointed time [the *moed*] I will return to you, according to the time of life, and Sarah shall have a son (Genesis 18:13-14).

God had already promised this along with the covenant promise: "My covenant will I establish with Isaac," God said, "which Sarah shall bear unto thee *at this set time* [*moed*] in the next year" (Genesis 17:21).

So Isaac (his name means "laughter") was to be born at the *moed*, and in the spring, thus at what would later be the Passover season. The expression, "time of life," is suggestive of the season when things come alive, hence a spring festival. [v] The serving of unleavened bread here and then a day or so later by Lot in Sodom [vi] might even suggest that the Feast of Unleavened Bread is older than Moses, though I can't imagine what significance it would have had. [vii] What it does suggest is that the thread we are following was already visible at this early date.

So God appears to Abraham at the time of the spring festival, and when he returns at the next spring festival, Abraham will have a son. Now we can follow the thread forward to the time of Moses.

Thanks to Charlton Heston as Moses, nearly everyone knows the story of the Exodus. But there are little things about that story that you may not have noticed. You know that God sent Moses to Pharaoh to say "Let my People go," but hardly anyone takes notice of the *reason* Moses offered to Pharaoh.

"Let my people go," demanded God, "that they may *hold a*

feast unto me in the wilderness" (Exodus 5:1). Now this may be nothing but a ruse, an excuse, but it may also be that one of God's very old festivals was approaching – one of his appointments with history.

Keep in mind that God is constant. He isn't one way today and another way tomorrow. He spoke to Malachi and said, "For I am the LORD, I change not; therefore ye sons of Jacob are not consumed" (Malachi 3:6). Later, James would describe God as "the Father of lights, with whom is no variableness, neither shadow of turning" (James 1:17).

It should come as no surprise, then, that God would have had his "appointed times," if at all, right from the beginning. We know that there was a well developed system of law in effect prior to Moses.[viii] No one should be surprised, then, when Moses demands of Pharaoh: "Let my people go, that they may hold a feast unto me in the wilderness."

On this occasion, Moses does not call this an "appointed time," but a *chagag*, a sacred celebration, but such celebrations are later seen to be annual and to fit a calendar. This one is pointed squarely at the 14th day of the first month of spring, even though it could not yet have been known as the Passover. Since Pharaoh would not let them go, this spring "festival with no name" was observed in the middle of Egypt, to the eternal dismay of the Egyptians, and became known as the Passover.

What I am suggesting is that the occasions when God acted in history commonly took place at a *moed*, an appointed time. As a result of God's action, the day itself took on the meaning and even the name of the events. Thus, the festival Moses said they wanted to observe in the wilderness could have been on the 14th day of the first month. But that day was not the Passover before this time. It *became* the Passover because on that night God *passed over* the houses of the Israelites and took all the firstborn of the land of Egypt.

All these appointed times of God took on names and customs which were related to the important events in Israel's history. They seem never to have imagined that there was any other meaning to these days. Jeremiah said that this would happen again. There will be another Exodus, so great that no one will remember the Exodus led by Moses:

"Therefore behold, the days are coming," says the LORD, "that it shall no more be said, 'The LORD lives who brought up the children of Israel from the land of Egypt,' but, 'The LORD lives who brought up the children of Israel from the land of the north and from all the lands where He had driven them.' For I will bring them back into their land which I gave to their fathers" (Jeremiah 16:14-15).

Traditional explanations say that the festivals came in with the old covenant and went out with the old covenant, that they were purely Jewish and only had application to the Jewish people. But there is good reason to question that. The feasts of the Lord are transcendent, and from the very beginning were pointed, not so much at Israel's history, but at the very work and ministry of Jesus Christ in history. For after all, it was Christ who was with Israel from the very first day.[ix] For a time, the festivals took on an Israelite historical meaning, but it seems apparent that they were pointing toward something transcendent all along.

A Christian Passover?

The best place to pick up the thread is with the first of the holydays in the year, the Passover. There is a passage in one of Paul's letters that long ago should have caused us to rethink this question. It was written to a Gentile church, and commentators tell us it was written during the Passover season. Paul is dealing with a serious problem in the church and in the process, he makes a connection to the Passover.

Therefore purge out the old leaven, that you may be a new lump, since you truly are unleavened. For indeed *Christ, our Passover, was sacrificed for us.* Therefore let us keep the feast, not with old leaven, nor with the leaven of malice and wickedness, but with the unleavened bread of sincerity and truth (1 Corinthians 5:7-8).

Conybeare and Howsen (1962), recognized authorities on Paul and his letters, acknowledge that this Christian church was observing Passover and the Days of Unleavened Bread. They had this to say about Paul's letter:

> In spite of the opinion of some eminent modern commentators, which is countenanced by Chrysostom [*A.D. 407*], we must adhere to the interpretation which considers these words as written at the Paschal season, and suggested by it. The words leaven, lump, Paschal Lamb, and feast all agree most naturally with this view. It has been objected, that St. Paul would not address the Corinthians as engaged in a feast which he, at Ephesus, was celebrating; because it would be over before his letter could reach them. Any one who has ever written a birthday letter to a friend in India, will see the weakness of this objection. It has also been urged that he could not address a mixed church of Jews and Gentiles as engaged in the celebration at a Jewish feast. Those who urge this objection must have forgotten that St. Paul addresses the Galatians (undoubtedly a mixed church) as if they had all been formerly idolaters (Gal. iv.8), and addresses the Romans sometimes as if they were all Jews (Rom. vii.1), sometimes as if they were Gentiles (Rom. xi.18). If we take 'as ye are leavened' in a metaphorical sense, it is scarcely consistent with the previous 'cast out the old leaven;' for the passage would then amount to saying, 'Be free from leaven (metaphorically) as you are free from leaven (metaphorically);' whereas on the other view, St. Paul says, 'Be free from leaven (metaphorically) as you are free from leaven (literally).' There seems to be no difficulty in supposing that the Gentile Christians joined with the Jewish Christians in celebrating the Paschal feast after the Jewish manner, at least to the extent of abstaining from leaven in the love-feasts. And we see that St. Paul still observed the 'days of

unleavened bread' at this period of his life, from Acts
xx:6. Also, from what follows, we perceive how
naturally this greatest of Jewish feasts changed into
the greatest of Christians festivals. [x]

Throughout most of history, the Passover has been a Jewish
festival dealing with a great event in Israel's history that took place
on this day. But here is a letter to a Gentile church, identifying the
Passover with the sacrifice of Christ and urging them to keep the
feast properly. I will have more to say about the Corinthian crisis
later, but Paul presents us with a classic example of the transcendent
nature of God's appointments with history.

I think readers generally assume that the 14th day of the first
month in the Jewish Calendar became important because that's when
Israel was delivered from Egypt. But what if Israel was delivered on
this day because it was *already* one of the "appointed times" of God,
one of the benchmarks of history, when he will act? When it comes to
the sacrifice of Christ, that day did not become a Christian festival
because Christ was crucified on that day. Christ died on that day
because he was the Passover Lamb, and the Passover, one of God's
appointments with history, had come.

There is a thread that runs all the way through the Bible, and
the thread is unbroken, not cut into bits and pieces. God has had a
plan and has been working the plan *from the start.* His appointments
with history mark places where we can pick up the thread, and those
appointments are marked by festivals.

I know that some of these things may seem complicated and
difficult. But maybe if we pick up the thread and follow it along,
things will become clearer. The "Festivals of Jehovah" mark places
where we can most easily find the thread.

Paul, in his letter to the Corinthians cited above, identified
Jesus with the Passover lamb. But when we follow the thread back,
we find it doesn't end where we thought it might, with what we
thought was the original Passover. It continues back further into the
past. One pointer is a scripture familiar to every student of the New
Testament – I think it may have been the first verse I ever
memorized:

7

> For God so loved the world, that he gave his only
> begotten Son, that whosoever believeth in him should
> not perish, but have everlasting life (John 3:16 KJV).

The thread from Paul's "Christ our Passover" runs right through this passage and continues back, not merely to the Passover of the Exodus, but to an event long before Moses. It continues to Father Abraham and to the day when God decided to put him to the ultimate test. He called Abraham and gave him this command:

> Take now your son, your only son Isaac, whom you
> love, and go to the land of Moriah, and offer him
> there as a burnt offering on one of the mountains of
> which I shall tell you (Genesis 22:2).

God only knows, and I choose my words carefully, what a crushing blow this was to Abraham. Abraham was a very old man who had no children. In the process of time, Sarah came to Abraham and offered her handmaid as a surrogate mother so they could have a child. They got the child, but that was their solution, not God's. That child and his mother became nothing but trouble – then and now.

Then God promised him a son through Sarah, his wife, and a year after that promise, Isaac was born. It is hard to imagine what it would be like to go so long without children, and then to finally have a son. Abraham would have loved this boy like his own life. This command from God to sacrifice him had to be the most terrible moment of his life. [xi]

Abraham rose up early in the morning on the fateful day and made his preparation. He saddled his animal, split the wood, took two of his servants and Isaac his son, and started toward the place. A careless reader might assume that Abraham had so much faith that he just did what God said without a second thought. He would be wrong. Abraham had plenty of second thoughts, and every one of them was fraught with pain. It took a movie, *The Bible*, and George C. Scott's portrayal of Abraham, to make this more real to me. This was hard for Abraham. It was sheer agony, but Abraham followed through.

It was a three day journey to the mountain, and they were surely the hardest three days of Abraham's life. He instructed his servants to wait while he and Isaac went forward to worship. He had Isaac carry the wood for the fire, and brought along a fire starter and knife. As they walked, Isaac asked, "My father, we have the fire and the knife and the wood, but where is the lamb for a burnt offering?"

This must have cut Abraham to the heart, but he replied, "My son, God will provide himself a lamb for a burnt offering." And they walked on. That short phrase, "God will provide himself a lamb," echoes down through history to this day. Christians write songs that apply that very phrase to Jesus Christ, whom Paul identifies as "our Passover."

So, they came to the place and Abraham built an altar there and laid the wood in order. Then came the moment of truth. He bound Isaac his son and laid him on the altar on the wood. He took the knife in hand to slay his son. This had to be one of the greatest movie scenes of all time, especially if you knew what it meant. Abraham reaches out to take the knife in his hand, with that beautiful boy bound and laid out on the wood, and prepares to actually do the deed. It was only at this last moment that an angel spoke to him and stopped him.

> And He said, "Do not lay your hand on the lad, or do anything to him; for now I know that you fear God, since you have not withheld your son, your only son, from Me." Then Abraham lifted his eyes and looked, and there behind him was a ram caught in a thicket by its horns. So Abraham went and took the ram, and offered it up for a burnt offering instead of his son (Genesis 22:12-13).

Why would God do a thing like this? Why would he put Abraham through it? I think I finally begin to understand. We can identify with Abraham easier than we can with God. Abraham was a man. Theologians haven't helped, presenting us with an impassible God who cannot be touched.[xii] What we learn in Abraham is what Jesus really meant when he said to Nicodemus, "For God so loved the world, that he gave his only begotten Son." This is not a gift lightly given, nor is it a gift without cost.

God allowed Abraham to play the role of the Father who

makes the greatest sacrifice, his son, his only son. It was a great honor to Abraham, though he may not have seen it that way. His agony was that of a man whose faith was so strong that he would do it, but whose pain was so great that he would have taken his own life rather than that of his son.

This was much more than a test of Abraham's faith. This is one segment of the thread that runs all through history, one significant moment of the plan of God laid out before the foundation of the world. And down through history, the Israelites offered animals again and again as substitutes for their own lives.

> Then the Angel of the LORD called to Abraham a second time out of heaven, and said "By Myself I have sworn, says the LORD, because you have done this thing, and have not withheld your son, your only son; blessing I will bless you, and multiplying I will multiply your descendants as the stars of the heaven and as the sand which is on the seashore; and your descendants shall possess the gate of their enemies. In your seed all the nations of the earth shall be blessed, because you have obeyed My voice" (Genesis 22:15-18).

In the words, "Your son, your only son," we hear the echo of John 3:16, "For God so loved the world, that he gave his *only* begotten Son, that whosoever believeth in him should not perish, but have everlasting life." And that "only begotten Son" was our Passover.

I can only believe that this day, the date of Abraham's near sacrifice of his son, was one of God's appointments with history. Surely, it is a day to remember in the history of every man of faith. This may have been the day, generations later, when the Israelites killed a lamb, struck its blood on the doorposts of their houses, and ate the Passover lamb, while the firstborn in all of Egypt were dying. It may have been the very day when Israel was delivered from the bondage of Egypt, just as Christians are delivered from the bondage of sin by the blood of *our* Passover Lamb.

And this may have been the very day, generations later, when

Jesus Christ, the Son of God, was pierced in the side and bled and died, while in the Temple, the Passover lambs were being slain. The thread we are following is very long and sometimes faint, but it is there.

In the next chapter, the thread will lead us to Egypt and the fateful days before the first Passover.

---

i. Genesis 22:2.

ii. "The two biggest holidays in the church year are Easter and Christmas – the bookends of Christianity. Both are preceded by a special time that prepares us to worship Christ in a deeper way. Lent moves us toward identifying with Jesus' sacrifice. Advent gets us ready for a birthday celebration." (*Group* magazine, November-December 2005, page 50.)

iii. This verse is missing in some ancient manuscripts, but at the very least, it represents an ancient tradition of the first Christians. It may have been a marginal note that found its way into the text, but if so, it was very early and is highly suggestive that this was indeed Paul's reason for haste.

iv. Jehovah: Most versions of the Bible use the small caps LORD to represent the Hebrew name of God, *YHWH*. There are numerous variations of pronunciation due to the fact that there are no vowels in Hebrew, and the Jewish people strenuously avoid speaking the divine name. One variant is "Jehovah," which uses the vowel points of *Adonai*, Lord, and was probably intended to be pronounced, *Yehovah*. The Y becomes J in Germanic languages, as in German and English. Most scholarly sources use *Yahweh*, but I prefer the more familiar, "Jehovah." There are some passages in the Bible that become startlingly clearer when the reader recognizes the name that is behind the word, "LORD."

v. "The LORD said, 'I will surely return to you *in the spring*, and Sarah your wife shall have a son.' And Sarah was listening at the tent door behind him" (Genesis 18:10 RSV).

vi. Genesis 19:3.

vii. On the other hand, no sacrifice to God was to be offered with leaven, which was considered a kind of corruption, as sourdough bread (Exodus 34:25). It may be that one does not serve sourdough bread to divine beings. Leaven would come to be seen as a symbol of sin – at least during the Days of Unleavened Bread.

viii. "Because that Abraham obeyed my voice, and kept my charge, my commandments, my statutes, and my laws" (Genesis 26:5). This does not merely suggest that Abraham was a moral man, but that he lived according to a known system of law.

ix. "Moreover, brethren, I would not that ye should be ignorant, how that all our fathers were under the cloud, and all passed through the sea; And were all baptized unto Moses in the cloud and in the sea; And did all eat the same spiritual meat; And did all drink the same spiritual drink: for they drank of that spiritual Rock that followed them: *and that Rock was Christ*" (1 Corinthians 10:1-4).

x. "The Life and Epistles of Paul" by Conybeare and Howsen, 1962, Page 389.

xi. I once heard Angel Martinez, an influential Baptist evangelist preach that this event took place on the 10th day of the first month, when the Passover lamb was later chosen (Exodus 12:3). I think his vision of this was based on the three day journey to the place of sacrifice. He also made a connection to the day of the triumphal entry of Jesus into Jerusalem, and the decision of the leadership to kill him. I mention this only to point out that some *Christian* preachers see the thread of Jesus' sacrifice leading back to the Passover and beyond.

xii. Impassible: "incapable of suffering or of experiencing pain." I can understand why theologians described God as "impassible," but I think they are missing something very important. Jesus said it to Nicodemus, cited above: "God so loved the world." This does not describe an emotionless God, one who cannot be touched with a feeling of our infirmities. He who has seen Jesus has seen the Father, and Jesus was not "impassible." He was moved with compassion, and he suffered pain for us. In Abraham, we are asked to see the meaning of "God so loved the world."

2

Judging Egypt

But Pharaoh shall not hearken unto you,
That I may lay my hand upon Egypt,
and bring forth mine armies,
and my people the children of Israel,
out of the land of Egypt by great judgments (Exodus 7:4).

Not long ago, a woman asked me a hard question about the Exodus. "Why did God have to kill all the firstborn children in Egypt?" she asked. "After all, he is God. He is sovereign. He can do anything he wants. Wasn't there a better way of getting Israel out of Egypt than killing innocent children?" [i]

It's a fair question. God is all powerful, merciful, kind and gracious. He is forgiving and gentle. So why the death of innocents?

God is all of those things, but none of that would matter if God were not *just*. Justice is a quality of the divine nature that we are tempted to avoid, never considering that mercy is meaningless without justice. If justice does not demand punishment, then there is no need for God's mercy. Oddly, it was from a sense of justice that the woman asked this question. Was it *just* for God to kill all the firstborn of Egypt? That is the question we have before us, and it lies right along the thread we are following.

The story is told in the book of Exodus. All of the children of Jacob, whose name would be changed to Israel, had migrated to the land of Egypt in a time of famine, but then they made a fatal mistake. When the famine was over, they stayed in Egypt instead of returning home. In the early years, the government of Egypt was dominated by one of their own, a man named Joseph. But after his death, and the death of the Pharaoh who admired Joseph, things began to change for the worse.

For a few generations, the Israelites prospered and multiplied. They were a strong and influential people, and "the land was filled with them" (Exodus 1:7). They were bearing children at a much higher rate than the Egyptians. At length, this became a concern to the Egyptians. And they began to take measures to protect themselves and to advance their own interests at the same time. The latest King of Egypt said to his people:

> Look, the people of the children of Israel are more
> and mightier than we; come, let us deal shrewdly with
> them, lest they multiply, and it happen, in the event of
> war, that they also join our enemies and fight against
> us, and so go up out of the land (Exodus 1:9-10).

Not only were the Israelites outnumbering the Egyptians, they were physically stronger. After all, they were doing all the work. The Egyptians had two concerns. One was a rebellion and the other was the loss of a very effective work force. So they set out to make slaves of the Israelites as they built some of the great treasure cities of Egypt on the backs of Israelite slaves. In the years to come, Egypt owed their entire economy to the success of a slave labor program. This would come back to haunt them later.

The Egyptians did everything in their power to suppress the Israelites, "But the more they afflicted them, the more they multiplied and grew. And they were in dread because of the children of Israel" (Exodus 1:12). The dominant feeling was fear, and one wonders if fear still lies at the roots of anti-Semitism.

> So the Egyptians made the children of Israel serve
> with rigor. And they made their lives bitter with hard
> bondage; in mortar, in brick, and in all manner of
> service in the field. All their service in which they

made them serve was with rigor (vv. 13,14).

Since that wasn't working, Pharaoh resorted to more drastic measures. He called in the Hebrew midwives and gave them specific instructions: "When ye do the office of a midwife to the Hebrew women, and see them upon the stools; *if it be a son, then ye shall kill him*: but if it be a daughter, then she shall live" (v. 16).

Inconvenient children have always been victims in human society. The state has an obligation to protect the weakest and most helpless of its citizens. Here, the state was the instrument of their destruction. It was the closest thing to selective abortion that the technology of the age allowed. The midwives were to crush the skull of any male child as he was being born.

It didn't work. The midwives refused to do it and lied to the king about it. "The Hebrew women," they said," are not like Egyptian women, and they give birth before we get there." But that only worked briefly.

So Pharaoh commanded *all his people*, saying, "Every son who is born you shall cast into the river, and every daughter you shall save alive" (Exodus 1:22).

Sometimes the Bible does not belabor the obvious, so I will. Note carefully, that it was not just the government that was involved in infanticide. It was *all the people* who were charged with taking little Hebrew boys by the ankles and throwing them into the river to drown and it was all the people who were involved in this infanticide.

It is amazing how readily people will come to accept and then participate in such vile acts. We had a horrible example of it in our own time with the participation of the German people in the persecution of the Jews. And the German people, like the Egyptians, ultimately suffered terribly for it. Divine justice finally descended on them in the form of the armies of America, Britain and Russia.

God only knows how many Israelite babies were thrown to the crocodiles of the Nile by that generation of Egyptians. Now here is the question which you must answer if you are going to understand what is yet to come. What is a just God to do about this record of callous infanticide? Can he ignore it? Let it slide? And if he is to punish the nation for it, what punishment is just? Remember, this was not merely the sin of a few. The whole nation was involved in it.

There is an incredible irony in the next phase of this story. There was a young couple, both of the tribe of Levi, who had a son in this terrible time. Not willing to see her son thrown into the river, she hid him as long as she could. But when it became clear that would not work indefinitely, she made a little boat, placed the child in it, and laid it among the tall plants along the river. In a sense, she followed Pharaoh's command. She put him in the river.

The daughter of this good woman, sister of the child, hid herself and watched from a distance to see what would happen to her little brother.

> Then the daughter of Pharaoh came down to bathe at the river. And her maidens walked along the riverside; and when she saw the ark among the reeds, she sent her maid to get it. And when she had opened it, she saw the child, and behold, the baby wept. So she had compassion on him, and said, "This is one of the Hebrews' children" (Exodus 2:5-6).

This woman knew what she was doing. And in making the decision to save this child's life, she saved the man who would be the undoing of her own people. She named the little boy "Moses" and brought him up in Pharaoh's household as a prince in Egypt.

God's justice is sometimes a long time coming, and in this case it had to wait for Moses to grow up. The story of Moses from this day until his exile from Egypt to his return to Egypt is a great story in itself, but we will pass over it for the moment to stay close to our thread.

When Moses returned to Egypt with his staff in his hand and God's instructions ringing in his ears, he marched into Pharaoh's presence with a message. "Thus saith the Jehovah, God of Israel, Let my people go, that they may hold a feast unto me in the wilderness" (Exodus 5:1). Implicit in this is the idea that there was a known festival approaching, which the Israelites were expected to observe.

Pharaoh replied, "Who is Jehovah, that I should obey his voice to let Israel go? I know not Jehovah, neither will I let Israel go"

(Exodus 5:2). There is no surprise here.

But Moses and Aaron persisted, and in the process tell us something very important about this festival: "The God of the Hebrews has revealed himself to us; let us go a three days' journey into the wilderness to sacrifice to the LORD our God, *or he will fall upon us with pestilence or sword"* (v.3 RSV).

Note well, this is not a voluntary holiday. It has divine sanctions connected with nonobservance. Yes, it was a deliberate provocation on God's part, but there is no reason to assume this festival was new. There is reason to believe that this is a festival that *became* the Passover after the terrible events to follow.

Pharaoh, of course, refused and made the burden on the Israelites that much worse. At length, God speaks to Moses and brings this issue into sharp focus.

> So the LORD said to Moses: "See, I have made you as God to Pharaoh, and Aaron your brother shall be your prophet. You shall speak all that I command you. And Aaron your brother shall speak to Pharaoh to send the children of Israel out of his land. And I will harden Pharaoh's heart, and multiply My signs and My wonders in the land of Egypt. But Pharaoh will not heed you, so that I may lay My hand on Egypt and bring My armies and My people, the children of Israel, out of the land of Egypt *by great judgments"* (Exodus 7:1-4).

One of the most common questions I am asked about this story is, "Why did God harden Pharaoh's heart?" The answer is clear. God is just. He hardened Pharaoh's heart to make him, and all the people of Egypt, pay for what they had done. They had committed wholesale murder most foul. They had killed the weakest of the Israelites in a callous and hateful manner. They had held a people captive generation after generation. They had grown wealthy by the use of slave labor. Justice *demanded* that a price be paid. Don't overlook the last three words of the above passage: "by great judgments," because that is what this is all about.

In the plagues that followed, Egypt's entire slave-built economy would be left in shambles and the firstborn of every family in Egypt dead. It is chilling when you consider the implications of this. In our own country, we held men slaves through several generations and built our wealth on the backs of slave labor. God only knows how many millions of captive blacks were killed outright in the slave trade. Only God knows how many died on the voyage across the Atlantic and were thrown over the side into the sea.

And it is a tragic irony that, as a direct result of this shameful crime, we fought one of the bloodiest and most insane wars in our history – the American War between the States. Even then, I don't know that we killed as many of our brothers as we did slaves in the trade. This country paid a terrible price for slavery in shed blood and economic loss. And it was *just*. It may have even been the judgment of God. We paid. God knows how we paid.

How can I be so sure that the plagues on Egypt were divine justice? This is not at all hard to see. What was the very first plague that fell on Egypt? God turned the river into blood and gave the Egyptians blood to drink. Why the river? Why blood? Because this is the place where the blood of the innocents was shed. This is where countless hundreds of little baby boys were thrown to the crocodiles. They wanted blood? God gave them blood to drink. This was the most symbolic thing Moses could have done as a first act, to point to the crimes of Egypt – in particular to the bloody murder of countless tiny Israelite boys.

And let me tell you what makes my blood run cold. In our country today, there is a different kind of infanticide going on. It is called "intact dilation and extraction." You may know it as partial birth abortion. There isn't a lot of difference between this procedure and what Pharaoh wanted the midwives to do. As soon as the baby was far enough out to determine that it was a boy, the midwives were supposed to whack its little head on the leg of the birthing stool and kill it. In the modern procedure, a doctor delivers all of the little fellow except the head and then he inserts scissors into the skull and sucks out the brains.

Senator Patrick Moynihan called it *infanticide*. And there is not a lot of difference between this procedure and other third-term abortions. Sometimes the babies survive the abortion and are killed afterward. And most people in this country seem content to have it so. I can't help wondering how long God is going to wait before he avenges the blood of the innocents on us as he did on the Egyptians.

Anyone who takes justice into his *own* hands on this issue is worse than a fool. Moses tried that early in life and it didn't work. God's justice will transcend anything you and I can imagine. Just be sure you are on the right side of the river when it all comes down.

Nine plagues later, with the Egyptian economy in a shambles, all the people awaited the final judgment of God. They couldn't find a way to repent and avoid it because Pharaoh wouldn't let them. God had hardened Pharaoh's heart to the end that *justice* might be done.

I have told you this story because it is here that we can again pick up our thread. There is a direct line from Abraham to Paul, and it runs right through Egypt. By the time we reach the near end of the thread, we will see the connection as clear as day. But we are not finished yet with Pharaoh.

> Then Pharaoh summoned Moses and said, "Go, worship the LORD. Even your women and children may go with you; only leave your flocks and herds behind." But Moses said, "You must allow us to have sacrifices and burnt offerings to present to the LORD our God. Our livestock too must go with us; not a hoof is to be left behind. We have to use some of them in worshiping the LORD our God, and until we get there we will not know what we are to use to worship the LORD" (Exodus 10:24-26 NIV).

This may have been true, but it was also a deliberate provocation on Moses' part. Pharaoh tried to negotiate some standoff that would allow him to save face and keep his slaves. God was not having any of it.

> But the LORD hardened Pharaoh's heart, and he was not willing to let them go. Pharaoh said to Moses, "Get out of my sight! Make sure you do not appear before me again! The day you see my face you will die." "Just as you say," Moses replied, "I will never

appear before you again" (vv. 27-29).

Pharaoh had come a long way in the concessions he was willing to make, but it would never be enough. Because God intended to punish Egypt for what they had done. He refused to grant repentance to the Egyptians.[ii]

The Lord spoke to Moses and told him that there was one more plague coming upon Pharaoh and the land of Egypt. This one will be final, he said. Not only will he let you go, he will *force* you all to leave. When that happens, you will ask the Egyptians for their jewels, their gold, their silver, and they will give them gladly. There is another irony in this, because the Lord gave the people favor in the sight of the Egyptian *people*. "Moreover the man Moses was very great in the land of Egypt, in the sight of Pharaoh's servants, *and in the sight of the people*" (Exodus 11:3).

This plague could not come without warning, so Moses told Pharaoh what God was about to do.

> Then Moses said, "Thus says the LORD: About midnight I will go out into the midst of Egypt; and all the firstborn in the land of Egypt shall die, from the firstborn of Pharaoh who sits on his throne, even to the firstborn of the female servant who is behind the handmill, and all the firstborn of the animals" (vv. 4-5).

What a cold, hard sentence God passed upon these people. From top to bottom, from high to low, no social strata were excluded. Not even the animals escaped. But remember that *all* of the people of Egypt were involved in the destruction, not merely of the firstborn of the Israelite children, but every single male child. God's justice did not extend to taking all the males of that generation as the Egyptians had done. He only took the firstborn.

> Then there shall be a great cry throughout all the land of Egypt, such as was not like it before, nor shall be like it again. But against none of the children of Israel shall a dog move its tongue, against man or beast, that

you may know that the LORD does make a difference between the Egyptians and Israel (Exodus 11:6-7).

There is a bright line between us now, said Moses, and you will see it. "And all of these your servants," said Moses, sweeping his hand around the assembly, "shall come to me and bow down to me and say 'Get out.' And Moses went out from Pharaoh's presence in great anger" (Exodus 11:8). That is easy to understand after all the vile acts of the Egyptians and then the final confrontation.

So, we have our answer to the original question. The firstborn of Egypt died and the economy of the nation was destroyed because of their horrible sins against the Israelites. And the people of Egypt knew this as well as anyone. Justice was served.

Out of it came the ancient Feast of Passover. How it became a great Christian holyday is a story not many have heard. But first, we must follow the thread to the first Passover.

---

i. The question may overlook the fact that it was not merely the children of the Egyptians who were taken, but the firstborn, whatever age he might have been. And to say they were all innocent begs the question.

ii. Compare 2 Timothy 2:25 and Romans 2:4. For man to repent, God must grant it. And despite many efforts to end slavery, it still exists today. Some 27 million people worldwide are enslaved or work as forced laborers. That's more people than at any point in the history of the world. Social Studies Understanding Slavery, Discovery Education, discoveryschool.com.

3

The Passover, Old and New

When I see the blood, I will pass over you (Exodus 12:13).

How is it possible that a Christian church, about 25 years after the ascension of Christ, was observing the oldest known Jewish holyday? That they were is easily demonstrated. And this wasn't a Jewish church. It was mostly Gentile.

We have a letter that the Apostle Paul wrote to the church in Corinth about 55 A.D. Scholars generally agree that the letter was written about Passover season (see chapter 1). Paul was addressing a problem that was disgracing the church, and almost in passing, as though he took it for granted, he remarked on the observance of the Passover.

> Your glorying is not good. Do you not know that a little leaven leavens the whole lump? Therefore purge out the old leaven, that you may be a new lump, since you truly are unleavened. For indeed Christ, our Passover, was sacrificed for us. Therefore let us keep the feast, not with old leaven, nor with the leaven of malice and wickedness, but with the unleavened bread of sincerity and truth (1 Corinthians 5:6-8).

There is no way to misunderstand this. The Corinthian church, mostly Gentile, was observing the Passover and the Feast of Unleavened Bread. How is the sacrifice of Christ connected to the Old Testament Passover, why was this church observing it, and why was Paul advocating it?

There is a clue to this in a statement made by John the Baptist. One day as he was baptizing people along the Jordan River, he looked up and saw Jesus walking toward him. And he said, "Behold the Lamb of God, which taketh away the sin of the world" (John 1:29).

As a Christian, you might hear that statement and say, "So?" But if you had been a Jew standing near John at the time, this would likely have been the first time you had heard anything like this. What do you mean, "Lamb of God"? It was not that they weren't familiar with the idea of a lamb as a sin offering. The law made provision for that.[i] So the idea of a lamb taking away one man's sins was not strange to John's companions.

But the idea of a *man* as a sacrificial lamb was utterly foreign. And just as foreign was the idea of taking away the sins of *the whole world*. Judaism was not a world evangelizing faith. It was a *Jewish* faith. And contrary to anything in the Law and the Prophets, Judaism had become an exclusive faith. For Jewish Christians, that was about to change, and the key to that change was the Lamb of God that takes away the sin, not of a man, but of the world.

That theme is also found in one of the favorite scriptures of the Christian faith: "For God so loved the world, that he gave his only begotten Son, that whosoever believeth in him should not perish, but have everlasting life" (John 3:16).

But gave him how? He gave him as "the Lamb of God that takes away the sin of the world." He gave him as "Christ our Passover." But we still haven't established the *Passover* connection. To do that, we have to take a step back into what appears to be the original Passover observance. The story is told in detail in Exodus 12.

On the tenth day of the first month, every household was to select a male lamb or kid. They were then to keep it up until the 14th day and kill it in the evening. They would then take a little blood of the lamb and strike it on the lintels and doorposts of their houses. They would eat the lamb on that night, roasted, with *unleavened bread* and bitter herbs. They were to leave none of it to the morning. And then there is this curious bit: "And thus shall ye eat it; with your loins girded, your shoes on your feet, and your staff in your hand; and ye shall eat it in haste: it is the LORD'S Passover."

These people were not even going to bed that night. And by the time they got the lamb killed, dressed and roasted, they were eating it very late. The events to follow were not going to give them much time for leisure.

> For I will pass through the land of Egypt on that night, and will strike all the firstborn in the land of Egypt, both man and beast; and against all the gods of Egypt I will execute judgment: I am the LORD. Now the blood shall be a sign for you on the houses where you are. And when I see the blood, I will pass over you; and the plague shall not be on you to destroy you when I strike the land of Egypt (Exodus 12:12-13).

And from this comes the name of this great festival, the *Passover*. As I noted earlier, this day may well have been one of the appointed times of Yahweh even before this time, but the events of this occasion stamped themselves indelibly on the feast. The day was declared to be a memorial, to be observed by a feast, forever. The Passover is not going to go away. It will take on new form and meaning with Jesus Christ, but it will never stop being celebrated.

> Seven days you shall eat unleavened bread. On the first day you shall remove leaven from your houses. For whoever eats leavened bread from the first day until the seventh day, that person shall be cut off from Israel. On the first day there shall be a holy convocation, and on the seventh day there shall be a holy convocation for you. No manner of work shall be done on them; but that which everyone must eat; that only may be prepared by you (Exodus 12:15-16).

The seven days of unleavened bread run from the 15th through the 21st of the first month of the Hebrew calendar. The first and the last days are actually Sabbath days, no matter what day of the week they fall on.

> For seven days no leaven shall be found in your houses, since whoever eats what is leavened, that same person shall be cut off from the congregation of Israel, whether he is a stranger or a native of the land. You shall eat nothing leavened; in all your dwellings you shall eat unleavened bread (Exodus 12:19-20).

Hence, Paul's statement to the Corinthians:

> Therefore purge out the old leaven, that you may be a new lump, since you truly are unleavened. For indeed Christ, our Passover, was sacrificed for us. Therefore let us keep the feast, not with old leaven, nor with the leaven of malice and wickedness, but with the unleavened bread of sincerity and truth (1 Corinthians 5:7-8).

There was no thought of doing away with the festival. Paul was rather explaining the meaning of the season to Gentiles who otherwise might not know. But the Passover is still connected to the original *in name and in practice.*

Moses gave his instructions to all the elders: "And ye shall take a bunch of hyssop, and dip it in the blood that is in the basin, and strike the lintel and the two side posts with the blood that is in the basin; and none of you shall go out at the door of his house until the morning" (Exodus 12:22).

Why not? "For the Lord will pass through to smite the Egyptians; and when he seeth the blood upon the lintel, and on the two side posts, the Lord will pass over the door, and will not suffer the destroyer to come in unto your houses to smite you."

The implications of this are far reaching. It is the blood of the Lamb *applied* that enables God to pass over us and spare us the destruction around us. Some Christians have long understood the connection between the blood of the Passover Lamb and the blood of

Jesus. There is an old hymn I remember singing in church when I was a boy:

Christ our redeemer died on the cross
Died for the sinner, paid all his due,
All who receive him need never fear
Yes, He will pass, will pass over you.
When I see the blood, when I see the blood,
when I see the blood,
I will pass, I will pass over you.

This hymn represents an understanding of the Bible by an earlier generation of Christians that seems to have faded with time. There was a time when the great hymn writers had more of a sense of connection between old and new. They realized that there is a strong tie between the death of Jesus and the Passover of the Jews, and it often found expression in the hymns of the church. But just as that connection presented problems for the early church, it presents problems today as well. Some Christian folk don't like the idea of anything Jewish connected with their Christianity. Yet here is this old hymn that ties Christ firmly to the Passover.

It seems a shame to me that some churches have lost touch with this great festival. They see Christ in it when they bother to look. But somewhere in their history, they stopped observing it annually *on the anniversary*. In observing communion, or the Lord's Supper every Sunday, or monthly or quarterly, they forgot that it was originally an *annual* observance. And subsequently, they seemed to forget altogether that it was the Passover.

Moses told the elders of Israel:

And you shall observe this thing as an ordinance for you and your sons forever. It will come to pass when you come to the land which the LORD will give you, just as He promised, that you shall keep this service. And it shall be, when your children say to you, "What do you mean by this service?" that you shall say, "It is the Passover sacrifice of the LORD, who passed over the houses of the children of Israel in Egypt when He struck the Egyptians and delivered our households." So the people bowed their heads and worshiped (Exodus 12:24-27).

The lesson was passed on from generation to generation as the curiosity of children was answered year by year by the retelling of the story.

At midnight on that fateful night, the Lord smote all the firstborn in the land of Egypt, from the firstborn of the captive in prison to the firstborn of Pharaoh himself and even of all cattle. There was not a house where there was not one dead.

Immediately Pharaoh "called for Moses and Aaron *by night*, [ii] and said, "Rise up, and get you forth from among my people." Get out, he said, lest we all be dead men. This does not suggest that the people could have gone to bed and waited until daylight to leave. In every way, they had to be ready for immediate departure.

So the people took their dough before it was leavened, having their kneading bowls bound up in their clothes on their shoulders. Now the children of Israel had done according to the word of Moses, and they had asked from the Egyptians articles of silver, articles of gold, and clothing. And the LORD had given the people favor in the sight of the Egyptians, so that they granted them what they requested. Thus they plundered the Egyptians. Then the children of Israel journeyed from Rameses to Succoth, about six hundred thousand men on foot, besides children. A mixed multitude went up with them also, and flocks and herds; a great deal of livestock. And they baked unleavened cakes of the dough which they had brought out of Egypt; for it was not leavened, because they were driven out of Egypt and could not wait, nor had they prepared provisions for themselves (vv. 34-39).

I think a lot of people look no further than this in considering why the feast is called the Feast of Unleavened Bread. We will look into this later, but first, there is this to consider.

> Now the sojourn of the children of Israel who lived in Egypt was four hundred and thirty years. And it came to pass at the end of the four hundred and thirty years; *on that very same day*; it came to pass that all the armies of the LORD went out from the land of Egypt (Exodus 12:40-41).

This is a remarkable statement, for it gives singular significance to a *given day* 430 years earlier. That day could not have been the day they came into Egypt, because the chronology does not work. The Septuagint version of Exodus says that "the sojourning of the Children of Israel, who dwelt in Egypt *and in Canaan*, was four hundred and thirty years." It isn't clear exactly what that day was 430 years prior, but it lends credence to the idea that the Festivals of Jehovah are much older than the days of Moses. We can't be certain, but if once again we follow the thread back in time, we come to a day that may well serve as a precursor of the Passover.

The word of the Lord came to Abram (later called Abraham) in a vision saying "Fear not, Abram: I am thy shield, and thy exceeding great reward." But Abraham had something of a complaint. How, he wondered, could God fulfill his promises seeing that he was old and childless? God went on to promise him an heir, but he did something more. He promised him descendants beyond number along with the entire land over which he traveled. "Lord GOD," Abraham asked, "whereby shall I know that I shall inherit it?" (Genesis 15:8).

What follows falls strangely on modern ears, but it is a crucial point in our story. It is a prophecy of the sojourn of Israel in Egypt, and also of the judgment of Egypt. It is also one more thing. It is the *moment of the covenant* with Abraham.

> So the LORD said to him, "Bring me a heifer, a goat and a ram, each three years old, along with a dove and a young pigeon." Abram brought all these to him, cut

them in two and arranged the halves opposite each other; the birds, however, he did not cut in half. Then birds of prey came down on the carcasses, but Abram drove them away. As the sun was setting, Abram fell into a deep sleep, and a thick and dreadful darkness came over him. Then the LORD said to him, "Know for certain that your descendants will be strangers in a country not their own, and they will be enslaved and mistreated four hundred years. But I will punish the nation they serve as slaves, and afterward they will come out with great possessions. You, however, will go to your fathers in peace and be buried at a good old age. In the fourth generation your descendants will come back here, for the sin of the Amorites has not yet reached its full measure" (Genesis 15:9-16 NIV).

Here is the prophecy of Israel's sojourn in Egypt, of the time lapse of 400 years, of Israel becoming slaves, the eventual judging of Egypt, and the return to their home land.

When the sun had set and darkness had fallen, a smoking firepot with a blazing torch appeared and passed between the pieces. On that day the LORD made a covenant with Abram and said, "To your descendants I give this land, from the river of Egypt to the great river, the Euphrates . . ." (vv. 17-18).

To understand what is happening here, we need to understand the customs surrounding ancient covenants. Everyone is familiar with the idea of blood brotherhood, even among American Indians. In ancient times, they went a little further than cutting themselves and mingling their blood with another. They sometimes actually drank the blood of their new brother, thus creating a new blood kinship. In later years, they shared the blood of a sacrificial animal or shared the meat from a sacrifice. [iii] What is described in Genesis 15 is the beginning point of the covenant between God and Abraham.

The events of the Exodus are the fulfillment of this promise, so I suspect this *is the very day*, 430 years before the Exodus, when the promises were made and the covenant entered.

This day of Abraham's covenant was, in an important way, a precursor of the Passover. And because of the symbolism involved, I suspect it was on an anniversary of this date that Abraham was sent to offer his only son as a sacrifice. It was a day when Abraham had an annual appointment with God.

> And it came to pass, on that very same day, that the LORD brought the children of Israel out of the land of Egypt according to their armies (Exodus 12:51).

The very same day as what? Well, it would make sense if it was the very same day of the year that God told Abraham he would do this very thing. *"And also that nation, whom they shall serve, will I judge: and afterward shall they come out with great substance."* (Genesis 15:14 KJV)

Everything of importance seems to take place along this thread. Even the Passover of Christ.

---

i. See Leviticus 4:32-35.

ii. After midnight, when the destroyer had done his work, it was safe to go out. The Israelites were told not to go out of their houses until morning but, in a manner of speaking, it is morning after midnight. They did not go to bed that night.

iii. See the *International Standard Bible Encyclopedia*, article "Covenant in the Old Testament," for a complete explanation of how covenant customs developed. Two types of covenants are discussed, covenants between men and between God and man.

4

The Body of Christ

*The Lord Jesus on the same night
in which He was betrayed took bread;
and when He had given thanks, He broke it and said,
"Take, eat; this is My body which is broken for you;
do this in remembrance of Me" (1 Corinthians 11:23-24).*

Sometimes the simplest answers are the best. I keep asking why it was, 25 years after the ascension of Christ, long after everything that was "nailed to the cross" was nailed there, that a Gentile church was observing the Passover and the Days of Unleavened Bread that go with it? The simple answer? Because the season is all about Christ. Paul made this plain enough in his letter to the Corinthians.[i]

According to Paul, the Passover and the seven days of unleavened bread are *all* about Christ. But what does that mean? I doubt there is a Christian in the world who doesn't understand that the wine taken at what they call Communion, or the Lord's Supper, symbolizes the shed blood of Jesus. We all know that Jesus died for our sins.

But there was a question that nagged my conscience for years. I understood fully that Jesus had to die for my sins. I had taken Communion with tears running down my face in deep repentance for what I had done. But what I didn't understand was why Jesus had to suffer so. Why, I wondered, couldn't they have just killed Jesus outright? A quick execution would have shed his blood and effectively paid for my sins. Or so I thought.

I knew all the songs about the blood of Jesus. Even today, I can sing from memory, "When I see the blood, I will pass, I will pass over you." But the wine is only half of the Lord's Supper. What about the bread?

Even as a teenager, I was profoundly moved by the suffering of Jesus in that long night and day of his Passion. He was despised, spit on, beaten, and a crown of thorns was placed on his head. And then there was the horror of the crucifixion. It took a long time, but finally I made the connection. From Luke:

> And when He had taken some bread and given thanks, He broke it, and gave it to them, saying, "This is My body which is given for you; do this in remembrance of Me" (Luke 22:19 NASB).

And from Paul:

> And when He had given thanks, He broke it and said, "Take, eat; this is My body which is broken for you; do this in remembrance of Me" (1 Corinthians 11:24).

So the bread of the Christian Passover represents the body of Christ, given for us, broken for us. Paul felt the Corinthians weren't getting the point about the Lord's body. More than once I have given thanks for the obstreperous Corinthians and their problems. Without them, we would not know a lot of things that Paul sees fit to tell us. So Paul went on:

> Therefore whoever eats this bread or drinks this cup of the Lord in an unworthy manner will be guilty of the body and blood of the Lord. But let a man examine himself, and so let him eat of the bread and drink of the cup. For he who eats and drinks in an unworthy manner eats and drinks judgment to himself, not discerning the Lord's *body*. For this

reason many are weak and sick among you, and many
sleep (vv. 27-30).

It is noteworthy that Paul didn't say that men fail to discern
the Lord's blood in the wine taken in the service. Like me, it was the
body they didn't get. But what is really surprising is the connection of
that failure with sickness and even death.

Now we can consider what we are to make of that. There was
an incident in the ministry of Jesus that may shed some light on the
question before us. Jesus was teaching in a man's house, and there
were so many people present that no one could even get to the door.
Four men came to the house carrying a paralyzed man on a kind of
stretcher hoping that Jesus might heal him. They couldn't get to the
door, so they went up on the roof of the house and broke through so
they could lower the man before Jesus. It was an act of remarkable
determination.

> When Jesus saw their faith, he said unto the sick of
> the palsy, Son, thy sins be forgiven thee. But there
> were certain of the scribes sitting there, and reasoning
> in their hearts, Why doth this man thus speak
> blasphemies? who can forgive sins but God only?
> (Mark 2:5-7).

Who indeed? The men who had struggled to let this poor
fellow down in front of Jesus may not have had a thought in their
heads about getting the poor fellow forgiven of his sins. They wanted
him healed of his disease. As for the lawyers, they were scandalized.

> And immediately Jesus, aware in His spirit that they
> were reasoning that way within themselves, said to
> them, "Why are you reasoning about these things in
> your hearts? Which is easier, to say to the paralytic,
> 'Your sins are forgiven'; or to say, 'Arise, and take up
> your pallet and walk'? But in order that you may
> know that the Son of Man has authority on earth to
> forgive sins" – He said to the paralytic – "I say to
> you, rise, take up your pallet and go home." And he

> rose and immediately took up the pallet and went out
> in the sight of all; so that they were all amazed and
> were glorifying God, saying, "We have never seen
> anything like this" (Mark 2:8-12 NASB).

No, I am sure they had not. But this astonishing example of healing may be the most revealing of all Jesus' miracles. It reveals an unexpected connection between sin and sickness. This is not to say that a sick person is a worse sinner than a well person. It does not draw a direct line between sin and disease *in the individual*. But it does suggest that sickness and disease are in the world because of sin and that the healing of disease involves, in some unexplained way, the forgiveness of sin.

Jesus said, "The Son of Man has authority on earth to forgive sins. Rise, take up your pallet and go home." How can there be any way of misunderstanding what this means? The Authorized Version says that Jesus has the *power* to forgive sins, which assumes only that he is able to do so. The NIV follows the Greek in saying that Jesus has the *authority*, to forgive sins. There is a significant difference between these two ideas.

Jesus had already made it clear to the most casual observer that he had the power to heal. But it was not so clear how he had the *right* to do it. If it had been, the Jews would not have asked this question:

> Then they came again to Jerusalem. And as He was
> walking in the temple, the chief priests, the scribes,
> and the elders came to Him. And they said to Him,
> "By what authority are You doing these things? And
> who gave You this authority to do these things?"
> (Mark 11:27-28).

I found this question incomprehensible. If a man has the ability to say the words and make the blind see, the deaf hear, the lame walk, and demons depart, it would never cross my mind to ask where he got the *authority* to do it. One would think that the authority is implicit in the act. But there must be more to it than that or the Jews would never have asked this question.

Jesus' disciples, following conventional wisdom and considering the link between sin and sickness, asked Jesus about a man who had been *born* blind. "Rabbi, who sinned, this man or his parents, that he was born blind?" (John 9:2). To them, this was a simple causeéffect equation. Someone sinned or this man would not have been born blind.[ii] Jesus' answer must have been a surprise: "Neither this man nor his parents sinned, but that the works of God should be revealed in him." And then there was another occasion when Jesus brushed this idea aside.

> Or those eighteen on whom the tower in Siloam fell and killed them, do you think that they were worse sinners than all other men who dwelt in Jerusalem? "I tell you, no; but unless you repent you will all likewise perish" (Luke 13:4-5).

This doesn't dismiss the possibility of dire consequences falling on man as a result of sin, but rather it dumps us all into the same bag. We are all sinners, and just because we escaped this disaster does not mean we are better than those who did not. We need to repent before our own tower falls on us.

I have taken this small digression to point out that there was, in the thinking of the time, a belief that men who suffer a catastrophe are under God's judgment for sin. That idea persists to this day in that we find ourselves wondering, when a crisis befalls us, what exactly we did to deserve this.

And this is the significance of the question asked of Jesus: "Who gave thee this authority to do these things?" What they were really asking was, "*Who has the authority to suspend God's judgment on sinners*, to heal the sick and diseased people who are suffering the results of sin? Who gave it to him? Where does he get the *right* to do it?" With this in mind, we can think about the Last Supper in a way that is perhaps new to us.

In another place, Paul[iii] turns to the office of Jesus as our High Priest. We all know he is our Lord, our Master, our Savior. Now we see another role, and in the process, we learn something about Jesus' suffering.

> Seeing then that we have a great High Priest who has
> passed through the heavens, Jesus the Son of God, let
> us hold fast our confession. For we do not have a
> High Priest who cannot sympathize with our
> weaknesses, but was in all points tempted as we are,
> yet without sin (Hebrews 4:14-15).

Jesus came to this last Passover with some unfinished business in hand. On this last night, there were ways in which Jesus had not yet been tempted – temptations that are familiar enough to all of us. And Jesus was not merely to die for our sins, he had to suffer for them as well, and in ways we might not understand.

The whole process of suffering began with a despicable act of betrayal. And there is something important here to consider. It isn't your enemies that betray you. You expect them to do what they can to oppose you. It is only your friends who can betray you, and most of us have had occasion to know how painful that can be.

The story of Judas is familiar enough. He was right there at the Last Supper pretending he was another faithful disciple. But Jesus knew, and he let Judas know that he knew. When he had told the disciples that one of them would betray him, Judas asked, "Rabbi, is it I?" Jesus answered in the idiom of the time, "You have said it."[iv]

Knowing what lay ahead of him, Jesus took his disciples with him to Gethsemane to pray. And it is in Gethsemane that we get a dramatic look into the heart and soul of Jesus.

> And they came to a place named Gethsemane; and He
> said to His disciples, "Sit here until I have prayed."
> And He took with Him Peter and James and John, and
> began to be very distressed and troubled. And He said
> to them, "My soul is deeply grieved to the point of
> death; remain here and keep watch" (Mark 14:32-34
> NASB).

It may be hard to imagine how the Savior could have been so troubled. He was God. He could do anything he wanted. That is true enough, because he said plainly that he could have called legions of angels to his defense. Therefore, he was in this place voluntarily.

That did not mean it was easy for him. The dread of this had been growing in him for days.

> And He went a little beyond them, and fell to the ground, and began to pray that if it were possible, the hour might pass Him by. And He was saying, "Abba! Father! All things are possible for Thee; remove this cup from Me; yet not what I will, but what Thou wilt." And He came and found them sleeping, and said to Peter, "Simon, are you asleep? Could you not keep watch for one hour? Keep watching and praying, that you may not come into temptation; the spirit is willing, but the flesh is weak." And again He went away and prayed, saying the same words (vv. 35-39).

Luke adds a detail to the story:

> Now an angel from heaven appeared to Him, strengthening Him. And being in agony He was praying very fervently; and His sweat became like drops of blood, falling down upon the ground (Luke 22:43-44 NASB).

I don't believe for a moment that Jesus was afraid of death. But death was not all he faced on this night. He faced being betrayed by a close friend, being forsaken by *all* his friends and being left entirely alone. He faced humiliation and mocking – degradation of the highest order men could devise. He faced false accusations and lying. He faced a terrible beating, a scourging, and long hours on the stake, in agony the whole time. And because it was necessary that he suffer, he would refuse the narcotic they offered him at the moment of crucifixion. The sufferings of Jesus on this day were terrible, and they were voluntary. Now think about the Last Supper:

> That the Lord Jesus the same night in which he was betrayed took bread: And when he had given thanks, he brake it, and said, Take, eat: this is my body,

which is broken for you: this do in remembrance of me (1 Corinthians 11:23-24).

On that day when they broke up the roof of the house and let that paralyzed man down in front of Jesus that he might be healed, Jesus knew something that none of those assembled seemed to know. He knew that sin had a terrible price that came with it, and he knew that he was going to have to pay that price. No one present knew what Jesus knew as the man got up and walked – that Jesus would have to pay for that healing with his own body.

It is worth pondering why healing played such a large part in Christ's ministry. To us, it is a mere conjunction of power and compassion. If we had the power to heal, we would do it out of mere compassion for the sick. But Jesus did not heal every sick person he met. When he healed, it had a purpose, a meaning. And the meaning was that he had not only the power to forgive sin and triumph over it, but the *authority* as well. Nevertheless, every time he did it, he knew there was a price that he alone must pay.

I asked before why a Gentile church would be observing the Passover and the Days of Unleavened Bread some 30 years after Christ's ascension. Maybe it was because they knew something we don't know. Perhaps to them, the Days of Unleavened Bread were not merely about the Exodus from Egypt. The thread led them naturally to the body of Christ and the Bread of Life.

---

i. 1 Corinthians 5:6-8.

ii. There was a similar thought relative to poverty and wealth. The rich have God's blessing and the poor did not. Compare Matthew 19:24-25.

iii. After considerable reflection, and taking into account all the arguments on the issue, I still think Paul wrote the book of Hebrews. Others will differ. Almost any Bible handbook will have a complete discussion of the authorship of Hebrews.

iv. Matthew 26:25.

5

The Bread of Life

And Jesus said unto them, I am the bread of life:
he that cometh to me shall never hunger;
and he that believeth on me shall never thirst
(John 6:35).

The thread has now taken us to one of the singular
peculiarities of the Passover, and one that carried over into Christian
observance. Why did the Jews, and later the Corinthian Christians,
eat unleavened bread during the seven days of the Passover season?

When Paul wrote his first letter to the Corinthians, it was at
the Passover season, and he had to tackle a regrettable problem in the
church. A man who was a brother in the church was committing
fornication, so openly that it was commonly known in the city. The
leadership of the Corinthian church, who knew what was going on,
had done nothing about it. Since they would not judge the matter,
Paul did.

> For though absent in body, I am present in spirit; and
> as if present I have already pronounced judgment in
> the name of the Lord Jesus on the man who has done
> such a thing. When you are assembled, and my spirit
> is present with the power of our Lord Jesus, you are to
> hand this man over to Satan for the destruction of the

flesh, so that his spirit may be saved in the day of the
Lord (1 Corinthians 5:3-5 NRSV).

Having judged the leadership of the church as arrogant
("puffed up" in the KJV), Paul goes on to develop the theme of the
season. "Your glorying is not good," he said. "Do you not know that
a little leaven leavens the whole lump?" (1 Corinthians 5:6).

The NIV uses the word "yeast" instead of "leaven" here, but
the Greek word, *zume*, means "to ferment". The bread was
sourdough. When baking bread, the sourdough baker preserves a
small lump of starter. When the time comes to bake a fresh loaf of
bread, he takes the starter and works it into the new lump of dough
and sets it aside to rise. Before he bakes it, he saves a small lump to
start the next loaf of bread. A baker's starter can sometimes have
years of history, and each may have a distinctive taste.

The bread of the Israelites in Egypt was also sourdough,
fermented, bread. Perhaps the image of corruption, of souring, was
the reason the law did not permit the offering of any sacrifice with
leaven.[i] So if the lamb is a sacrifice, it must be eaten with unleavened
bread. Thus, there is not even nominal corruption connected with the
Lord's sacrifice.

From the idea of fermentation, Paul develops the idea of one
corrupt individual corrupting the whole. "Purge out therefore the old
leaven," he said, "that ye may be a new lump, as ye are unleavened"
(v. 7). The expression "old leaven" is a reference to the old lump of
starter which was used to leaven a new batch of dough. The man who
was corrupt was having the effect of souring the whole church
(hence, the puffed up leadership). Paul acknowledges that they were
unleavened in the matter of ordinary bread ("as you are unleavened")
but that spiritually, they were far from it.

"Therefore let us keep the feast," Paul continued, "not with
old leaven, neither with the leaven of malice and wickedness; but
with the unleavened bread of sincerity and truth" (v. 8).

Paul told them to get the man who was sinning out of the
church like they had gotten leaven out of their houses. So leaven
symbolized corruption, and there was to be no corruption connected
with the Lamb of God or his church.

Part of the understanding we are looking for focuses on the

curious question of unleavened bread. The impression one gets from Exodus is that it was merely a matter of the haste of the Israelites fleeing Egypt who had no time for their bread to rise. Thus the days of unleavened bread following the Passover were merely commemorative of one aspect of the Exodus from Egypt. But that doesn't explain why Paul was urging the Gentiles in Corinth to keep the Feast of Unleavened Bread. Egypt had nothing to do with their history. So there had to be more to it than that, especially in the light of what Jesus said on a day early in his ministry.

John, who tells us the story, notes that this was just before the Passover (see John 6:4). Jesus had gone up into a mountain, and he was followed by a great company of people because of the miracles he had done for sick people. It isn't surprising that Jesus would draw a crowd wherever he went. It was all but impossible for him to get away from crowds.

When he saw so many of them there, so far from anything to eat, he asked Philip, "Where shall we buy bread, that these may eat?" There was no such place, which both of them knew well enough. So Jesus had the people sit down in ranks, and fed the whole multitude of people with only a few loaves and fish. It was a classic example of Middle Eastern hospitality. Jesus had the means to feed them, so feed them he did. But in doing so, he posed a problem for himself.

> Then those men, when they had seen the miracle that Jesus did, said, This is of a truth that Prophet that should come into the world. When Jesus therefore perceived that they would come and take him by force, to make him a king, he departed again into a mountain himself alone (John 6:14,15 KJV).

At this point, Jesus did his best to get away from these people. They were ready to start a revolution with him as king, and he wanted no part of it. They, for their part were not ready to take no for an answer. He crossed the Sea of Galilee, and they followed.

> And when they found Him on the other side of the sea, they said to Him, "Rabbi, when did You come here?" Jesus answered them and said, "Most

> assuredly, I say to you, you seek Me, not because you saw the signs, but because you ate of the loaves and were filled. Do not labor for the food which perishes, but for the food which endures to everlasting life, which the Son of Man will give you, because God the Father has set His seal on Him" (vv. 25-27).

Jesus saw through all of this. People who have seen a miracle will only want to see another one. Jesus ignored the question and pointed them away from food to what is really important.

> Then they said to Him, "What shall we do, that we may work the works of God?" Jesus answered and said to them, "This is the work of God, that you believe in Him whom He sent." Therefore they said to Him, "What sign will You perform then, that we may see it and believe You? What work will You do? Our fathers ate the manna in the desert; as it is written, 'He gave them bread from heaven to eat'" (vv. 28-31).

They were still looking for the miracle, demonstrating that Jesus was right in judging their motives. And, of course, they wanted their bellies filled. Nevertheless, it opened the door for Jesus to clarify a crucial issue that shed light on the approaching Passover and the Days of Unleavened Bread.

> Then Jesus said to them, "Most assuredly, I say to you, Moses did not give you the bread from heaven, but My Father gives you the true bread from heaven. For the bread of God is He who comes down from heaven and gives life to the world." Then they said to Him, "Lord, give us this bread always" (vv. 32-34).

Now Jesus is ready to make the crucial point: "And Jesus said unto them, *I am the bread of life:* he that cometh to me shall never hunger; and he that believeth on me shall never thirst" (v.35). And it is right here that we find a hint of the connection with the Feast of Unleavened Bread which is fast approaching.

But I said to you that you have seen Me and yet do not believe. All that the Father gives Me will come to Me, and the one who comes to Me I will by no means cast out. For I have come down from heaven, not to do My own will, but the will of Him who sent Me. This is the will of the Father who sent Me, that of all He has given Me I should lose nothing, but should raise it up at the last day (vv. 36-39).

This did not please many of his listeners, for he plainly said that he was the bread that *came down from heaven*. That can't be true, they said. We know his father and mother. How can he claim to have come down from heaven?

Jesus therefore answered and said to them, "Do not murmur among yourselves. No one can come to Me unless the Father who sent Me draws him; and I will raise him up at the last day. It is written in the prophets, "And they shall all be taught by God." Therefore everyone who has heard and learned from the Father comes to Me. Not that anyone has seen the Father, except He who is from God; He has seen the Father. Most assuredly, I say to you, he who believes in Me has everlasting life." (vv. 43-47).

And here we approach the mystery of the meaning of the unleavened bread of Passover. Jesus went on to say, "I am that bread of life" (v. 48). Now it may not be immediately apparent, but the command in the law is that *you shall eat* unleavened bread for seven days. It is not that we must merely abstain from leavened bread, we are to do the positive act of eating unleavened bread (Exodus 12:15). For the Christian, that unleavened bread would symbolize Jesus, the Bread of Life. Because leaven will be seen as a symbol of sin, and because Jesus was sinless, then the bread of life is unleavened.

Your fathers ate the manna in the wilderness, and are dead. "This is the bread which comes down from heaven, that one may eat of it and not die. I am the

> living bread which came down from heaven. If
> anyone eats of this bread, he will live forever; and the
> bread that I shall give is My flesh, which I shall give
> for the life of the world" (vv. 49-51).

When I read this passage, I can't help reflecting on all the years I thought about, read about, sang about, and trusted the blood of Christ to take away my sins. This is fundamental, woven into the fabric of the Christian faith. But I never gave a thought to the *flesh* of Jesus which he said he would give for the life of the world. I did not grasp the importance of the flesh of Jesus in the New Covenant. It is odd that this has never made it very far into the consciousness of the Christian church. The blood of Christ has made it there. The blood of the Lord is everywhere in Christian hymnals. We all understand this. But Jesus said he would give his *flesh* for the life of the world, and there is an important distinction here.

The Jews who were listening did not much like this idea. "How," they wondered, "can this man give us his flesh to eat?" (v. 52). Jesus did not stop there, he went on to say something that they should have understood but did not.

> Then Jesus said to them, "Most assuredly, I say to
> you, unless you eat the flesh of the Son of Man and
> drink His blood, you have no life in you. Whoever
> eats My flesh and drinks My blood has eternal life,
> and I will raise him up at the last day. For My flesh is
> food indeed, and My blood is drink indeed. He who
> eats My flesh and drinks My blood abides in Me, and
> I in him" (vv. 53-56).

Anyone should immediately see the connection with the Lord's Supper in this saying. We take a little wine as a symbol of the blood of Christ, and a little bread as a symbol of his body. This is why, at the Last Supper, Jesus handed them the cup and said, "Take this and drink it. It is my blood of the covenant" (Matthew 26:28 NIV).

Even Jesus' disciples had a problem with this, calling it a hard saying. They should have recognized that this was language symbolic of a covenant, but they seem to have missed it. Some of his disciples went home and ceased to follow Jesus.

> Then Jesus said to the twelve, "Do you also want to go away?" But Simon Peter answered Him, "Lord, to whom shall we go? You have the words of eternal life. Also we have come to believe and know that You are the Christ, the Son of the living God" (vv. 67-69).

What is inescapable in this passage is the connection between the Passover, the Days of Unleavened Bread, and the Christian Passover which he will soon thereafter institute with his disciples.

---

i. *"Thou shalt not offer the blood of my sacrifice with leaven; neither shall the sacrifice of the feast of the Passover be left unto the morning" (Exodus 34:25).*

6

The Passover by Any Other Name

*And when the hour was come, he sat down,
and the twelve apostles with him. And he said unto them,
With desire I have desired to eat this Passover with you before I
suffer: For I say unto you, I will not any more eat thereof,
until it be fulfilled in the kingdom of God (Luke 22:14-16).*

If it seems strange that the early church was still observing the Passover and the Feast of Unleavened Bread some 30 years after the ascension of Christ, consider this. The vast majority of the Christian world still observes the "Passover," in their own way.

The word for the celebration of the resurrection of Jesus, in Greek, Latin, Spanish, Italian, and all the romance languages is *Pasca.* And *Pasca* is the Greek and Latin word for Passover. This is also the word that is usually translated "Easter," in English. So in Latin or Spanish, Resurrection Sunday is not called Easter. It is called "Passover." Now why is that? And what is the connection of the Jewish Passover to Christianity?

The connection comes straight out of the ministry and work of Jesus himself. First and foremost, there is this simple fact. Jesus observed the Passover with his disciples.

Now it came to pass, when Jesus had finished all these sayings, that He said to His disciples, "You know that after two days is the Passover, and the Son of Man will be delivered up to be crucified" (Matthew 26:1-2).

Let me point out some peculiarities of language that cause a little confusion to the modern reader. The term "Passover" is used in a broad variety of applications in the New Testament. For example, the term can refer to the lamb that was sacrificed on the day of Passover. The lamb is sometimes called, simply, "the Passover," without a qualifying word. Moses told the Israelites to "kill the Passover," i.e., kill the lamb.[i] And Jesus said that he wanted to "*eat* the Passover" with his disciples.[ii] Hold on to this thought, because while we can kill time, we can't really kill a day. We certainly cannot eat a day.

That said, the term "Passover" can also refer to the day the lamb was sacrificed, or it can refer to the entire festival of seven days in which unleavened bread was to be eaten. It even seems to be used for the season. In the Old Testament, the 14th day of the first month is called "The Lord's Passover." [iii] It was the day the Passover Lamb was killed. But the seven day feast, which is also called the Passover, begins on the 15th and continues for seven days.

It doesn't take long to realize that this could lead to some confusion for the modern reader. It didn't seem to confuse anyone in the first century, but the Passover was a part of their lives. They recognized the ambiguity of the term "Passover" and took its meaning from the context. They drew a distinction, though, when it came to the first day of unleavened bread. That was called "the Feast Day."

Then assembled together the chief priests, and the scribes, and the elders of the people, unto the palace of the high priest, who was called Caiaphas, And consulted that they might take Jesus by subtilty, and kill him. But they said, Not on the feast day, lest there be an uproar among the people (Matthew 26:3-5 KJV).

"Not on the feast day." This is important. The "feast day" was the 15th day of the first month of their calendar. It was a holyday, one of the "appointed times of Jehovah," and it was a Sabbath day – that is, a day when no ordinary work was to be done and the people were to assemble. It was also called, "The Passover." The 14th, the day the lambs were killed and the day Jesus was crucified, was *not* a Sabbath day, but it also was "The Passover." [iv]

It was a day of preparation for the Feast. The priests made a deliberate decision not to kill Jesus on the holyday but to get it out of the way before the feast.[v] The effect of this was to bring about the crucifixion and death of Jesus at the hour the Passover lambs were being killed in the Temple. This underlines Paul's expression, "Christ our Passover is sacrificed for us." [vi]

But there is still room for the modern reader to misunderstand.

> Now on the first day of the Feast of the Unleavened Bread the disciples came to Jesus, saying to Him, "Where do You want us to prepare for You to eat the Passover?" And He said, "Go into the city to a certain man, and say to him, 'The Teacher says, My time is at hand; I will keep the Passover at your house with My disciples.'" So the disciples did as Jesus had directed them; and they prepared the Passover. When evening had come, He sat down with the twelve (Matthew 26:17-20).

There is a parallel passage in Luke that is revealing. Luke puts it this way: "Now the feast of unleavened bread drew near, which is called the Passover" (Luke 22:1). Note that the entire festival is called the Passover. Luke continues to say, "Then came the day of unleavened bread, when the Passover must be killed" (v. 7).

It is very clear from the law, that the first day of unleavened bread was the 15th while the day the Passover was killed was on the 14th. Why then is the 14th called a day of unleavened bread? It is merely a matter of custom and usage. The custom of the Jews was to get all the leavening out of their homes on the evening before the Passover lamb was killed. Bear in mind that in Jewish custom, a day began at sunset, so the 14th day of the month, the Lord's Passover, began at sunset. So in popular usage, the 14th was a day of unleavened bread as well. The law called for seven days. The Jewish custom led to eight days of Unleavened Bread. The entire time, the season, is also called "The Passover."

> And He sent Peter and John, saying, "Go and prepare the Passover for us, that we may eat." So they said to Him, "Where do You want us to prepare?" And He said to them, "Behold, when you have entered the city, a man will meet you carrying a pitcher of water; follow him into the house which he enters. Then you shall say to the master of the house, 'The Teacher says to you, Where is the guest room where I may eat the Passover with My disciples?' Then he will show you a large, furnished upper room; there make ready."
> So they went and found it just as He had said to them, and they prepared the Passover. When the hour had come, He sat down, and the twelve apostles with Him. Then He said to them, "With fervent desire I have desired to eat this Passover with you before I suffer; for I say to you, I will no longer eat of it until it is fulfilled in the kingdom of God" (Luke 22:8-16).

There is no question but that Jesus called this meal they were eating "The Passover." And this has posed a conundrum for scholars ever since. Why? Because the Passover lambs were not to be killed until the next afternoon, and the prevailing Jewish custom of the day was to eat the Passover the following night.

Samuele Bacchiocchi has a fascinating discussion of the problem of sacrificing all the Passover lambs in time for the beginning of the feast.[vii] When you take into account that, according to Josephus, there were between two and three million people in Jerusalem for the Passover, it should be obvious that not all the lambs could be killed at the time specified in the law. Dr. Bacchiocchi does the math and concludes that to finish sacrificing the lambs by Friday sunset, the priests might have had to start the task Thursday noon.

The priests naturally had to make judgments in how the law was carried out. The original Passover was sacrificed at every household and could be done all at once, at even, at the time of the evening sacrifice. When the sacrifices were later centralized, that became, quite simply, impossible. The priests would have begun the sacrifice of the lambs whenever it was necessary for them to be ready in time to be eaten the night of the Feast. Thus, it's apparent that a Passover lamb might well have been available for Jesus and his disciples a night earlier than the time the Jews ate the Passover.

Jesus' emphasis on "this Passover" and "before I suffer" may indicate that this was an exceptional Passover, eaten a night early because of his impending death. The unusual expression, "With desire I have desired," (KJV) is very strong. Continuing:

> Then He took the cup, and gave thanks, and said, "Take this and divide it among yourselves; for I say to you, I will not drink of the fruit of the vine until the kingdom of God comes." And He took bread, gave thanks and broke it, and gave it to them, saying, "This is My body which is given for you; do this in remembrance of Me." Likewise He also took the cup after supper, saying, "This cup is the new covenant in My blood, which is shed for you" (Luke 22:17-20).

I hope the significance of this is not lost on us. This ceremony which we may call "The Lord's Supper" or "Holy Communion," in its origins was "The Passover." And this carries with it some important implications regarding the frequency of observance. The Passover was an annual observance. It was not done weekly or quarterly, or whenever you got around to it. The dropping of the name of the observance has allowed a variety of times of observance. The Passover, which should draw us all together on the same day, got changed to "The Lord's Supper," or some variant, and an important aspect of the day was lost.

Paul addresses this issue in his letter to the Corinthians. They were observing the feast, but observing it improperly.

> Now in giving these instructions I do not praise you, since you come together not for the better but for the worse. For first of all, when you come together as a

church, I hear that there are divisions among you, and in part I believe it. For there must also be factions among you, that those who are approved may be recognized among you. Therefore when you come together in one place, *it is not to eat the Lord's Supper*. For in eating, each one takes his own supper ahead of others; and one is hungry and another is drunk (1 Corinthians 11:17-21).

It is from this accidental reference that the term "The Lord's Supper" passes into the language as the name of the event. But Paul is making the point that they are eating their *own* supper instead of the Lord's Supper which, as we will see, is the Passover.

What! Do you not have houses to eat and drink in? Or do you despise the church of God and shame those who have nothing? What shall I say to you? Shall I praise you in this? I do not praise you. For I received from the Lord that which I also delivered to you: that the Lord Jesus on the same night in which He was betrayed took bread (vv. 22-23).

Note well. Paul establishes the authority for this observance by quoting Jesus' instructions given personally to him. An important part of what he received of the Lord was the *time* of Jesus' observance: "the same night in which he was betrayed." The Jewish day began at sunset, and Jesus was betrayed in the night leading up to the day of the 14th, the day of his crucifixion. Paul and his readers understood that this is an annual event, not an occasional event.

And when He had given thanks, He broke it and said, "Take, eat; this is My body which is broken for you; do this in remembrance of Me." In the same manner He also took the cup after supper, saying, "This cup is the new covenant in My blood. This do, as often as you drink it, in remembrance of Me." For as often as you eat this bread and drink this cup, you proclaim the Lord's death till He comes (vv. 24-26).

51

Once the observance is cut loose from its identity in the Passover, this can be taken to mean that you can do it often. But when you start from the premise that it is an *annual* observance, which the Passover was, then the passage doesn't support occasional observance. The emphasis is on the meaning, not the time. Paul is simply saying that *"When* ye eat this bread, and drink this cup, ye do show the Lord's death till he come." And of course, the time to do this is on the anniversary of the Lord's death.

> Therefore whoever eats this bread or drinks this cup of the Lord in an unworthy manner will be guilty of the body and blood of the Lord. But let a man examine himself, and so let him eat of the bread and drink of the cup. For he who eats and drinks in an unworthy manner eats and drinks judgment to himself, not discerning the Lord's body. For this reason many are weak and sick among you, and many sleep (vv. 27-30).

As noted in a previous chapter, this passage poses some problems. I think a lot of Christian folk observe this ceremony with full understanding of the Lord's blood. But in many churches, not much is said about the Lord's body, nor about Paul's cryptic statement: "For this cause many are weak and sickly among you, and many sleep." The failure to discern the Lord's body, strangely, had led to death. How on earth could that be?

When I finally came to think this through, my search took me to Isaiah 53, which is widely understood to be a prophecy of Christ's Passion. It is important, because it underlines the very question that bothered me. Why did Jesus have to suffer? Why wasn't dying for us enough?

> Who has believed what we have heard? And to whom has the arm of the LORD been revealed? For he grew up before him like a young plant, and like a root out of dry ground; he had no form or majesty that we should look at him, nothing in his appearance that we should desire him. He was despised and rejected by

others; a man of suffering and acquainted with infirmity; and as one from whom others hide their faces he was despised, and we held him of no account (Isaiah 53:1-3 NRSV).

The prophet places himself among the Jewish leadership who, when the Messiah came into their midst, rejected him, despised him, held him of no account. Jesus himself was "a man of suffering," but not for his own sins.

Surely he has borne *our* infirmities and carried *our* diseases; yet we accounted him stricken, struck down by God, and afflicted. But he was wounded for our transgressions, crushed for our iniquities; upon him was the punishment that made us whole, and by his bruises we are healed (vv. 4-5).

It is almost as though men look at Jesus and say, "Oh, he must have done something very bad. God has stricken him," as though it had nothing to do with us. Yet he was wounded for our transgressions and by his bruises, by the stripes laid on his back, we are healed. Generally, when people look at this, they spiritualize it, they conclude that we are healed spiritually. But when you think about it, throughout his earthly ministry, one of the most important aspects of Jesus' ministry was all the people he healed. People came from everywhere to be healed, people were carried on litters to him for healing. Jesus healed person after person, and the lame were not merely made to feel better, they were made to walk and run.

On one occasion, they tore up a roof to let a man down on ropes before Jesus. They couldn't get through the crush at the door. When Jesus saw this man and the faith demonstrated by his friends, he said, "Son, your sins be forgiven you." [viii]

This generated an immediate question among those present. How can this man forgive sins? Jesus replied, "For whether is easier, to say, Thy sins be forgiven thee; or to say, Arise, and walk? But that ye may know that the Son of man hath power on earth to forgive sins" (Matthew 9:5-6). Jesus makes the point that he has the power to forgive sins, and right here he connects it to the power to heal people who were sick.

What it means is this. We mess up our lives in so many ways. We hurt ourselves in so many ways, and so many of the ways we hurt ourselves are *physical*. It was necessary that in bearing our sins and iniquities, Jesus not only had to die for us, he had to bear our suffering as well. He suffered, not only to give us eternal life, but so he could heal us.

> All we like sheep have gone astray; we have all turned to our own way, and the LORD has laid on him the iniquity of us all. He was oppressed, and he was afflicted, yet he did not open his mouth; like a lamb that is led to the slaughter, and like a sheep that before its shearers is silent, so he did not open his mouth. By a perversion of justice he was taken away. Who could have imagined his future? For he was cut off from the land of the living, stricken for the transgression of my people.

> They made his grave with the wicked and his tomb with the rich, although he had done no violence, and there was no deceit in his mouth. Yet it was the will of the LORD to crush him with pain. When you make his life an offering for sin, he shall see his offspring, and shall prolong his days; through him the will of the LORD shall prosper (Isaiah 53:6-10 NRSV).

All this is said so you and I could understand. So that I, even as a teenager, could understand that it was necessary, not only that Jesus die for my sins, but that he suffer for my sins as well. When you think about the night in which he was betrayed, what was the first thing that happened to him, that sometimes happens to us as well? He was betrayed by one of his closest friends.

What else happened on that night? He was arrested, all of his friends ran away, one of them leaving his clothes behind, he was in such haste. Unfortunately, this sort of thing happens to us as well. We are betrayed, sometimes by friends who are close to us. We find ourselves in trouble, with the whole world coming down on our shoulders, and we look around for our friends and find that they are all gone.

On this night, Jesus suffered in all the ways in which you and I suffer. Through that long night he was beaten, he was humiliated, he was spit on. Why? Because those things happen to you and me. We, through our sins and our foolishness, put ourselves in situations where we are mocked, we are humiliated, where our lives come crashing down around our heads. And Jesus suffered the same way, on our behalf.

Never forget this. The thread links the Passover inexorably to the suffering and death of your Savior. And the thread comes directly to you.

---

i. Exodus 12:21.

ii. Mark 14:14.

iii. Leviticus 23:5.

iv. Leviticus 23:5.

v. It was about this time, when the priests were planning judicial murder, that Judas Iscariot came to them and cut a deal to betray Jesus for 30 pieces of silver.

vi. 1 Corinthians 5:7.

vii. Samuele Bacchiocchi, *God's Festivals in Scripture and History, Part 1, The Spring Festivals*, (1995), pp. 63-65.

viii. Matthew 9:2.

7

Three Days and Three Nights

*Now the LORD had prepared a great fish to swallow
up Jonah. And Jonah was in the belly of the fish three
days and three nights (Jonah 1:17).*

Nearly the whole Christian world believes that Jesus was crucified on Friday and rose from the dead Sunday morning. But if you have read the New Testament with any care at all, you may have a lingering question about this. Jesus said plainly that he would be in the grave for three days *and* three nights. How can we squeeze three days and three nights into the time between Friday, about sunset, and Sunday morning before daybreak? Here is what Jesus said:

> But He answered and said to them, "An evil and adulterous generation seeks after a sign, and no sign will be given to it except the sign of the prophet Jonah. For as Jonah was three days and three nights in the belly of the great fish, so will the Son of Man be three days and three nights in the heart of the earth" (Matthew 12:39-40).

Now, how do we get three days *and three nights* between late Friday afternoon and early Sunday morning – a period of about 36 hours? We can count this off on our fingers: Friday night, Saturday,

Saturday night, and we end up with one day and two nights. Yes, I know some people think it is a Greek idiom, but you don't have to be a scholar to check that out. If you know how to use a concordance, you can take a Bible and easily walk through the usage of these terms. "Three days" may be ambiguous, but when you toss in the expression "and three nights" you add an emphasis to the expression that really requires that third night.

Let me suggest an alternative for you to consider. Suppose Jesus was not crucified on Friday. Suppose he was crucified on a Wednesday. That would mean that in the year Jesus was crucified, the 14th day of the first month of the Jewish calendar would have been on a Wednesday. In that case he would have been buried late on Wednesday afternoon. You can then count them on your fingers. Wednesday night, Thursday, Thursday night, Friday, Friday night, Saturday – three days and three nights. So why does the whole Christian world think otherwise? This is a fascinating story, so settle back and let's take a look.

Late in the afternoon on the day of his crucifixion, Jesus finally ended his suffering and died. From Mark's account:

> And Jesus cried out with a loud voice, and breathed His last. Then the veil of the temple was torn in two from top to bottom. So when the centurion, who stood opposite Him, saw that He cried out like this and breathed His last, he said, "Truly this Man was the Son of God!" There were also women looking on from afar, among whom were Mary Magdalene, Mary the mother of James the Less and of Joses, and Salome, who also followed Him and ministered to Him when He was in Galilee, and many other women who came up with Him to Jerusalem. Now when evening had come, because it was the Preparation Day, that is, *the day before the Sabbath,* Joseph of Arimathea, a prominent council member, who was himself waiting for the kingdom of God, coming and taking courage, went in to Pilate and asked for the body of Jesus (Mark 15:37-43).

Now everyone knows the Sabbath is Saturday, so this had to be Friday, the preparation day, right? Well, no, not necessarily. Continuing from Luke's account of the same events:

> And behold, a man named Joseph, who was a member of the Council, a good and righteous man (he had not consented to their plan and action), a man from Arimathea, a city of the Jews, who was waiting for the kingdom of God; this man went to Pilate and asked for the body of Jesus. And he took it down and wrapped it in a linen cloth, and laid Him in a tomb cut into the rock, where no one had ever lain. And it was the preparation day, and the Sabbath was *about to begin* (Luke 23:50-54 NASB).

So it was firmly established that this is a preparation day followed closely by a Sabbath day. Backing up just slightly, here is what *John* says about the death of Jesus.

> After this, Jesus, knowing that all things had already been accomplished, in order that the Scripture might be fulfilled, said, "I am thirsty." A jar full of sour wine was standing there; so they put a sponge full of the sour wine upon a branch of hyssop, and brought it up to His mouth. When Jesus therefore had received the sour wine, He said, "It is finished!" And He bowed His head, and gave up His spirit. The Jews therefore, because it was the day of preparation, so that the bodies should not remain on the cross on the Sabbath (for that Sabbath was a high day), asked Pilate that their legs might be broken, and that they might be taken away (John 19:28-31 NASB).

The Sabbath in question was a *high day* because it was the First Day of Unleavened Bread. The 15th day of the first month was a Sabbath day in the Jewish calendar, no matter what day of the week it fell on. So if Jesus was crucified on the 14th, on a Wednesday, then Thursday would have been a Sabbath day. See Leviticus 23:24-39, where annual holydays are called Sabbaths regardless of the day of the week. (All the holydays except one fall on calendar dates, not on particular days of the week.)

So nothing of what we have read so far *requires* a Friday crucifixion. Why is this so confusing in the New Testament? Because none of the Gospel writers anticipated our problem with this some 2000 years later. For them, it was as clear as crystal. Going back a little further in Mark's account:

> After two days it was the Passover and the Feast of Unleavened Bread. And the chief priests and the scribes sought how they might take Him by trickery and put Him to death. But they said, "Not during the feast, lest there be an uproar of the people." (Mark 14:1-2).

They wanted to get this whole mess out of the way before the high day, the 15th. It would be a Sabbath, no matter if it was on a Thursday, which it appears to have been in this year. Continuing with John's account:

> And after these things Joseph of Arimathea, being a disciple of Jesus, but a secret one, for fear of the Jews, asked Pilate that he might take away the body of Jesus; and Pilate granted permission. He came therefore, and took away His body. And Nicodemus came also, who had first come to Him by night; bringing a mixture of myrrh and aloes, about a hundred pounds weight. And so they took the body of Jesus, and bound it in linen wrappings with the spices, as is the burial custom of the Jews. Now in the place where He was crucified there was a garden; and in the garden a new tomb, in which no one had yet been laid. Therefore on account of the Jewish day of preparation, *because the tomb was nearby*, they laid Jesus there (John 19:38-42 NASB).

Why was the location of the burial important? Because a Sabbath day was coming on. They had to get the body of Jesus down off the stake and the work of burial finished before sundown, when the Sabbath began. There is no slack in here. I have included all this information to establish that Jesus' body went into the tomb in the last moments before the sun went down, beginning the Sabbath day.

So our question is, was this late on Friday, just before the Sabbath, or late on Wednesday, just before the *festival* Sabbath? The latter of these alternatives would give us our three days and three nights.

Now notice two fascinating items. It was the custom of the time to wrap a body with spices, mummy-style, before burial. The problem in this case was that there was no time. Joseph and Nicodemus did a hasty job of preparing the body. The women wanted to do more in the way of burial customs and planned to do so. Luke, from a slightly different perspective, notes: "And the women also, which came with him from Galilee, followed after, and beheld the sepulchre, and how his body was laid. And they returned, and prepared spices and ointments; and *rested the sabbath day* according to the commandment" (Luke 23:55-56).

If you are reading carefully, you will realize that there is a problem here. They had to bury Jesus in haste because there was no time. How then could these women go home and do the work of preparing more spices before the Sabbath began?

There is another account of this in Mark's gospel. It isn't a major point with Mark. It is almost an aside: "*When the Sabbath was over*, Mary Magdalene, Mary the mother of James, and Salome bought spices so that they might go to anoint Jesus' body" (Mark 16:1 NIV

So they bought their spices when the Sabbath was over, prepared their ointments and spices and *then* rested the Sabbath day. It is easy to miss since the details of the sequence of events are spread over four gospels. But the women saw Jesus buried in the last minutes before sundown beginning the Sabbath. [i] Then, when the Sabbath was over, they bought spices, prepared them, and then rested the Sabbath day according to the commandment. This second Sabbath was indeed Saturday.

When these men wrote all this down, more than thirty years

had passed since the events. Each of them told part of the story, but neither saw any reason to explain to us that there were two Sabbaths that week with a day in between – Thursday and Saturday. If we have this right, then we have no problem at all in finding three days and three nights between Jesus' burial and resurrection.

But perhaps we should also ask why three days and three nights even matter. How did they get into the picture? To answer that, we can start by looking at another remarkable resurrection. There was a family in Bethany who were very special to Jesus. He loved Lazarus, Mary and Martha, and no doubt had spent a lot of time with them. So when they sent word to Jesus that Lazarus was dying, they expected him to come to them right away. But when word came to Jesus, he delayed for two more days. He told his disciples, "This sickness is not unto death, but for the glory of God, that the Son of God may be glorified through it" (John 11:4).

After delaying these extra days, waiting deliberately for Lazarus to die, Jesus said to his disciples, "Our friend Lazarus sleeps, but I go that I may wake him up." The disciples didn't catch his drift at first, so Jesus spoke more plainly: "Lazarus is dead. And I am glad for your sakes that I was not there, that you may believe. Nevertheless let us go to him" (vv. 11-15).

It is clear enough right from the start that Jesus intended, not merely to heal Lazarus, but to raise him from the dead. The whole episode, though, was terribly hard on Mary and Martha.

When Martha heard Jesus was coming, she left the house to meet him, Mary staying behind. Then Martha said to Jesus, "Lord, if You had been here, my brother would not have died. But even now I know that whatever You ask of God, God will give You" (vv. 21-22).

The pain of this moment is palpable. And that last phrase of Martha's seems to imply that she thought Jesus might indeed raise Lazarus from the dead. Jesus replied: "Thy brother shall rise again." It is the answer we hear at funeral after funeral of people we love. Your loved one will rise again, you will be reunited in the day of resurrection.

"I know," said Martha, "that he shall rise again in the resurrection at the last day." Jesus' answer to this plaintive cry is the hope that all of us carry:

> I am the resurrection and the life. He who believes in
> Me, though he may die, he shall live. And whoever
> lives and believes in Me shall never die. Do you
> believe this? (John 11:25-26).

Martha did believe, and she returned to the house and quietly told Mary that Jesus had come at last. Mary got up quickly and went to Jesus. When she found him she fell down at his feet and said, "Lord, if you had only been here, my brother would not have died." That had to hurt, even though Jesus knew what he was going to do. Knowing what Mary and Martha had to suffer, "he groaned in the spirit and was troubled" (v. 33). Here was Mary crying like her heart would break, along with a collection of mourners also who had followed her from the house.

"Where have you laid him?" he asked. "Lord, come and see," they replied. "Jesus wept" (vv. 34-35).

These two words speak volumes about Jesus' humanity. Even knowing he was going to raise Lazarus from the dead, he hurt inside for the pain others were feeling. And there is something inside all of us, no matter how well prepared we think we are for the death of a loved one, that makes us weep in the face of death.

Still groaning, Jesus approached the cave where they had placed Lazarus. There was a stone across the entrance and Jesus told them to take it away. Martha protested, "But, Lord," she said, "by this time there is a bad odor, *for he has been there four days*" (v. 39).

And this begins to answer the question of Jesus' delay. It had to be established that Lazarus was truly dead before Jesus raised him. Otherwise it might have been argued that Lazarus only appeared to be dead. Jesus called out, "Lazarus, come forth!" And the man who had been dead staggered out of the tomb still wrapped in his shroud.

We tend to forget in this day and age when we can be more certain through science when a person is dead, that in ages gone by, they were not so sure. Some held a belief that the soul stayed with the body for three days after death. Here is one Jewish source:

> Tractate Semahot (Mourning) says: "One may go
> out to the cemetery for three days to inspect the dead
> for a sign of life, without fear that this smacks of

heathen practice. For it happened that a man was inspected after three days, and he went on to live twenty-five years; still another went on to have five children and died later." [ii]

Other Jewish sources believe they should only use wood coffins, and they do not embalm the dead. The reason offered is that "as the body decays, the soul ascends to Heaven." [iii] The decay was assumed to begin *after three days*. So if Jesus had been buried at sunset on Friday and rose while it was still dark Sunday morning, he would have been in the tomb less than 36 hours. The Pharisees and others might have argued that he had not been dead, that this was no miracle. He had merely lapsed into a coma and then recovered. So the three days and three nights turn out to be more important than one might think.

But now we have raised yet another problem. This sequence suggests that Jesus rose from the dead on Saturday evening instead of Sunday morning. How do we deal with that little anomaly? This may come as a surprise to you, but there is no passage in the Bible that tells us precisely when Jesus rose from the dead. There is a reason for that: there were no witnesses to the actual event. The first people who saw Jesus alive saw him on Sunday morning, but that does not mean that was *the time of the resurrection.*

But wait. What about Mark's statement, "Now when Jesus was risen early the first day of the week, he appeared first to Mary Magdalene, out of whom he had cast seven devils"? (Mark 16:9). Bear in mind that no one witnessed the actual resurrection of Jesus, so no one could testify as to the moment. Thus, this passage is describing, not the time of the resurrection, but the time of Jesus' appearing to Mary. The Greek texts have no punctuation, so all the commas and periods are left to the translators. Just put the comma in the right place and all becomes clear. "Now when Jesus was risen, early the first day of the week he appeared first to Mary Magdalene." Also note in Mark's testimony that the first person to see Jesus alive was Mary. That confirms that no one saw the moment of the resurrection of Jesus.

There is nothing in the Gospel accounts to dispute that Jesus rose from the dead Saturday evening rather than Sunday morning.

Three days and three nights from his burial would naturally take us to an evening. But there is something else that is highly suggestive.

Remember that I have been telling you that the Passover and the Days of Unleavened Bread are all about Christ. There was, at this season, a little noticed ceremony in the Temple service that was also all about Christ. This was the season of the first ripe barley. But the people were not allowed to eat any of that year's crop until a small portion of it had been offered to God by the priest. It is called "the wave sheaf" in the King James Version, and the ceremony is described in Leviticus.

> And the LORD spoke to Moses, saying, "Speak to the children of Israel, and say to them: 'When you come into the land which I give to you, and reap its harvest, then you shall bring a sheaf of the firstfruits of your harvest to the priest. He shall wave the sheaf before the LORD, to be accepted on your behalf; on the day after the Sabbath the priest shall wave it'" (Leviticus 23:9-11).

This could not be done on the Sabbath because it was an act of work, of harvesting and preparing the grain offering. So it was done when the Sabbath ended. The ceremony is also described in Alfred Edersheim's well known book, *The Temple, Its Ministry and Service.*[iv] The ceremony had to take place after the Sabbath day according to the law. It was an act of work to "harvest" the wave sheaf.

So, just after sundown, at the end of the three days and three nights that had passed since Jesus was buried, a noisy little procession of people made their way down from the Temple carrying torches and no doubt passing around a little wine. This is a festival, and a harvest festival to boot. They are having a good time. They came to a field that had been selected ahead of time where there were several bundles of grain already tied together, but not yet cut from the ground.

One of the sheaves was selected, and a man stood over it holding a sickle over his head. He shouted a series of questions to the crowd gathered around him and they shouted their answers back at him:

"Is the sun down?" he shouted. The crowd answered, "Yes!" "This sheaf?" "Yes!" "With this sickle?" "Yes!" "Shall I reap?" "Yes!"

And with a stroke, he cut the sheaf from the ground. That may have been the moment that Jesus, who is also called "the Firstfruits," opened his eyes in the tomb. Through that night, the sheaf was prepared for offering. The grain was threshed from it and parched in a pan over fire. Early the next morning, it was presented to God in the Temple. This sheaf is the very first of the firstfruits from the fields around Jerusalem. Now consider this very *New* Testament idea:

> But now Christ is risen from the dead, and has become the *firstfruits* of those who have fallen asleep. For since by man came death, by Man also came the resurrection of the dead. For as in Adam all die, even so in Christ all shall be made alive. But each one in his own order: Christ the *firstfruits*, afterward those who are Christ's at His coming (1 Corinthians 15:20-23).

No grain could be harvested until the wave sheaf of the firstfruits was presented to God. Jesus Christ was the firstfruits and, according to the book of Revelation, the first *born* from the dead. [v] So the connection is made to the moment of Jesus' resurrection.

Then there was a striking instance on the morning of Jesus' first appearance to his disciples. The very first to see the risen Christ was none other than the broken hearted Mary Magdalene. She stood at the entrance to the tomb, weeping and stooped down to look inside. There, she saw two angels in white robes. They said "Woman, why are you weeping?" Thinking they were the men who had removed Jesus' body, she replied: "Because they have taken away my Lord, and I do not know where they have laid Him" (John 20:13).

In frustration, Mary turned around and saw a man she thought was the gardener. He also asked her, "Woman, why are you weeping? Whom are you seeking?"

"Sir," Mary replied, "if You have carried Him away, tell me where You have laid Him, and I will take Him away" (v. 15). At that point, Jesus called her by name and for the first time, she realized that Jesus was alive.

> She turned and said to Him, "Rabboni!" (which is to
> say, Teacher). Jesus said to her, Do not cling to Me,
> for I have not yet ascended to My Father; but go to
> My brethren and say to them, 'I am ascending to My
> Father and your Father, and to My God and your
> God'" (John 20:16-17).

Later that day, Jesus would allow his disciples to touch him.
The implication is that between the time Mary saw him and the time
he met with his disciples, he had ascended to the Father and returned.
There is a minor difference in translation from the King James
version, which reads, "Touch me no t; for I am not yet ascended to
my Father." [vi]

In either case it is plain that between the time Jesus saw Mary,
and later his disciples, he ascended to the Father and returned. This
would have been very near to the moment when the sheaf of
firstfruits was being offered in the Temple. The parallel with the
wave sheaf cannot be ignored. In the symbolism of the events, Jesus
came to life when the sheaf was cut, was prepared during the night, [vii]
and was presented to the Father the next morning.

Now there is another curious thing about this incident. It took
place on the first day of the week, right? Well, yes, but there is more
to it than that. Remember that these people were Jews, and nowhere
in the Bible do they refer to the day after the Sabbath as "the first day
of the week." To a Jew, what we call Sunday would *always* be called
the "morrow after the Sabbath." [viii]

So why do we read this in the New Testament: "Now after the
Sabbath, as it began to dawn toward the first day of the week, Mary
Magdalene and the other Mary came to look at the grave" (Matthew
28:1 NASB)? The normal way for a Jew to say this would be "Now
after the Sabbath, as it began to dawn, Mary Magdalene and the other
Mary came to look at the grave."

What is the significance of the "first day of the week"? There
is no word for "week" in this passage. Literally it is "the first of the
Sabbaths" and it is *plural*. Where in the Bible do we have a series of
Sabbaths described? We were close to it before:

You shall eat neither bread nor parched grain nor fresh grain until the same day that you have brought an offering to your God; it shall be a statute forever throughout your generations in all your dwellings. And you shall count for yourselves from the day after the Sabbath, from the day that you brought the sheaf of the wave offering: seven Sabbaths shall be completed. Count fifty days to the day after the seventh Sabbath; then you shall offer a new grain offering to the LORD (Leviticus 23:14-16).

This 50th day is the day Christians know as Pentecost. So the day of the firstfruits offering was day one of the seven weeks of harvest leading up to Pentecost, also known as the "Feast of Weeks" because it comes at the end of seven weeks.

So when we find this expression in the New Testament: "Now after the Sabbath, as it began to dawn toward the first day of the week," it is a reference to the first day of the seven weeks leading up to Pentecost. It is not merely a day of the week, but a singular day of the *year*. So how and when did this get changed to the first day of the week? And how did Christians come to observe "Easter" instead of the Day of Firstfruits?

---

i. Jewish days ran from sunset to sunset, so the Sabbath would begin at sunset rather than at midnight.

ii. jacksonsnyder.com/arc/2005/stinkest.htm

iii. www.jdcc.org/sepoct97/doc1.htm.

iv. All of Edersheim's work is available on the Internet at www.studylight.org/his/bc/edr/.

v. "and from Jesus Christ, who is the faithful witness, *the firstborn from the dead*, and the ruler of the kings of the earth. To him who loves us and has freed us from our sins by his blood" (Revelation 1:5 NIV

vi. I think the King James Version is correct here. The Greek word is *haptomai*, which in many applications can only mean "touch." See Matthew 9:21 for one example among many.

vii. We know nothing of what Jesus was doing in the time between his resurrection and his appearance to Mary Magdalene. The wave sheaf was taken, threshed, parched and a small basket of it taken into the Temple to be waved before God. Perhaps angels ministered to Jesus in those hours, preparing him for his presentation to the father. He had, after all, been severely mistreated in the hours before his burial. It is plain enough that his appearance was altered. Mary didn't recognize him at first. All this is highly suggestive of the bodily resurrection of Jesus.

viii. In the Old Testament, the word "week" is the Hebrew *shabua*, "seven." The days of the week could only be designated in relation to the Sabbath. Hence, Sunday is "the morrow after the Sabbath," in the Old Testament. See Leviticus 23:15. In the New Testament, the same usage is found. There, the word translated "week" is *Sabbaton*, the genitive *plural* of "Sabbath." The writers of both Testaments were Hebrew in their usage, and what we call the first day of the week, they would call the morrow after the Sabbath.

8

From Passover to Easter

But now is Christ risen from the dead,
and become the firstfruits
of them that slept (1 Corinthians 15:20).

Occasionally, when I have said that "Easter" is nowhere mentioned in Bible, someone reminds me of the incident where Herod has arrested Peter and put him in prison, "intending after *Easter* to bring him forth to the people" (Acts 12:4). The problem is that the Greek word translated "Easter" is the Greek *Pascha* which, everywhere else it is used in the New Testament, is translated "Passover." So why, 1600 years later, did the King James translators use Easter instead of Passover here?

As early as the third century, the entire church had begun to confuse Easter and Passover. How did it happen that the early church stopped observing the Passover and began observing Easter?

First, realize that at the beginning, this was not a Passover/Easter controversy. It was a calendar controversy. It was a question of *when* the church would observe *Pascha,* which is the Greek and Latin word for Passover. The issue is confusing, because even modern English works, when citing early Greek and Latin documents, translate *Pascha* as "Easter." When discussing the Jewish observance, they render *Pascha* as "Passover."

But what was at issue in the second century was whether they would observe Passover on any day of the week, as the Hebrew calendar allowed, or only on a Sunday. Later the issue became *which* Sunday.

The issue is further confused by a misunderstanding of the significance of the Sunday following the crucifixion of Jesus. This was an important day in the Jewish calendar. As noted in the previous chapter, it was the day of offering the firstfruits of the barley harvest. It was also the first day of the countdown to Pentecost, 50 days later.

Pentecost is a Greek word, and therefore it is not found in the Old Testament. There, the day is called the Feast of Harvest,[i] the Feast of Weeks (i.e., sevens)[ii] and the Feast of Firstfruits.[iii] On the Feast of Firstfruits, two leavened loaves of bread were lifted up to God, loaves made of the harvest of the firstfruits.[iv]

So here is the pattern. On the evening after the Sabbath was over, the very first sheaf of grain of the early harvest was cut from the ground. It was prepared that night by threshing the barley from the chaff and then parching it over a fire. The next morning, the priest lifted an omer[v] of the grain to God as the presentation of the firstfruits of the harvest. Now, compare this to Christian theology of the resurrection.

> But now is Christ risen from the dead, and become the firstfruits of them that slept. For since by man came death, by man came also the resurrection of the dead. For as in Adam all die, even so in Christ shall all be made alive. But every man in his own order: Christ the firstfruits; afterward they that are Christ's at his coming (1 Corinthians 15:20-23 KJV).

It is clear enough, in referring to "Christ the firstfruits," that Paul is referring directly to that first sheaf offered on the morning after the Sabbath by the priest. His wording leaves no room for doubt.

James will follow up on what is to follow: "Of His own will He brought us forth by the word of truth, that *we* might be a kind of firstfruits of His creatures" (James 1:18). What we see here is Christ as the first of the firstfruits in the resurrection, with the remainder of the firstfruits to follow at his coming.

So this particular Sunday was important to both Jews and Christians. To Jews, it was the day of the offering of the firstfruits, the first day of the seven weeks to the Feast of Firstfruits. To Christians, it was the morning of Jesus' presentation to the Father and of his first appearance to his disciples after his resurrection from the dead. And it was the first day of the seven weeks to Pentecost.

For the first Christians, the symbolism of the Jewish observance was seen to point directly to Christ. The connection was clear and strong from the start. The early church had not adopted a calendar different from that of the Jewish majority in the first century,[vi] so the comparison between liturgy and events was, to them, even more apparent.

Now consider this carefully. This Sunday was celebrated early on as the day of Christ's first appearance after his resurrection. It was an anniversary that appeared on the Jewish calendar on the first Sunday after Passover every year. As explained in the previous chapter, every place in the New Testament where you see the expression "the first day of the week," it is referring, not to a Sunday, but to a singular day of the *year*. It is the first day of the *weeks* leading up to Pentecost. It is an annual, not a weekly observance. It was, for want of a better term, "wave sheaf Sunday." How it got confused with Easter is an interesting story all in itself.

It is well established, both in the Bible and in history, that late in the first century the entire Christian church still observed *Pascha* on the 14th day of the first month of the Jewish calendar. This meant that *Pascha,* the Christian Passover, could fall on any day of the week. Meanwhile, much of the visible Christian church observed "resurrection Sunday" on the Sunday following the Passover.[vii] And, because it was the Passover season, they called the Sunday observance *Pascha.*

A controversy arose between the Western Christians, who observed *Pascha* on wave sheaf Sunday and the Eastern Christians, who observed it on the 14th day of the month. It is called the *Quartodeciman* controversy and is discussed at some length in the *Catholic Encyclopedia.* The controversy became important around A.D. 190.

But Easter is still not in the picture. These people were writing in Greek and Latin, and the word in both languages was

Pascha, Passover. The Sunday observance of *Pascha* won out in most of the known churches, but early in the fourth century a second controversy arose. They had mostly settled on Sunday, but now the question was *which* Sunday.

Through the intervening years, the churches had increasingly distanced themselves from the Jews, dropping as many links as they could.[viii] The council of Nicea, in the year 325 made the following rulings:

1. Easter must be celebrated by all throughout the world on the same Sunday;
2. This Sunday must follow the 14th day of the Paschal moon;
3. That moon was to be accounted the Paschal moon whose 14th day followed the spring equinox;
4. That some provision should be made, probably by the Church of Alexandria as best skilled in astronomical calculations, for determining the proper date of Easter and communicating it to the rest of the world (see St. Leo to the Emperor Marcian in Migne, P.L., LIV, 1055). [ix]

What they had done at first was to move *Pascha* to the Sunday following the Jewish Passover. Now they moved *Pascha* to the first Sunday after the first full moon after the spring equinox. It was still, to them, the *Pascha*, but they had, by accident or design, moved the Passover to coincide with an ancient pagan festival called Easter. The name, Easter, comes from the Anglo-Saxon goddess of the dawn. In pagan cultures, an annual spring festival was held in her honor. She was also a fertility goddess, hence the fertility symbols of eggs and rabbits.

So the celebration of Easter, with a sunrise service for the goddess of the dawn, and all the Easter egg hunts, and bunnies and stuff, is an entirely different holiday from the Passover. But because the church moved the Passover from its original date to the date of Easter, the two holidays have become conflated to this day.

> The name Easter comes from Eostre, an ancient Anglo-Saxon goddess, originally of the dawn. In pagan times an annual spring festival was held in her honor. Some

Easter customs have come from this and other pre-Christian spring festivals. Others come from the Passover feast of the Jews, observed in memory of their deliverance from Egypt. The word paschal comes from a Latin word that means belonging to Passover or to Easter. Formerly, Easter and the Passover were closely associated.

The resurrection of Jesus took place during the Passover. Christians of the Eastern church initially celebrated both holidays together. But the Passover can fall on any day of the week, and Christians of the Western church preferred to celebrate Easter on Sunday the day of the resurrection. [x]

Easter, as such, has absolutely nothing to do with Christianity. Wave Sheaf Sunday has somewhat to do with Christianity, because it is the day Jesus first appeared to his disciples, and it is the day when Jesus was presented to the Father as the firstfruits from the dead. This lies along our thread, because Wave Sheaf Sunday is the day when the priests in the Temple waved a sheaf of the firstfruits of the barley harvest before God. It is on the day after the Sabbath following *Pascha*, regardless of when the equinox takes place.

The days from Wave Sheaf Sunday to Pentecost were days of harvest, an idea somewhat foreign to a reader who is divorced from the land. But to the first readers of the New Testament books, the imagery was vivid. The resurrection of Jesus as the *firstfruits* revealed something very important – he was not going to be the only one resurrected from the dead. So the resurrection of the saints was a vital doctrine of the early church.

But the idea was not without its detractors. In these early days of the faith, heresies sprang up like weeds. One of the earliest dismissed the idea of a resurrection. It isn't entirely surprising, because even among the Jews there was a division between Pharisees and Sadducees on this very issue.[xi] Somehow, this schism made its way to Corinth.

Now if Christ be preached that he rose from the dead,

> how say some among you that there is no resurrection
> of the dead? But if there be no resurrection of the dead,
> then is Christ not risen: And if Christ be not risen, then
> is our preaching vain, and your faith is also vain. Yea,
> and we are found false witnesses of God; because we
> have testified of God that he raised up Christ: whom he
> raised not up, if so be that the dead rise not (1
> Corinthians 15:12-15 KJV).

Paul threw down the gauntlet. There was no middle ground on
this question. He and others had testified to the resurrection of Jesus.
They were not merely misguided enthusiasts. If the dead didn't rise,
then they were liars. This is precisely what is at issue in some
quarters today. Jesus was a good man, a great teacher, they say, but
he wasn't raised from the dead. But if Jesus wasn't raised, all his
claims to divinity would brand him as a charlatan, or a madman. Paul
claims it goes even further than that. Following the thread through the
agricultural season of the spring harvest, Paul makes his way toward
Pentecost.

> For if the dead rise not, then is not Christ raised: And if
> Christ be not raised, your faith is vain; ye are yet in your
> sins. Then they also which are fallen asleep in Christ are
> perished. If in this life only we have hope in Christ, we
> are of all men most miserable. But now is Christ risen
> from the dead, and become the firstfruits of them that
> slept. For since by man came death, by man came also
> the resurrection of the dead. For as in Adam all die, even
> so in Christ shall all be made alive. But every man in his
> own order: Christ the firstfruits; afterward they that are
> Christ's at his coming (vv. 16-23).

The season of the grain harvest was Jesus' chosen metaphor.
There were two major harvest seasons in Palestine. The grain harvest
in the spring, and the fruit harvest in the autumn. The spring harvest,
which started with barley and ended with wheat, took place between
Passover and Pentecost. Pentecost is also called the Feast of
Firstfruits because the season begins and ends with an offering of the

firstfruit harvest – the first, barley, the second, wheat. So it is only natural that Jesus would use the harvest as an analogy for saving people.

> Then Jesus went about all the cities and villages, teaching in their synagogues, preaching the gospel of the kingdom, and healing every sickness and every disease among the people. But when He saw the multitudes, He was moved with compassion for them, because they were weary and scattered, like sheep having no shepherd. Then He said to His disciples, "The harvest truly is plentiful, but the laborers are few. Therefore pray the Lord of the harvest to send out laborers into His harvest" (Matthew 9:35-38).

The harvest metaphor is very strong in all of Jesus' teaching, and it is also strong in the holydays of the Bible. The firstfruits of Wave Sheaf Sunday and Pentecost are especially meaningful to Christians. I noted above that James spoke of the disciples as "a kind of firstfruits of his creatures" (James 1:18). We find the same metaphor in Revelation.

> Then I looked, and behold, a Lamb standing on Mount Zion, and with Him one hundred and forty-four thousand, having His Father's name written on their foreheads. And I heard a voice from heaven, like the voice of many waters, and like the voice of loud thunder. And I heard the sound of harpists playing their harps. They sang as it were a new song before the throne, before the four living creatures, and the elders; and no one could learn that song except the hundred and forty-four thousand who were redeemed from the earth. These are the ones who were not defiled with women, for they are virgins. These are the ones who follow the Lamb wherever He goes. These were redeemed from among men, *being firstfruits to God and to the Lamb* (Revelation 14:1-4).

The pattern is clear enough. Christ is the first of the firstfruits. The saints are the rest. It is a crying shame that the Christian churches have lost the thread of the holydays of the Bible. For in the annual observance of these days, the study and preaching of them in their seasons, there is so much to be learned about God and his plan for man.

---

i. Exodus 23:16.

ii. There is no word for "weeks," per se in Hebrew. The word commonly translated "weeks" is *shabuwa*, from *sheba*, the cardinal number seven. It is the past participle of *shaba*, "to seven," as in "to complete." So it is properly a "feast of sevens;" i.e. the seven weeks leading up to the Feast of Firstfruits.

iii. Exodus 34:22.

iv. Leviticus 23:17.

v. A dry measure of about two quarts.

vi. The calendar was crucial, because it defined the time of observance of the feasts. There is not a word in the New Testament to suggest any change from the Jewish observance. This comes from the *Catholic Encyclopedia*, article "Easter Controversy":

> The first was mainly concerned with the lawfulness of celebrating Easter on a weekday. We read in Eusebius (Hist. Eccl., V, xxiii): "A question of no small importance arose at that time [i.e., the time of Pope Victor, about A.D. 190]. The dioceses of all Asia, as from an older tradition, held that the fourteenth day of the moon, on which day the Jews were commanded to sacrifice the lamb, should always be observed as the feast of the life-giving pasch . . ."

vii. Ibid. It is of passing interest that in the *Catholic Encylcopedia's* citation of Eusebius and Irenaeus, they translate *Pascha* as "Easter."

viii. Samuele Bacchiocchi, in his landmark book, *From Sabbath to Sunday*, includes a thorough discussion of what he calls an "anti-Judaism of separation." See pp 170 ff.

ix. *Catholic Encyclopedia* (Online), article, "Easter."

x. *Funk & Wagnalls Knowledge Center Online*, article, "Easter."

xi. And when he had so said, there arose a dissension between the Pharisees and the Sadducees: and the multitude was divided. For the Sadducees say that there is no resurrection, neither angel, nor spirit: but the Pharisees confess both (Acts 23:7-8).

9

Pentecost

And when the day of Pentecost was fully come,
they were all with one accord in one place (Acts 2:1).

Pentecost is the exception. It is the one biblical holiday that many Christians *do* observe. In England, it used to be a national holiday, called Whitsunday, or White Sunday, because of the custom of wearing white after baptism. We were surprised on one visit to London when even the West End theaters were closed on Monday night after Whitsunday. Pentecost was a two-day holiday in England.

But many American churches seem to remain blissfully unaware of the Festival. "Pentecostal" is a word they connect with a charismatic movement that includes speaking in tongues, but has little to do with the Feast of Pentecost. Few think of it as a day to observe, and yet Pentecost is plainly a Christian holiday. It is the day the Holy Spirit fell on the church with power and the day the disciples baptized 3000 people. Some even call it the birthday of the church. You would think all Christians everywhere would have a major celebration on this day, if on no other.

As explained earlier, the word "Pentecost" is a Greek word that means "fiftieth," because it is the fiftieth day from the day the firstfruits of the harvest were presented to God (see chapter seven). One curious thing about Pentecost is that unlike all the other biblical festivals, it was not originally established as a date on the calendar (see appendix one). But for the Christian, the resurrection of Jesus trumped everything. The day he first appeared to his disciples after his resurrection, as the firstfruits from the dead, was day one of the countdown to Pentecost, and so it has remained.

The first forty days from Jesus' resurrection were days of learning for the disciples. Many things they had seen and heard from Jesus they had not understood. Now many of these questions were clarified and distilled. By the time they wrote their accounts of the Gospel, they had throughly digested what Jesus told them.

Among the things he told them was this: "Do not leave Jerusalem," he said, "but wait for the gift my Father promised, which you have heard me speak about. For John baptized with water, but in a few days you will be baptized with the Holy Spirit" (Acts 1:4-5 NIV).

It is hard to imagine what the disciples thought Jesus meant by that. They could not have been completely clueless. The Holy Spirit had come upon men in time past, usually leading to significant prophecy. But there was no precedent for what would happen to them, a mere ten days later.

On their last day with Jesus, they asked a question which betrayed their expectations of what the Messiah would do. "Lord," they asked, "are you at this time going to restore the kingdom to Israel?" (v. 6). The conventional wisdom was that the Messiah would come, he would deliver them from the Romans, and establish an earthly kingdom right then and there. Jesus dismissed the question. "It is not for you to know the times or the seasons, which the Father hath put in his own power," he said. "But ye shall receive power, after that the Holy Ghost is come upon you: and ye shall be witnesses unto me both in Jerusalem, and in all Judaea, and in Samaria, and unto the uttermost part of the earth" (vv. 7, 8).

One wonders what they thought of that last phrase, "unto the uttermost part of the earth." To them, God was the God of the Jews and their religion was a Jewish religion. They had, for the most part, lived their lives in isolation from Gentiles, not associating with them nor worshiping with them. Their tradition did not even allow them to eat with Gentiles.[i] They kept themselves completely apart.

And most Jews would have thought that the work of spreading the Gospel of Jesus Christ would have been a work that they were supposed to do among *Israelites*. Not so. He said "you are going to be witnesses in Jerusalem, in Judaea, in Samaria [God forbid, the Jews despised the Samaritans] and the *uttermost parts of the earth.*" That last includes the Gentiles. We also know that Jesus told his disciples explicitly, "Go you, therefore, and make disciples of the *Gentiles*" (Matthew 28:19).

I know, every major translation of Matthew says, "Go and make disciples of all nations." But if you read Greek, you will see it immediately, the word that is translated "nations" is *ethnos*, a word that is elsewhere translated "Gentiles." This will be pivotal to what comes later.

When Jesus had finished his instructions, while they watched, he was taken up and disappeared into a cloud. As they stood there, gaping, two "men" appeared by them, both clothed in white. "You men of Galilee," they said, "why are you standing here gazing up in to heaven? This same Jesus which was taken up from you into heaven shall so come in like manner as you have seen him go unto heaven" (Acts 1:11).

So the disciples returned from the Mount of Olives to Jerusalem to wait. Meanwhile, they had some unfinished business. They had to replace Judas to retain the number of apostles at 12, and, of course, there was Pentecost, fast approaching. There was hardly any point in returning home, because their attendance was required for the feast.[ii] And besides, the Master had told them to wait. They doubtless awaited Pentecost with some expectation. God always seemed to act in history on the dates of the festivals, his appointments with history.

So, it was only natural that when that day came, they would all be assembled together. They were where they were supposed to be, doing what they were supposed to be doing. It was a time of one of the appointments of God. They had only ten days to wait.

There is, in some quarters, a fundamental misunderstanding of what happened next in Acts 2. The assumption seems to be that the disciples began to speak in unknown tongues, at least that is the impression conveyed by the tongues movement in charismatic Christianity. Speaking in tongues is seen in some quarters as evidence of the baptism of the Holy Spirit. It is also seen as a kind of prayer language. It isn't uncommon to hear some charismatic preachers lapse into tongues as they speak. Sometimes there is an interpreter present, sometimes not. As a rule, the person speaking in tongues has no idea what he is saying. For the most part, modern ideas on speaking in tongues are based on an interpretation of Paul's letter to the Corinthians.[iii]

But what happened on that first Christian Pentecost was something entirely different and is in no way related to what takes place among charismatic groups today. The first thing one should know in reading this account is that the common Greek word for one's tongue, *glossa*, is a synonym for "language," just as it is in English. And as the story proceeds, more information becomes available.

> And there were dwelling in Jerusalem Jews, devout men, from every nation under heaven. And when this sound occurred, the multitude came together, and were confused, because everyone heard them speak *in his own language* (Acts 2:5-6).

The word for "language" here is the Greek *dialektos*, or dialect. These were Jews who had migrated back to the Holy Land from all over the Roman Empire. The question naturally arises, didn't these folks all speak Hebrew? Apparently not. They had been born in, say, Arabia, and had grown up speaking Arabic. In any case, these men, born elsewhere in the empire, spoke other languages. Whatever you may believe about speaking in tongues, this event is not an incident of unknown tongues. These were recognized, identifiable languages and regional dialects, and they are named.

> Utterly amazed, they asked: "Are not all these men who are speaking Galileans? Then how is it that each of us hears them in his own native language? Parthians, Medes and Elamites; residents of Mesopotamia, Judea and Cappadocia, Pontus and Asia, Phrygia and Pamphylia, Egypt and the parts of Libya near Cyrene; visitors from Rome (both Jews and converts to Judaism); Cretans and Arabs – we hear them declaring the wonders of God in our own tongues!" (Acts 2:7-11 NIV).

There are 15 named languages here, one of them a regional dialect. What is even more important, the message was understood: "We hear them declaring the wonders of God in our own tongues."

The gift of languages on this occasion was significant because it defined where the Gospel was supposed to go, and these were the languages of the nations, the *ethnos*, the Gentiles. This sharply underlines the meaning of the event. Jesus told them to wait until they were endued with power. The only power on display on this day was the power to proclaim the Gospel in lands and among people who did not speak Aramaic or Hebrew or even Greek, the *lingua franca* of the empire.

And so the instructions were clear. And the miracle was clear. And the miracle underlined the instructions. And I hate to disappoint, but there's nothing in this passage that supports speaking in unknown tongues. That's not what this was about. What it was about was left for Peter to explain to the assembled crowd.

---

i. Galatians 2:11-12.

ii. "Three times a year all your men must appear before the LORD your God at the place he will choose: at the Feast of Unleavened Bread, the Feast of Weeks and the Feast of Tabernacles. No man should appear before the LORD empty-handed" (Deuteronomy 16:16 NIV).

iii. See 1 Corinthians 14.

10

Baptized with Fire

*And it shall come to pass afterward,
that I will pour out my spirit upon all flesh;
and your sons and your daughters shall prophesy,
your old men shall dream dreams, your young men shall see
visions: And also upon the servants and upon the handmaids
in those days will I pour out my spirit (Joel 2:28-29 KJV).*

Imagine yourself sitting in a room with 120 of the first disciples of Jesus. You have been through an emotional roller coaster the past two months, from the triumphant entry into Jerusalem of the Messiah, to his ignominious torture and death, to his resurrection. All of you saw him alive, some of you saw him ascend to heaven.

You are expectant, but you really have no idea what is coming. He told you to wait in Jerusalem until you were empowered, but what did that mean? Now, it is Pentecost, the fiftieth day after Christ's resurrection. You have all come together to observe the Feast of Pentecost as you have all your lives.

Suddenly, with no warning, the room is filled with a great roaring sound, something very much like fire shimmers across the ceiling of the room, and a little stream of that fire descends upon each of you sitting in the room.

This would surely be the epitome of what we would call "a hair-raising experience." Each of you finds yourself with the ability to speak in a language you have never spoken before and bursting with a message about the wonderful works of God. It would be an unforgettable experience. It would be energizing, empowering.

But the experience is not what this was about. The experience only lasted for a day, and then the disciples were left to ponder what the experience was all about and what it meant. It was clear enough right from the start that what was important was not so much the experience, but the *meaning* of the experience. What the disciples were coming to understand was that the Temple was a stage upon which a drama was played out, and that drama, from the beginning, was the story of Christ. Every year of their lives, they had observed a set of holydays, in all of which they were seeing, not only the history of God's interaction with Israel, but of God's interaction in the person of Jesus Christ. And here, on the day of Pentecost, one of the greatest movements in the history of God and man began.

The holidays of the Bible had an Israelite historical meaning, but they also foreshadowed the work of Christ. They sit in the Scriptures like rocks in the stream from which we can look back over history and forward into the future.

One of the really great losses to the nominal Christian faith was the abandonment of the holydays of the Bible, their dismissal as merely "Jewish" institutions. And surely, one of the greatest of the Christian holydays is Pentecost, because it was on this day that the church was empowered to do its work. Some even call Pentecost the birthday of the church.

But on that first Pentecost of the New Testament church, no one even thought of abandoning this festival. They were too high with the experience. But on this day, one question had to be dominant in every mind. Once you look past the incredible experience of the day, *what did it all mean?*

As word spread, men came running together to see what had happened, and as they listened to the disciples speaking, they were all amazed, and were in doubt, saying one to another, "What does this mean?" Some, to be sure, mocked and accused the disciples of being drunk, they were that excited. Peter stilled the crowd and explained what was happening.

> Men of Judea and all who dwell in Jerusalem, let this
> be known to you, and heed my words. For these are
> not drunk, as you suppose, since it is only the third
> hour of the day. But this is what was spoken by the
> prophet Joel: And it shall come to pass in the last
> days, says God, That I will pour out of My Spirit on
> all flesh; Your sons and your daughters shall
> prophesy, Your young men shall see visions, Your old
> men shall dream dreams. And on My menservants and
> on My maidservants I will pour out My Spirit in those
> days; And they shall prophesy. (Acts 2:14-18).

It seems doubtful that Peter, even here, fully understood all the implications of Joel's prophecy. He was seeing with his own eyes part of the phenomenon, but in the light of his later conduct, it is doubtful that he considered the implications of the phrase, "all flesh." For Peter and the others still had not absorbed the truth that God was breaking the faith loose from the Temple, from Jerusalem, and in particular, from the control of the religious establishment. It would later become apparent to Peter that when God said "all flesh," he meant precisely that.

And in the event, the pouring out of the Spirit was all encompassing – old, young, male, female. And I have to conclude, based on Peter's citation of Joel, that there were women present who received this same gift and who spoke as well. Peter went on:

> I will show wonders in heaven above And signs in the
> earth beneath: Blood and fire and vapor of smoke.
> The sun shall be turned into darkness, And the moon
> into blood, Before the coming of the great and
> awesome day of the LORD. And it shall come to pass
> That whoever calls on the name of the LORD Shall be
> saved (vv. 19-21).

This passage also kicked the door wide open for taking the Gospel to the Gentiles. That last phrase was all inclusive. "Whoever" included Gentiles. So here we go all the way back to the Prophet Joel, and he was not the only one. The Old Testament prophets, Isaiah in particular, foresaw the conversion of the Gentiles to God, something all the Jews, and even some of the disciples, had a lot of trouble dealing with in the early years of the church.

The difficulty with this passage, though, is that Joel is plainly dealing with an end time event – the Day of the Lord. The confusing thing about prophecy is its dreamlike quality. You know how it is when you dream. All the normal rules of time and space are suspended. You can be acting out events in one location and finish them in another. In a dream, anything can happen. In prophecy, you can start out in one dimension of time and end up in another.

So attempts to interpret prophecy in conscious, literal terms is, in the main, futile. Peter was sure that he was seeing a fulfillment of Joel's prophecy. What he could not know was how soon or in what manner the rest of the prophecy might come to pass.

The references to these signs in the book of Revelation place these events well into the future. But the empowering of the disciples and the opening of the door to the Gentiles was a *right now* event. But apart from taking the Gospel to the Gentiles, what did Pentecost mean? Peter continues:

> Men of Israel, hear these words: Jesus of Nazareth, a Man attested by God to you by miracles, wonders, and signs which God did through Him in your midst, *as you yourselves also know* (v. 22).

Peter did not have to recount all the events of Jesus' ministry. The men in front of him on this day knew them. Even though they were from another part of the empire and spoke those languages, they had been in Jerusalem during Jesus' ministry.

> Him, being delivered by the determined purpose and foreknowledge of God, you have taken by lawless hands, have crucified, and put to death (v. 23).

Yes, but *they* didn't do it, did they? Didn't the Romans crucify Jesus? Yes, but they cannot escape responsibility. They had been there, they knew. They may even have been in the crowd that yelled, "Let him be crucified!"

> Whom God raised up, having loosed the pains of death, because it was not possible that He should be held by it. For David says concerning Him: I foresaw the LORD always before my face, For He is at my right hand, that I may not be shaken. Therefore my heart rejoiced, and my tongue was glad; Moreover my flesh also will rest in hope. For You will not leave my soul in Hades, Nor will You allow Your Holy One to see corruption. You have made known to me the ways of life; You will make me full of joy in Your presence (vv. 24-28).

Peter here cites a Psalm,[i] written by David, who serves in the Bible as a type of Christ. Because he was anointed of God to be King, he was a kind of Messiah in his own right.[ii] Often in the Psalms, he speaks in the first person as God's anointed, and he is speaking for Christ.

Now Peter comes to the crux of the matter, and it could not be denied. There were 120 witnesses present who had seen Jesus alive after his death and burial. And Peter does not rely only on the phenomenon to establish his point. His audience was Jewish and well trained to reject mere miracles as proof of anything.[iii] They expected matters like this to be established by Scripture, so Peter cites Scripture.

> Men and brethren, let me speak freely to you of the patriarch David, that he is both dead and buried, and his tomb is with us to this day. Therefore, being a prophet, and knowing that God had sworn with an oath to him that of the fruit of his body, according to the flesh, He would raise up the Christ to sit on his throne, he, foreseeing this, spoke concerning the resurrection of the Christ, that His soul was not left in Hades, nor did His flesh see corruption (vv. 29-31).

David knew. This comes as a bit of a surprise. We know David as a poet and king, but the role of the prophet seems unexpected. Yet so many of his Psalms are prophetic, especially Psalms about the Messiah. Peter continued:

This Jesus God has raised up, of which we are all witnesses. Therefore being exalted to the right hand of God, and having received from the Father the promise of the Holy Spirit, He poured out this which you now see and hear. For David did not ascend into the heavens, but he says himself: "The LORD said to my Lord, 'Sit at My right hand, Till I make Your enemies Your footstool.'" Therefore let all the house of Israel know assuredly that God has made this Jesus, whom you crucified, both Lord and Christ (vv. 32-36).[iv]

Peter's speech was tough and to the point. There was no denying the resurrection of Jesus in the face of 120 witnesses, all nodding their heads and for all we know, giving amens to what Peter was saying. And it was the resurrection of Jesus that trumped everything and led to the climax. The Lord has made this same Jesus *whom you have crucified*, both Lord and Christ.

Now when they heard this, they were cut to the heart, and said to Peter and the rest of the apostles, Men and brethren, what shall we do? (vv. 32-37).

Cut to the heart is probably putting it mildly. To come to the realization that you had crucified the Christ, that he was now raised from the dead, would have crushed a man's soul. Peter offers the crowd a way to resolve the pain.

Then Peter said to them, "Repent, and let every one of you be baptized in the name of Jesus Christ for the remission of sins; and you shall receive the gift of the Holy Spirit. For the promise is to you and to your children, and to all who are afar off, as many as the Lord our God will call." And with many other words he testified and exhorted them, saying, "Be saved from this perverse generation." Then those who gladly received his word were baptized; and that day about three thousand souls were added to them. And they continued steadfastly in the apostles' doctrine and fellowship, in the breaking of bread, and in prayers (vv. 38-42).

So, what did Pentecost mean, to these disciples, in this time and place? To the Jew, Pentecost was not a stand alone festival. It was the fiftieth day of the harvest that had begun seven weeks ago. In the Jewish economy, it started with "the first day" of seven "weeks" of harvest. It started with the offering of the first of the firstfruits to God at the same moment that the resurrected Jesus was presented to the Father on the morning after his resurrection.

To the disciples of Jesus, Pentecost was the Feast of Firstfruits, and the baptism of 3000 souls on that day was a sharp reminder of what they were about.

Now, what is the Christian connection to the Feast of Firstfruits? That's our question. As is so often the case, Paul comes to our rescue.

> But Christ has indeed been raised from the dead, the firstfruits of those who have fallen asleep. For since death came through a man, the resurrection of the dead comes also through a man. For as in Adam all die, so in Christ all will be made alive. But each in his own turn: Christ, the firstfruits; then, when he comes, those who belong to him (1 Corinthians 15:20-23 NIV

So for the early Christians the connection was almost automatic. They saw very clearly and very quickly what all this meant. We walked through this earlier, but consider it again from their perspective:

> You shall eat neither bread nor parched grain nor fresh grain until the same day that you have brought an offering to your God; it shall be a statute forever throughout your generations in all your dwellings. And you shall count for yourselves from the day after the Sabbath, from the day that you brought the sheaf of the wave offering: seven Sabbaths shall be completed (Leviticus 23:14-15).

Note this well. There was a countdown of seven Sabbaths. So when Matthew says that Mary first saw Jesus on "the first day of the week," what he said in Greek is that Jesus appeared to Mary on the "first of the Sabbaths." Now we know it was a Sunday morning, so it had to be on the first day of the weeks, the first day of the seven.

> Count off fifty days up to the day after the seventh Sabbath, and then present an offering of new grain to the LORD. From wherever you live, bring two loaves made of two-tenths of an ephah of fine flour, baked with yeast, as a wave offering of firstfruits to the LORD (Leviticus 23:16-17 NIV

Now we encounter a marked difference. When we thought of Jesus as the Bread of Life, we were speaking of unleavened bread, bread that is absent the symbolism of sin. Now we have an anomaly. We have two loaves of *leavened* bread presented to God as an offering of the firstfruits to God. These are offered on Pentecost, on the day the Holy Spirit was poured out in great power, and the day they baptized 3000 people.

What would the first Christians have made of all this? Seven weeks after Jesus rose from the dead as the firstfruits, yet another offering is made that is also called firstfruits. How would they have understood it? We know how James understood it because he states it outright in his letter.

> Every good and perfect gift is from above, coming down from the Father of the heavenly lights, who does not change like shifting shadows. He chose to give us birth through the word of truth, that we might be *a kind of firstfruits* of all he created (James 1:17-18 NIV

Make no mistake about it. James, like all the apostles, was well versed in the Scriptures, and this comparison to the Feast of Firstfruits is deliberate. Not only is Christ the firstfruits, so are we. So when we make our way into the Temple on Pentecost and see the priests with the two "wave loaves" of leavened bread to offer before God, we have closed up the season of the firstfruits. But now it is not about the resurrection of Christ. It is about the resurrection of the saints.

You may not realize this, but in Revelation 14, the 144,000 that you've probably heard about, are called the firstfruits unto God and to the Lamb. The church surely would have connected these two loaves of the firstfruits to the three thousand people they baptized at Pentecost. In a sense, Pentecost looks to the Day of the Lord – the return of Christ and the resurrection of the dead when the firstfruits are presented to God.

But there's a joker in the deck, and I wonder if you've caught it. Mind you, we have made our way down to the time of the resurrection of the dead, the 144,000 are standing there along with the rest of us, and they are the *firstfruits* of God. The very term "firstfruits" suggests that there are later fruits, doesn't it? Otherwise, why are they the first?

There are later fruits to be harvested after the firstfruits which, in Christian doctrine, come at the return of Christ, the Day of the Lord, and the resurrection. Sobering thought, isn't it? You see, in Palestine, there were two major harvests: grain in the spring, fruit in the fall. We are left to ponder the significance of firstfruits and then later fruits. We will come back to that later, but for now, we have to consider how Jesus spoke of this.

> Jesus went through all the towns and villages, teaching in their synagogues, preaching the good news of the kingdom and healing every disease and sickness. When he saw the crowds, he had compassion on them, because they were harassed and helpless, like sheep without a shepherd. Then he said to his disciples, "The harvest is plentiful but the workers are few. Ask the Lord of the harvest, therefore, to send out workers into his harvest field" (Matthew 9:35-38 NIV

You don't have to be a scholar to see what Jesus is talking about. He is talking about people, not grain. It was the people who were scattered and leaderless. There were so many of them, and so few to provide help and direction. The harvest of lives is out there in great abundance, Jesus told his disciples. Pray to God that he would send more workers out into the harvest. There is much work to be done. In the New Testament, the harvest is a repeated analogy for evangelizing the people of the world so they can be harvested as the firstfruits to God.

So Pentecost brings us up to the resurrection – the harvesting of the saints for the kingdom of God. Where does the thread take us next in the year? It takes us to the Feast of Trumpets on the first day of the seventh month. Of the seven Christian holidays in the Bible, the Feast of Trumpets is the fourth. The Old Testament tells us surprisingly little of the festival.

---

i. Peter is citing Psalm 16:8-11.

ii. "Messiah" in the Hebrew is *Mashiyach* and means "Anointed." Thus every king and every priest, being anointed of God, was a messiah of sorts.

iii. See Deuteronomy 13:1-3.

iv. "Christ" comes from the Greek *Christos* and means "Anointed." It is the Greek translation of "Messiah."

11

The Feast of Trumpets

Judgment Day

As I live, saith the Lord, every knee shall bow to me,
and every tongue shall confess to God.
So then every one of us shall give account
of himself to God (Romans 14:11-12 KJV).

The first three festivals of the year, Passover, the Feast of Unleavened Bread, and Pentecost, can be seen clearly enough in both Jewish and Christian history. But now the scene begins to change. Of all these appointed festivals of God, the one with the least obvious connection to Christianity is the day the Jews call *Rosh Hashana,*[i] the Jewish New Year:

> Then the LORD spoke to Moses, saying, "Speak to the children of Israel, saying: In the seventh month, on the first day of the month, you shall have a sabbath-rest, a memorial of blowing of trumpets, a holy convocation. You shall do no customary work on it; and you shall offer an offering made by fire to the LORD" (Leviticus 23:23-25).

This is the Feast of Trumpets. Like any religious holiday, you take a day off from work and you go to church (a holy convocation is an occasion for assembling before God). That part is simple enough, but after that it becomes a little more complicated. Of all the holidays, this one is least attested to in Scripture as to meaning, for either Christians or Jews.

For example, the day is called a memorial. But a memorial of what? The Scripture doesn't say. And you may have noticed that this is the first day of the *seventh* month, not the first day of the first month. How then can it be the new year? This is especially curious when you realize that Passover falls in the month that God calls "The beginning of months."[ii] As it happens, that is six months earlier. I went to the Virtual Jerusalem website and this is what I found:

> Five thousand seven hundred and sixty years ago the world experienced the very first Rosh Hashanah. According to Rabbi Eliezer, it was on this day that Adam was created. God's creation was complete. Our sages tell us that on this very day, Adam violated the commandment that God gave him – the prohibition to eat from the tree of life [sic] On this day God said to Adam "As you were judged before me this day and emerged forgiven, so will your children be judged before me on this day and emerge forgiven." Thus, from the beginning of our history, Rosh Hashanah has been marked with judgment and forgiveness. On Rosh Hashanah we celebrate the creation of the world, we mark the Kingship of God, and we stand in judgment as His humble servants.

So in Jewish tradition (not to be confused with Scripture), this day is a memorial of creation. And it is also a day of judgment. Christian tradition also expects a day of judgment. Jesus spoke of this to his disciples as he sent them out to preach around Judea:

> And whoever will not receive you nor hear your words, when you depart from that house or city, shake off the dust from your feet. Assuredly, I say to you, it

93

will be more tolerable for the land of Sodom and Gomorrah *in the day of judgment* than for that city! (Matthew 10:14).

Jesus seems to speak of a day of judgment yet in the future. It is a little chilling to contemplate. On a speaking tour through the cities, Jesus rebuked town after town. They had seen so many of the miracles he had done, and yet they couldn't believe. "Woe to you," he said. "If I had done these works in Sodom, they would have repented long ago in sackcloth and ashes." He concluded by warning: "But I say to you that it shall be more tolerable for the land of Sodom in the day of judgment than for you" (Matthew 10:24).

In a way, this is a shocking thing to consider. Not merely that there is a day of judgment, but that Sodom and Gomorrah will be there and find a measure of tolerance. Not only that, but wicked Sodom, had she seen the works that Jesus did, *would have repented.* This last is among the more shocking things that Jesus ever said.

Jesus was a judge, even while he was here, and he could be very tough on occasion. In one instance, after the Pharisees had alleged that he cast out demons by the power of the devil, he had this to say in reply:

> Brood of vipers! How can you, being evil, speak good things? For out of the abundance of the heart the mouth speaks. A good man out of the good treasure of his heart brings forth good things, and an evil man out of the evil treasure brings forth evil things. But I say to you that for every idle word men may speak, they will give account of it in the day of judgment. For by your words you will be justified, and by your words you will be condemned (Matthew 12:34-37).

So the day of judgment is a day when we render an account for the things we have done and said. I think as Christians we lose sight of this. We may think we are saved, and then forget that we are held responsible for the things we continue to do. The Jews are reminded of it every year at the memorial of blowing of trumpets. Christians would do well to remind themselves of it as well. Some do, on the day they call "The Feast of Trumpets." This day of judgment loomed large in Jesus' teaching.

> Then some of the scribes and Pharisees answered, saying, "Teacher, we want to see a sign from You." But He answered and said to them, "An evil and adulterous generation seeks after a sign, and no sign will be given to it except the sign of the prophet Jonah. For as Jonah was three days and three nights in the belly of the great fish, so will the Son of Man be three days and three nights in the heart of the earth. The men of Nineveh will rise up in the judgment with this generation and condemn it, because they repented at the preaching of Jonah; and indeed a greater than Jonah is here" (vv. 38-41).

This presents an image of a judgment day sometime in the future, in which the men of Nineveh will stand right alongside the generation of Pharisees who heard Jesus and saw his works. They will be able to say, "Look, we repented at the preaching of Jonah. You heard the Lord himself and didn't repent."

> The queen of the South will rise up in the judgment with this generation and condemn it, for she came from the ends of the earth to hear the wisdom of Solomon; and indeed a greater than Solomon is here (Matthew 12:42).

It must have seemed incredible to the Jews on that day for Jesus to claim to be greater than Jonah and greater than Solomon, but as Christians, we know that indeed he was. There is a lot we don't know about the judgment day, but we keep getting little snippets of information that should give us pause. Some might well cause us to break out in a cold sweat.

One notable item is the implication that there is a resurrection connected with this judgment day. Probably some theologians think Jesus is speaking metaphorically here, but that is a little too convenient for me. Even a metaphor stands for something, and what if he is not speaking metaphorically? What if there is a real judgment day? When Jesus speaks of it, it doesn't sound like a metaphor. It sounds all too real.

On an occasion when the Jewish religious establishment were trying to have Jesus killed, he had this to say to them:

> Most assuredly, I say to you, the Son can do nothing of Himself, but what He sees the Father do; for whatever He does, the Son also does in like manner. For the Father loves the Son, and shows Him all things that He Himself does; and He will show Him greater works than these, that you may marvel. For as the Father raises the dead and gives life to them, even so the Son gives life to whom He will. For the Father judges no one, but has committed all judgment to the Son (John 5:19-22 NKJV

Once again, resurrection and judgment are connected. And the one who is going to be doing the judging is none other than Jesus himself. He continues to develop this theme in the verses following.

> Most assuredly, I say to you, the hour is coming, and now is, when the dead will hear the voice of the Son of God; and those who hear will live. For as the Father has life in Himself, so He has granted the Son to have life in Himself, and has given Him authority to execute judgment also, because He is the Son of Man. Do not marvel at this; for the hour is coming in which all who are in the graves will hear His voice and come forth; those who have done good, to the resurrection of life, and those who have done evil, to the resurrection of condemnation (John 5:25-29 NKJV

Again and again, we encounter two things at the same time. Resurrection and judgment. And who is the Judge? None other than Jesus. I don't know why the translators switched words here, because the word here translated "condemnation" is everywhere else translated "judgment." It is the Greek word, *krisis*, from which we derive "crisis," and I suspect it will represent a very real crisis for the people who find themselves there.

> I can of mine own self do nothing: as I hear, I judge: and *my judgment is just*; because I seek not mine own will, but the will of the Father which hath sent me (v. 30).

His judgment will be just, but it still sends a little shiver down the spine when we think about it. This theme continues throughout the New Testament. For example, when Paul wrote to the Romans:

> For to this end Christ died and rose and lived again, that He might be Lord of both the dead and the living. But why do you judge your brother? Or why do you show contempt for your brother? For we shall all stand before the judgment seat of Christ. For it is written: "As I live, says the LORD, Every knee shall bow to Me, And every tongue shall confess to God." So then each of us shall give account of *himself* to God (Romans 14:9-12 NKJV

Paul is addressing the nasty Christian habit of sitting in judgment of one another. If everyone doesn't live his life exactly as we think he should, we have an opinion about it, a judgment, even a condemnation for it. Paul wants to know why they are doing this. We shall all, he said, stand before the judgment seat of *Christ*. That really ought to be enough. When we all stand together before the judgment seat of Christ, there will not be an awful lot of difference between us.

When we stand in judgment before Christ, we will not be there to render an account for our brother. It will be for ourselves. You don't have to explain to God where your brother went wrong and why he did it. The one you are going to have to explain is yourself. We really do have to give an account of ourselves to God.

Now I know I have been forgiven. I know I have God's mercy. But this last verse still has to be dealt with. It is disappointing how carelessly a lot of Christian people live their lives. They trust in the blood of Christ to cover their sins and that is good. But does that mean we will not be in any way held responsible for what we do and don't do? Frankly, when we read the Bible, it would certainly seem that we will be.

This issue becomes rather more serious when we come to the book of Hebrews. Here Paul urges us to hold fast our profession of faith and to stay faithful to one another. Then he deals with what is commonly called the unpardonable sin. This becomes all the more urgent, he says, as we see "the *day* approaching" (Hebrews 10:25).

> For if we sin willfully after we have received the knowledge of the truth, there no longer remains a sacrifice for sins, but a certain fearful expectation of judgment, and fiery indignation which will devour the adversaries (vv. 26-27).

This is a hard saying, and it is frightening to consider that there is a sin for which the sacrifice of Christ can no longer atone. And this is all the more true for one who has received the knowledge of the truth, not so much for the person who doesn't know any better. At the end of the road lies a day of judgment.

> Anyone who has rejected Moses' law dies without mercy on the testimony of two or three witnesses. Of how much worse punishment, do you suppose, will he be thought worthy who has trampled the Son of God underfoot, counted the blood of the covenant by which he was sanctified a common thing, and insulted the Spirit of grace? (vv. 28-29).

It doesn't seem possible that one who had been sanctified by the blood of Christ should turn and sin willfully. But if it is not possible, why is it here?

> For we know Him who said, Vengeance is Mine, I will repay,'says the Lord. And again, The LORD will judge His people.'It is a fearful thing to fall into the hands of the living God (vv. 30-31).

Yes, I should think so. So now we know that there is a judgment day. When does it come? Where does it fit into all this? If this is a yet future thing, we might expect to find it in the book of Revelation. And in fact, we do. When the seventh angel sounds the seventh trumpet, great voices in heaven announce that "The kingdoms of this world are become the kingdoms of our Lord, and of his Christ; and he shall reign for ever and ever" (Revelation 11:15).

> And the twenty-four elders who sat before God on their thrones fell on their faces and worshiped God, saying: We give You thanks, O Lord God Almighty, The One who is and who was and who is to come, Because You have taken Your great power and reigned. The nations were angry, and Your wrath has come, *And the time of the dead, that they should be judged,* And that You should reward Your servants the prophets and the saints, And those who fear Your name, small and great, And should destroy those who destroy the earth. Then th e temple of God was opened in heaven, and the ark of His covenant was seen in His temple. And there were lightnings, noises, thunderings, an earthquake, and great hail (Revelation 11:16-19 NKJV

So Judgment Day comes at the last trump, at the same moment as the resurrection of the dead.

---

i. In Hebrew, "the head of the year."

ii. Exodus 12:2.

12

The Resurrection

For since by man came death,
by Man also came the resurrection of the dead.
For as in Adam all die,
even so in Christ all shall be made alive.[i]

Even if you are not Jewish, you are probably aware of the two main Jewish holidays in the autumn of every year: The Jewish New Year, and Yom Kippur. By now, you are beginning to suspect that these may also be Christian holidays.

The end of the first century saw a time of severe persecution of the Jews in and around Rome. It was no wonder that the Roman Christians began to differentiate themselves from the Jews in every way they could. Many practices that were very common in the early church disappeared in the smoke of the persecution of the Jews. But why would the early church have paid any attention to what we know as Jewish holidays in the first place? For one thing, Christians and Jews shared the same God. In its earliest years, Christianity was viewed by the world, not as a separate religion, but as a sect of Judaism. The earliest Christians were Jewish, and they had no consciousness of starting a new religion. Many saw what they were doing as a restoration of a purer faith. Judaism, in their view, had gone astray from the faith of Abraham and Moses.

There is nothing strange about that. Every new sect of religion sees itself as a restorer of lost paths. And so the first Christians, who were Jewish, continued to observe the holidays they had observed all their lives, and they taught the Gentile converts to do the same. But it was inevitable that they should begin to see new significance in these days, a significance that transcended the Jewish/historical meaning of the days. The early Christians saw Christ in the "Jewish holidays." And now, 2000 years later, you and I come along and wonder, "What did they see that led them to this conclusion?" When you look at the law on the question of the Jewish New Year, you don't get a lot of help.

> Then the LORD spoke to Moses, saying, Speak to the children of Israel, saying: "In the seventh month, on the first day of the month, you shall have a sabbath-rest, a memorial of blowing of trumpets, a holy convocation. You shall do no customary work on it; and you shall offer an offering made by fire to the LORD" (Leviticus 23:23-25).

There are two curious items here. First, why have your new year in the seventh month? That's easy enough. Israel had a religious year and a civil year. The civil year began in the seventh month of the religious year. It is not unlike a company that has a fiscal year that starts in July of a calendar year. But the other item runs a little deeper. This day is called "a *memorial* of blowing of trumpets," and there is nothing in the Bible to tell us what is memorialized. It is a memorial of what? In Christian thought, a memorial can be in terms of the future. In Jewish thought, memorials had to do with the past. There is a short aside in one of Paul's letters to the church in Colosse that illustrates this.

> So let no one judge you in food or in drink, or regarding a festival or a new moon or sabbaths, which are *a shadow of things to come*, but the substance is of Christ (Colossians 2:16-17).

Strangely, some use this passage to argue against the observance of the holydays. The truth is, this passage *assumes* the observance of the days by the Colossians and tells them not to let anyone condemn them for doing so. But more important than that, it shows that Christians thought of these days as shadows of things yet to come – a future memorial, as it were.

Now there is a curious ambiguity relative to the Feast of Trumpets, also known as the Jewish New Year.

> Speak to the children of Israel, saying: "In the seventh month, on the first day of the month, you shall have a sabbath-rest, a memorial of blowing of trumpets, a holy convocation" (Leviticus 23:24).

The word "trumpet" is absent from the text and is assumed by the translators. That assumption is correct, but still there is a point to be taken from it. The Hebrew says literally that this is a day of shouting or blasting. The term is used elsewhere of a trumpet blast, so the translation is appropriate enough. But the word "shouting" here is also commonly used of the shouting of a crowd. And if you trace the word through the Old Testament, you will gradually see that the sense of the word is better rendered, in modern terms, by the word "cheering."

A day of shouting is not a day we go around yelling at one another, it is a day of cheering. So what do we have to cheer about? In the Old Testament, the trumpet was used as a signal. Just as the military has used trumpets for reveille, taps, chow call, officers call, or to the colors, trumpets were used in the Old Testament in much the same way. They would use a distinct blast on the trumpet to call all the elders together for a meeting. They had yet another call to warn everyone that there was an enemy in sight. Still another sound was used to order the people to break camp and prepare to go on the march. And in the Scriptures, the *shofar*[ii] is called an alarm of war.

It is not clear how the trumpet passed into Christian theology, but it plainly did, in two significant places in Paul's letters and in a major section of the book of Revelation. I am sure that when we get the chance someday, we will want to ask Paul why he didn't say some of these things more clearly. But he would probably stare at us as much as to say, "You mean you didn't get that? It's as plain as day." He would also want to know why we didn't do our homework.

Take the first letter to the Thessalonians as a case in point. If we have read that portion of the book of Acts dealing with this, we will realize that the poor Thessalonian brothers had been persecuted beyond measure. Even reading between the lines of Paul's letter, we can see that in the very short time since Paul had left there, only a matter of weeks, some people had been killed. So in this first letter, he was at some pains to encourage everyone concerning their brothers who had died, who had "fallen asleep," to use Paul's euphemism.

> But I do not want you to be ignorant, brethren, concerning those who have fallen asleep, lest you sorrow as others who have no hope. For if we believe that Jesus died and rose again, even so God will bring with Him those who sleep in Jesus. For this we say to you by the word of the Lord, that we who are alive and remain until the coming of the Lord will by no means precede those who are asleep (1 Thessalonians 4:13-15).

As an interesting aside, this sounds very much as though Paul assumed the return of Christ was rather less than 2000 years in the future. But of course, he had not been told that, any more than had the rest of the disciples. We are not going to see Christ one moment before those who have died will see him.

> For the Lord Himself will descend from heaven with a shout, with the voice of an archangel, and with the trumpet of God. And the dead in Christ will rise first. Then we who are alive and remain shall be caught up together with them in the clouds to meet the Lord in the air. And thus we shall always be with the Lord. Therefore comfort one another with these words (vv. 16-18).

The connection between the trumpet of God and the Resurrection of the Dead is firmly established. Not only is there a blast on the trumpet, there is the shout of the Archangel. Knowing what Paul knew about the Feast of Trumpets (or shouting) the connection becomes even more obvious. In any case, in Christian theology, the shout and the trumpet are tied to the resurrection. Then there is yet another definitive statement on the subject in Paul's famous resurrection chapter – the first letter to the Corinthians. The first thing he does is to establish that the resurrection is heart and core of the Gospel, a message that he had delivered to the Corinthians right from the start.

> Moreover, brethren, I declare to you the gospel which I preached to you, which also you received and in which you stand, by which also you are saved, if you hold fast that word which I preached to you; unless you believed in vain.

> For I delivered to you first of all that which I also received: that Christ died for our sins according to the Scriptures, and that He was buried, and that He rose again the third day according to the Scriptures, and that He was seen by Cephas, then by the twelve. After that He was seen by over five hundred brethren at once, of whom the greater part remain to the present, but some have fallen asleep. After that He was seen by James, then by all the apostles. Then last of all He was seen by me also, as by one born out of due time (1 Corinthians 15:1-8).

So Paul establishes the first important thing. Christ died, he was buried, and he rose again the third day according to the Scriptures. Without this simple equation, there is no Gospel. The point had to be driven home, because the resurrection had been called into question by one or more heretics. Not only does he assert the truth of the resurrection, he cites the cloud of witnesses who could attest to the fact that Jesus was seen alive after he had died and been buried. It is easy to overlook the simple truth that all through these days, it was still fairly common to be able to sit down and talk with someone who was a witness of the resurrected Christ – there were 500 people who saw him on one occasion, and there may have been more. I strongly suspect that those people who could attest to Jesus' resurrection were in great demand and moved around a great deal. Corinth being the center of commerce that it was, it is not at all unlikely that Paul was not the only witness they had heard.

Nevertheless, there were those who still did not believe. It is an age old problem of any faith, that no matter how well established it may be, there will be someone who will challenge it. In this case, it may well have been a believing Sadducee. We don't hear very much about these people, but if there were Pharisees who believed, and there were, it seems likely there were Sadducees as well. And just as the Pharisees retained many of their core beliefs, so would the Sadducees who, from the start, did not believe in the resurrection of the dead.[iii]

> Now if Christ is preached that He has been raised from the dead, how do some among you say that there is no resurrection of the dead? But if there is no resurrection of the dead, then Christ is not risen. And if Christ is not risen, then our preaching is empty and your faith is also empty. Yes, and we are found false witnesses of God, because we have testified of God that He raised up Christ, whom He did not raise up; if in fact the dead do not rise (vv. 12-15).

Paul leaves no middle ground. You could not argue that Paul and the others were merely mistaken. Either they told the truth on this important issue or all 500 of the people who claimed to have seen Jesus alive, and all the people Paul has named above, were bald-faced liars.

> For if the dead do not rise, then Christ is not risen. And if Christ is not risen, your faith is futile; you are still in your sins! (vv. 16-17).

Now there is a remarkable statement. I suspect most Christian believers think that it was the death of Christ that took care of everything, his shed blood that covered their sins. The nailing of Jesus to the cross, his blood running down the sword of the Roman soldier who pierced his side, these are the things that took away our sins. When Christ died, was taken down from the tree and placed in the tomb, then we were forgiven and all our sins were gone.

According to Paul, that common belief is not true. If Christ was not raised from the dead, you are still in your sins. Being forgiven of your sins depended on something happening after the resurrection of Jesus. That something was Jesus being presented to the Father on that morning after as the Lamb of God that takes away the sin of the world. It also depends on Jesus' continual intercession for us in the Father's presence.

The point is thus established that it is not merely the death of Christ, but his *resurrection* that makes all the difference. Paul goes on to drive this home.

> Then also those who have fallen asleep in Christ have perished. If in this life only we have hope in Christ, we are of all men the most pitiable. But now Christ is risen from the dead, and has become the *firstfruits* of those who have fallen asleep. For since by man came death, by Man also came the resurrection of the dead. For as in Adam all die, even so in Christ all shall be made alive (vv. 18-22).

I don't know if, today, I could quite say what Paul said then. Even in this life alone, it is better for me to have known Christ, to have followed his teachings, to have walked in his ways, than not to have known him at all. But it was different then. A person took his life in his hands if he openly confessed Christ. People lost jobs, careers, friends, family. It was a hard time to be a Christian, and thus pointless if there is no resurrection from the dead.

And here is the nexus between Jewish and Christian belief. The Feast of Trumpets is to Jews the memorial of creation, specifically the creation of man. It is also believed to be the day that Adam sinned. And so the Jewish New Year is the first of ten days of repentance leading up to Yom Kippur, the Day of Atonement or reconciliation. It is a day of profound awareness of the first Adam, and of Adam's sin. Paul seems to be tapping into this ancient Jewish belief.

In Christian thought, the ultimate reconciliation of Adam's sin takes place at the resurrection from the dead, which is also a day of shouting and blowing of trumpets. So there is a Christian meaning to the Feast of Trumpets. There is naturally some uncertainty reading this some 2000 years later. It seems apparent that this Jewish belief prevailed as early as the first century and that Paul, a Pharisee of Pharisees, was well schooled in the first Adam and the Jewish doctrine of reconciliation. It is hard to imagine, knowing all this, that Paul was not drawing the Jewish doctrine of reconciliation into the picture of the resurrection.

> For as in Adam all die, even so in Christ shall all be made alive. But every man in his own order: Christ the firstfruits; afterward they that are Christ's *at his coming* (vv. 22-23).

So the resurrection takes place at the coming of Christ. Our thread emerges here again in that Christ is called the *firstfruits*, looking back to Pentecost, the Feast of Firstfruits.

> Then comes the end, when He delivers the kingdom to God the Father, when He puts an end to all rule and all authority and power. For He must reign till He has put all enemies under His feet. The last enemy that will be destroyed is death (vv. 24-26).

It is the resurrection that finally destroys death and the power of the grave. Paul delivers quite a polemic about the resurrection and then comes to some of the niggling questions others had raised about the resurrection. He does not suffer fools gladly. It seems surprising to me that the debate about bodily resurrection has raged for centuries. It is true enough that Paul does not answer every question we may have, but it is also true that he shouldn't have to.

> But someone will say, "How are the dead raised up? And with what body do they come?" Foolish one, what you sow is not made alive unless it dies. And what you sow, you do not sow that body that shall be, but mere grain; perhaps wheat or some other grain.

> But God gives it a body as He pleases, and to each seed its own body. All flesh is not the same flesh, but there is one kind of flesh of men, another flesh of animals, another of fish, and another of birds (1 Corinthians 15:35-39).

It is clear enough that what we put into the ground and what we take out of the ground is both similar and different. We sow a seed and get a plant. We are all different, as varieties of grain are different. We are distinct going into the ground, and distinct coming out of it. From what Paul says here, I derive an answer to an old question: Will we recognize one another in the resurrection? Of course we will. Just as a good farmer can look at a plant and know what seed it came from. But there is another way we are different in the resurrection from the way we are now.

> There are also celestial bodies and terrestrial bodies; but the glory of the celestial is one, and the glory of the terrestrial is another. There is one glory of the sun, another glory of the moon, and another glory of the stars; for one star differs from another star in glory. So also is the resurrection of the dead. The body is sown in corruption, it is raised in incorruption. It is sown in dishonor, it is raised in glory. It is sown in weakness, it is raised in power. It is sown a natural body, it is raised a spiritual body. There is a natural body, and there is a spiritual body (vv. 40-44).

All this is said in response to the question, "How are the dead raised up and with what body do they come?" From what Paul says, I would conclude that they come with glorified bodies and they are different – in other words, they can be recognized as distinct persons in the resurrection. When you think about it, if you know who you are, you can make yourself known to others. We sometimes have to do this when we encounter an old friend we haven't seen in many years. We do change with age.

Now Paul's awareness of the Jewish connection of the Feast of Trumpets, the creation of Adam, and Adam's sin, come back into play. It is almost as though the sin of Adam and the resurrection from the dead are the bookends of a very long story.

> And so it is written, "The first man Adam became a living being." The last Adam became a life-giving spirit. However, the spiritual is not first, but the natural, and afterward the spiritual. The first man was of the earth, made of dust; the second Man is the Lord from heaven. As was the man of dust, so also are those who are made of dust; and as is the heavenly Man, so also are those who are heavenly. And as we have borne the image of the man of dust, we shall also bear the image of the heavenly Man (vv. 45-49).

> Now this I say, brethren, that flesh and blood cannot inherit the kingdom of God; nor does corruption inherit incorruption. Behold, I tell you a mystery: We shall not all sleep, but we shall all be changed; in a moment, in the twinkling of an eye, at the last trumpet. For the trumpet will sound, and the dead will be raised incorruptible, and we shall be changed (vv. 50-52).

In saying "the last trump" is the time of the resurrection, Paul implies that there might be more trumpets, a veritable "feast" of trumpets. So where do we go to find the rest of them?

---

i. 1 Corinthians 15:21-22.

ii. Jeremiah 4:19. The shofar, the ram's horn "trumpet."

iii. "But when Paul perceived that one part were Sadducees and the other Pharisees, he cried out in the council, 'Men and brethren, I am a Pharisee, the son of a Pharisee; concerning the hope and resurrection of the dead I am being judged!' {7} And when he had said this, a dissension arose between the Pharisees and the Sadducees; and the assembly was divided. For Sadducees say that there is no resurrection; and no angel or spirit; but the Pharisees confess both (Acts 23:6-8).

13

Trumpets and the Resurrection

Behold, I tell you a mystery: We shall not all sleep,
but we shall all be changed; in a moment, in the twinkling of an
eye, at the last trumpet. For the trumpet will sound,
and the dead will be raised incorruptible,
and we shall be changed.[i]

There is no idea more central to the Christian faith than the resurrection of the dead. And yet, in these early days of Christianity, it had been called into question – in the church. It is in the great 15th chapter of Paul's first letter to the Corinthians that Paul wrestles with a group that claimed there was no resurrection from the dead.[ii] I presume they still held a doctrine of the Kingdom of God, but for them, it was a physical kingdom – something a lot of Jews believed and expected. They thought the Messiah would come, conquer the Romans, and set up his kingdom right then on the earth – a physical kingdom. But Paul made it plain that they had it wrong. "Now this I say, brethren, that flesh and blood cannot inherit the kingdom of God; neither doth corruption inherit incorruption" (1 Corinthians 15:50). For Paul, the whole discussion ends right there. He is not talking about a physical kingdom.

According to Paul, in the passage cited above, the resurrection and the change of living saints to spirit beings takes place at the same time, at an event he calls, "the last trumpet." Now in saying the last trumpet, he implies that there is more than one trumpet in a series. It is the last one that results in the resurrection from the dead.

There is only one place in the Bible where such a series of trumpets is described. It is in the book of Revelation. Revelation is not an easy book to interpret, and in fact, I think most Bible teachers try to over-interpret the book. They explain far too much.

Revelation is a description of a vision seen by the Apostle John. John merely tells us what he saw and what he heard, and he makes no real effort at interpreting those things. The problem is that what he saw was not, in itself, real. It was all highly symbolic and it didn't take place in real time anymore than your dreams do.

While Revelation is difficult, it does have something of an outline that helps us follow it. After some introductory letters, John comes to the core of the vision:

> After these things I looked, and behold, a door standing open in heaven. And the first voice which I heard was like a trumpet speaking with me, saying, "Come up here, and I will show you things which must take place after this." Immediately I was in the Spirit; and behold, a throne set in heaven, and One sat on the throne. And He who sat there was like a jasper and a sardius stone in appearance; and there was a rainbow around the throne, in appearance like an emerald. Around the throne were twenty-four thrones, and on the thrones I saw twenty-four elders sitting, clothed in white robes; and they had crowns of gold on their heads. And from the throne proceeded lightnings, thunderings, and voices. Seven lamps of fire were burning before the throne, which are the seven Spirits of God (Revelation 4:1-5).

By this time, I expect John's hair was standing on end. He had come into the very throne room of the universe. He was not in body, he was in spirit, which I take to mean that he was in vision. Something akin to this happened to Paul, and he couldn't even tell if he was in or out of the body.[iii] John saw a throne with one sitting on it, and a green light like an iris surrounding the throne. There was enormous power in the place with lightning, crackling thunder and voices rumbling in the background. John had come to the place where God was. That one sitting on the throne was none other than God himself.

> And I saw in the right hand of Him who sat on the throne a scroll written inside and on the back, sealed with seven seals. Then I saw a strong angel proclaiming with a loud voice, "Who is worthy to open the scroll and to loose its seals?" And no one in heaven or on the earth or under the earth was able to open the scroll, or to look at it. So I wept much, because no one was found worthy to open and read the scroll, or to look at it (Revelation 5:1-4).

This is so dream like. No time frame for the search is given, but John, like a lot of people in dreams, was just crying his heart out when he thinks they will be unable to open the scroll. This was not a book as we think of it, but a scroll. Scrolls were often written on only one side and then rolled up. This one was full, written on both sides, rolled up and sealed with seven seals. John could have merely said the scroll was sealed, but this one was sealed with the number of finality, of completion, seven.

> But one of the elders said to me, "Do not weep. Behold, the Lion of the tribe of Judah, the Root of David, has prevailed to open the scroll and to loose its seven seals." And I looked, and behold, in the midst of the throne and of the four living creatures, and in the midst of the elders, stood a Lamb as though it had been slain, having seven horns and seven eyes, which are the seven Spirits of God sent out into all the earth (vv. 5-6).

In Christian iconography, the Lamb is Christ. It is the Lamb slain and risen. There is something we should know about icons and iconography: A generation ago, icons meant little to us, but in the computer age, they are common. An icon is a little picture or image that stands for something. Instead of cluttering up the page with words and sentences telling us what this or that program will do, the designers use icons. On your computer screen, there may be a little image of a printer. Click on it and the print program is executed immediately. I counted on the screen of my computer this morning and saw some 65 separate icons. I was shocked that there were so many things I could do with one click of a mouse.

When you read the Bible, you find icons nearly everywhere. They are described by words in the Bible, but they are intended to evoke a mental image. A serious student of the Bible will have to do his own study of icons, his own iconography, so he can grasp what God, through the prophet, is trying to say. I believe that, in some cases, we have lost the significance of the icon. We read the description, but don't have a clue what it means. It is like an icon on your computer screen that you don't recognize. You may say to yourself, "I wonder what that does," click on it and get a rude surprise. I think it is possible that the icon was meaningful to the first generation that read this, but is lost after so long a time. But the icon of the slain lamb is well understood across all of Christian study. The Lamb is Jesus Christ.

> Then I looked, and I heard the voice of many angels around the throne, the living creatures, and the elders; and the number of them was ten thousand times ten thousand, and thousands of thousands, saying with a loud voice: "Worthy is the Lamb who was slain To receive power and riches and wisdom, And strength and honor and glory and blessing!" And every creature which is in heaven and on the earth and under the earth and such as are in the sea, and all that are in them, I heard saying: "Blessing and honor and glory and power Be to Him who sits on the throne, And to the Lamb, forever and ever!" Then the four living creatures said, "Amen!" And the twenty-four elders fell down and worshiped Him who lives forever and ever (Revelation 5:11-14).

There is no great difficulty in understanding what is happening here. The Father is there, the Son is there, and they are receiving the worship and adoration of, well, everybody and everything. Poor John must have been weak in the knees by this time. But there remains the question of why no one but the Lamb could open the seals. No one else was "worthy." How can that be? The answer will emerge: Jesus Christ, by his life, his suffering, his death and his resurrection, was the only one who had the *experience* to judge the earth. He had earned the right.

> Now I saw when the Lamb opened one of the seals; and I heard one of the four living creatures saying with a voice like thunder, "Come and see." And I looked, and behold, a white horse. He who sat on it had a bow; and a crown was given to him, and he went out conquering and to conquer (Revelation 6:1-2).

At first blush, one might think this icon was also Christ, who will return on a white horse (see Revelation 19). But the returning Christ has a sword. The horse, the bow, and the sword are all icons for warfare.[iv] This horseman carries a bow, the icon represents the Antichrist.

> When He opened the second seal, I heard the second living creature saying, "Come and see." Another horse, fiery red, went out. And it was granted to the one who sat on it to take peace from the earth, and that people should kill one another; and there was given to him a great sword (vv. 3-4).

The red horse is also an icon of war, which is borne out by the context. What is opening up here, seal by seal, is the judgment of the earth by the one to whom all judgment has been given (John 5:22).

> When He opened the third seal, I heard the third living creature say, "Come and see." So I looked, and behold, a black horse, and he who sat on it had a pair

of scales in his hand. And I heard a voice in the midst of the four living creatures saying, "A quart of wheat for a denarius, and three quarts of barley for a denarius; and do not harm the oil and the wine" (Revelation 6:5-6).

The icon of the black horse and the rider with the balances in his hand, is the icon for famine. Famine naturally follows on the heels of war. If this is a dream, it is a nightmare.

When He opened the fourth seal, I heard the voice of the fourth living creature saying, "Come and see." So I looked, and behold, a pale horse. And the name of him who sat on it was Death, and Hades followed with him. And power was given to them over a fourth of the earth, to kill with sword, with hunger, with death, and by the beasts of the earth (vv. 7-8).

The pale horse is the icon for pestilence, which follows war and famine like day follows night. It is our future that John is seeing here.

When He opened the fifth seal, I saw under the altar the souls of those who had been slain for the word of God and for the testimony which they held. And they cried with a loud voice, saying, "How long, O Lord, holy and true, until You judge and avenge our blood on those who dwell on the earth?" Then a white robe was given to each of them; and it was said to them that they should rest a little while longer, until both the number of their fellow servants and their brethren, who would be killed as they were, was completed (vv. 9-11).

Still more persecution falls on the heads of the saints, following hard on the heels of what are commonly called, "The Four Horsemen of the Apocalypse." At the time John saw this vision, the church had already endured much persecution and more was on the way. But this vision is for the very last days. It is hard to see a major persecution of Christians in the modern world from any other than an Islamo-Facist power. It is already underway in remote corners of the world, and it will reach a crescendo at the time of the end.

> I looked when He opened the sixth seal, and behold, there was a great earthquake; and the sun became black as sackcloth of hair, and the moon became like blood. And the stars of heaven fell to the earth, as a fig tree drops its late figs when it is shaken by a mighty wind. Then the sky receded as a scroll when it is rolled up, and every mountain and island was moved out of its place. And the kings of the earth, the great men, the rich men, the commanders, the mighty men, every slave and every free man, hid themselves in the caves and in the rocks of the mountains, and said to the mountains and rocks, "Fall on us and hide us from the face of Him who sits on the throne and from the wrath of the Lamb! For the great day of His wrath has come, and who is able to stand?" (Revelation 6:12-17).

What a description! It reminds me of what happens here in Texas when they decide to harvest pecans. They have a machine that grabs the tree high on its trunk and shakes the tree. All around them comes a "rainstorm," as it were, of pecans. John sees something like that, only global and with fire. It is something like a meteor shower of enormous proportions – an event that the earth has seen before, but long before there were any men to see it.

I don't know what the ancients thought about this vision, but scientists now have no difficulty in accepting it because they have found the evidence that it has happened before. When one or more really big meteors strike the earth, they throw up a cloud of dust that can block out the sun and change the climate over the entire earth. So can the eruption of a volcano.

Someone recently theorized that Mars at one time had considerable water and an atmosphere not unlike ours. But an asteroid of considerable size had a close encounter with Mars and stripped away much of its atmosphere. I suppose if that happened here, a prophet might describe it as the heavens departing like a scroll.

One can almost imagine God saying at this moment, "All right, world . . . do I have your attention now?"

> When He opened the seventh seal, there was silence in heaven for about half an hour. And I saw the seven angels who stand before God, and to them were given seven trumpets (Revelation 8:1-2).

After all that has happened up to this point, that silence would have been more than welcome, I should think. But now we come to the only meaningful series of trumpets in the Bible and along with it, an interesting view of the outline of the book of Revelation. The events of the last days are divided into sevens: Seven seals, seven trumpets, and seven bowls of God's wrath. The seventh seal, as it is opened, is composed of seven trumpets. And the last trumpet includes the seven bowls of God's wrath (Revelation 15:7 ff.). It is enough to make one shudder.

> So the seven angels who had the seven trumpets prepared themselves to sound. The first angel sounded: And hail and fire followed, mingled with blood, and they were thrown to the earth. And a third of the trees were burned up, and all green grass was burned up. Then the second angel sounded: And something like a great mountain burning with fire was thrown into the sea, and a third of the sea became blood. And a third of the living creatures in the sea died, and a third of the ships were destroyed. (vv. 6-9).

It boggles the mind to even think about it. What could possibly account for this kind of event? In recent years, movie makers have found new ways to show us what lies in our future, things that lay well beyond the knowledge or the experience of a first century prophet. Over a period of a few years, there were no less than four major films dealing with encounters with meteors, comets or asteroids. One introduced us to the idea of an "extinction event." It is generally assumed now that we have had events like that in the history of the planet; one ended the age of the dinosaurs. As awful as the events of Revelation sound, they are far from impossible. They are indeed certain to come and now we don't need a prophet to tell us they are in our future. We have science and Hollywood to tell us that. We need a prophet, though, to tell us why.

> Then the third angel sounded: And a great star fell from heaven, burning like a torch, and it fell on a third of the rivers and on the springs of water. The name of the star is Wormwood. A third of the waters became wormwood, and many men died from the water, because it was made bitter (vv. 10-11).

It is only natural to wonder as you read through some of these disasters, are they all natural disasters, like passing through the tail of a comet? Or are some of them man-made? The earlier trumpets do sound like cosmic events, but this third trumpet is different. One can imagine this "great star falling" as a missile coming in, carrying chemical or biological weapons – something well beyond John's horizon, but it could happen tomorrow with weapons now available.

> Then the fourth angel sounded: And a third of the sun was struck, a third of the moon, and a third of the stars, so that a third of them were darkened. A third of the day did not shine, and likewise the night. And I looked, and I heard an angel flying through the midst of heaven, saying with a loud voice, "Woe, woe, woe to the inhabitants of the earth, because of the remaining blasts of the trumpet of the three angels who are about to sound!" (vv. 12-13).

It is almost too much to think about. After all this, there are three more angels to sound their horns. The next chapter in Revelation includes the fifth and sixth angels and as you read them, the overwhelming impression is that these are not natural disasters. This is war. Human beings are engaged in the final acts of destruction from which, except for divine intervention, no flesh would be saved alive.[v]

You don't have to go back many generations to a place where, had you spoken of something putting an end to all life on the planet, men would have scoffed. Then we went through a time when man could do it, but he would have to work at it. Now we have come to the place where we could put an end to life without even intending to.

So two more angels sound with terrible disasters following, but we have only found six of the seven last trumpets, and only two of the three final "woes." It is not until chapter 11 that the seventh and last angel blows his trumpet.

> The second woe is past. Behold, the third woe is coming quickly. Then the seventh angel sounded: And there were loud voices in heaven, saying, "The kingdoms of this world have become the kingdoms of our Lord and of His Christ, and He shall reign forever and ever!" And the twenty-four elders who sat before God on their thrones fell on their faces and worshiped God, saying: "We give You thanks, O Lord God Almighty, The One who is and who was and who is to come, Because You have taken Your great power and reigned. The nations were angry, and Your wrath has come, *And the time of the dead, that they should be judged,* And that You should reward Your servants the prophets and the saints, And those who fear Your name, small and great, And should destroy those who destroy the earth." Then the temple of God was opened in heaven, and the ark of His covenant was seen in His temple. And there were lightnings, noises, thunderings, an earthquake, and great hail (Revelation 11:14-19).

Right here, at the last trumpet is the moment of the resurrection of the dead and the rapture [catching away] of the saints. It takes place at the *end* of the period the Bible calls "the Great Tribulation" and just before the period called "The Wrath of God." It is right here that we once again pick up the thread that has run from the beginning and through all the appointed times of God. It is Judgment Day.

I made the point previously that the early church had connected the Jewish New Year, or the Feast of Trumpets, to the resurrection. I also made the point that it is called in the Hebrew, a day of shouting, or cheering.

Someday you will gather up your feet into your bed, and you will die. It may be a heart attack that takes you. Or congestive heart failure. Or it may be the gradual shut down of your vital organs. And you will sleep. I doubt that you will be conscious of the passage of time at all.

Perhaps you will be "grinding at the mill." You may be working in your cubicle or cutting your grass. You may even be hiding out in a cave someplace. In a moment, in the twinkling of an eye, you will find yourself cut loose from the earth, rising upward, your body radically changed. And you will know. You will know that you are finished with the flesh and that you are about to meet the Glorified Christ. Do you think you will shout?

No pilot ever forgets his first solo flight. I recall one part of mine vividly to this day. After the take-off, the climb to pattern altitude, the setting up on the downwind leg, all of which required concentration, I turned around and looked at the empty seat behind me and shouted at the top of my voice. The part of that flight I remember most vividly is the moment of the shout.

Some of us have a saying when we land an airplane successfully. We grin and say, "Cheated death again." And I know that all that is nothing compared to the shout I will make when I know I have finally cheated death. It makes my hair stand on end to imagine the scene around Christ when we meet him in the air. I expect all of us, including Jesus himself, will be grinning from ear to ear and weeping at the same time. The cheer will be deafening. The celebration will be overwhelming.

I don't have a certain knowledge of the timing of events after that. But I suspect it will take us all of the ten days between trumpets and the Day of Atonement to settle down and see what Yom Kippur is really about.

My favorite TV commercial is one about the brave new world coming our way through technology, the internet, communications.

Voice after voice around the world asks, "Are you ready?" "Are you ready?" "Are you ready?" And finally, a little girl comes on the screen, looks me right in the eye and asks, "Are You?"

You see, in the end, we will face death and we will win. "O Death, where is your sting?" Paul asked. "O Grave, where is your victory now?" Thanks be to God, who gives us the *win* through our Lord Jesus Christ.

---

i. 1 Corinthians 15:51-52

ii. It is easy to forget that the very earliest Christians were Jewish and had been members of one or another of the Jewish sects of the day. The Pharisees and Sadducees are the two commonly encountered in the New Testament. One fundamental difference between these two sects was that the Pharisees believed in a resurrection of the dead, while the Sadducees did not. Apparently, the Sadducean error had crept into the church along with several other mistaken ideas.

iii. See 2 Corinthians 12:1 ff.

iv. In ancient times, horses were not used for agriculture, but for warfare, often pulling chariots, the "tanks" of the armies of old. Consequently, when kings came in peace, they rode mules or donkeys – icons for humility.

v. "For then there will be a great tribulation, such as has not occurred since the beginning of the world until now, nor ever shall. And unless those days had been cut short, no life would have been saved; but for the sake of the elect those days shall be cut short (Matthew 24:21-22 NASB).

14

The Day of Atonement

*For if, when we were enemies, we were reconciled to God by the
death of his Son, much more, being reconciled, we shall be saved
by his life. And not only so, but we also joy in God through our
Lord Jesus Christ, by whom we have now received the atonement
(Romans 5:10-11 KJV).*

In the Autumn of every year, the Jews celebrate their most
solemn festival, Yom Kippur, the Day of Atonement. Would it
surprise you to learn that Yom Kippur is a Christian holiday as well,
that the New Testament church observed the day, only with a
different sense of its meaning? Very few Christians take any note of
the day at all, and that is surprising, since the day is all about the
ministry of Christ. They cheerfully observe Easter which is not in the
Bible at all, and ignore the Day of Atonement which is not only
biblical, it lies right at the heart of the meaning of the Christian Faith.
Maybe it is because observing the Day of Atonement requires a fast,
but it is probably because no one ever thinks of it.

So, how can I say that Yom Kippur is a Christian holiday as well
as a Jewish holiday? I could point to Acts, where Luke mentions
that sailing in the Mediterranean was now dangerous because "the
fast" was already past. It is a reference to the fast of the Day of
Atonement, which comes at the beginning of the stormy season in
that part of the world (Acts 27:9).

But it is better, I think, to look at the Christian *significance* of the day. During the entire period in which the New Testament was written, the churches not only continued to observe the Sabbath, but the festivals and holydays of the Bible as well. That really shouldn't surprise anyone, since in the early years the church was almost entirely Jewish. But the new Christians began to see a new significance in those festivals as time went by. The peculiarity of the New Testament is that it is not a systematic dissertation on the theology of the early church. It is a collection of *ad hoc* writings originally intended for living, first century Christians, sometimes to solve problems that had arisen in the community. Imagine how much information would be lost to us if the Corinthian church had not been so problematic.

All those people had a background in the faith that is somewhat different from the modern Christian. The Gospels and letters of the New Testament fit into that background and made sense to them in connection with that background. They understood these documents somewhat differently from us. For one thing, they had no "New Testament" to cite. For them, the Old Testament was their Bible, their "Holy Scriptures." As Paul wrote to Timothy:

> But you must continue in the things which you have learned and been assured of, knowing from whom you have learned them, and that from childhood you have known the Holy Scriptures, which are able to make you wise for salvation through faith which is in Christ Jesus. All Scripture is given by inspiration of God, and is profitable for doctrine, for reproof, for correction, for instruction in righteousness, that the man of God may be complete, thoroughly equipped for every good work (2 Timothy 3:14-17).

Bear in mind that the only "Holy Scriptures" that Timothy knew from his childhood were those of what we call "The Old Testament," and that those Scriptures were able to make him wise for salvation. Moreover, when Paul says "all Scripture is given by inspiration of God," he is referring solely to the Old Testament. The New Testament is replete with references to the Old Testament, because it was the *only written authority they had.*[i] If Paul wanted a written Scriptural authority for what he said, the only source he could cite was the Old Testament. The only other source they had was the oral tradition of the words of Jesus. It may come as a surprise to realize that the four Gospels of the New Testament were written later than Paul's best known epistles. That in no way diminishes the importance or the authority of the Gospels. And the oral traditions that lay at the root of the Gospel were strong and finalized by eye witnesses. Memorization was much more commonly practiced in that world than in ours.

Occasionally, the writers of New Testament books launch into explanations of the Old Testament that open up avenues of thought we otherwise might never notice. In the Book of Hebrews, for example, there is a commentary on the Temple ceremony of the Day of Atonement. Here is where our thread once again comes into view. Scholars are not certain who wrote the book of Hebrews, but the most common attribution is to Paul. His subject throughout the book is Christ, his divinity, his priesthood, his works. He is at some pains to establish that Jesus is our High Priest even though, in the flesh, he comes from the tribe of Judah, not Levi. And in the process of explaining and developing the priesthood of Christ, he incidentally gives us a *Christian* commentary on the Day of Atonement, *Yom Kippur*, and tells us what it actually means to a Christian. Now for Paul to write to a group of Christians to explain the Christian meaning of a "Jewish holiday" should be suggestive. But before we go there, we need to take a look at the original commandment for the Day of Atonement:

> Also the tenth day of this seventh month shall be the Day of Atonement [i.e., Reconciliation]. It shall be a holy convocation for you [i.e., you go to church]; you shall afflict your souls [fast],[ii] and offer an offering made by fire to the LORD.

> And you shall do no work on that same day, for it is the Day of Atonement, to make atonement for you before the LORD your God. For any person who is not afflicted in soul on that same day shall be cut off from

his people. And any person who does any work on that same day, that person I will destroy from among his people. You shall do no manner of work; it shall be a statute forever throughout your generations in all your dwellings. It shall be to you a sabbath of solemn rest, and you shall afflict your souls; on the ninth day of the month at evening, from evening to evening, you shall celebrate your sabbath (Leviticus 23:27-32).[iii]

As an interesting aside, the precise limits of this day are prescribed with much more precision than they are on the other days. It may have something to do with impressing on one's mind not to cut the fast short, but it also limits the overly righteous who might think if one day is good, two is better. In any case, it is probably the fact that they are fasting on this day that leads to the precise delineation of the day.

So once a year, all Israel came together to be reconciled to God, and consequently to one another. What does all this have to do with Christianity? Fortunately for us, Paul fully develops the theme of this day in his letter to the Hebrew Christians. It is part of a longer discussion of the priesthood of Christ. Paul finds it necessary to digress from that theme and explain some things to us about the services in the Temple.

Then indeed, even the first covenant had ordinances of divine service and the earthly sanctuary. For a tabernacle was prepared: the first part, in which was the lampstand, the table, and the showbread, which is called the sanctuary; and behind the second veil, the part of the tabernacle which is called the Holiest of All, which had the golden censer and the ark of the covenant overlaid on all sides with gold, in which were the golden pot that had the manna, Aaron's rod that budded, and the tablets of the covenant; and above it were the cherubim of glory overshadowing the mercy seat. Of these things we cannot now speak in detail (Hebrews 9:1-5).

Paul takes pains to draw a mental image for his readers. The layout of the Tabernacle, and later the Temple, was simple enough. It was a rectangular structure comprising two equal squares, one was the Holy Place, the other was the Holy of Holies. The heart of all this was the Ark of the Covenant, with two giant golden Cherubs touching their wingtips over the Ark. The cover of the ark is called the "mercy seat," or the seat of mercy. In Hebrew, it is *Kippur*, hence *Yom Kippur*, the day of covering.

> Now when these things have been thus prepared, the priests are continually entering[iv] the outer tabernacle, performing the divine worship, but into the second only the high priest enters, once a year, not without taking blood, which he offers for himself and for the sins of the people committed in ignorance. The Holy Spirit is signifying this, that the way into the holy place has not yet been disclosed, while the outer tabernacle is still standing (Hebrews 9:6-8 NASB).

Paul reveals something of his method right here. He says that the Holy Spirit *signified* something by the order of service in the old Tabernacle. In this case, the service revealed that man did not have complete access to God in olden times, but now it is different. The Temple was like a stage, upon which the drama of the plan of God was played out in the ceremonies performed there. Everything they did had meaning. By the time the Epistle of Hebrews was written, the apostles were beginning to see, perhaps in ways they had never seen before, that all those ceremonies played out on the stage of the Temple pointed, of all places, to the ministry of Jesus Christ.

The Tabernacle, Paul said, was a figure, a metaphor. This, he said, "is an illustration for the present time, indicating that the gifts and sacrifices being offered were not able to clear the conscience of the worshiper" (v. 9). The entire structure of the Tabernacle and its service had meaning, meaning that reaches to "the present time."

> But Christ came as High Priest of the good things to come, with the greater and more perfect tabernacle not made with hands, that is, not of this creation. Not

with the blood of goats and calves, but with His own blood He entered the Most Holy Place once for all, having obtained eternal redemption (Hebrews 9:11-12).

If we are going to understand what Paul is talking about, we need to know a little more about the background. He is making an oblique reference to the ceremony that took place on the Day of Atonement, something his Hebrew readers would have understood. But lacking that background, we need a little more help.

The ceremony in question is described in considerable detail in the 16th chapter of Leviticus. These instructions come just after a tragic event when Aaron's two sons had decided to engage in some innovative worship at the Tabernacle. They had offered "strange fire" which simply meant burning incense that they had no instructions to offer, at a time when they had no business doing it. They got too close to the power in the Tabernacle and got burned to a crisp for their trouble. They were away, smoking, wrapped in their coats.

Now the LORD spoke to Moses after the death of the two sons of Aaron, when they offered profane fire before the LORD, and died; and the LORD said to Moses: "Tell Aaron your brother not to come at just any time into the Holy Place inside the veil, before the mercy seat which is on the ark, lest he die; for I will appear in the cloud above the mercy seat" (Leviticus 16:1-2).

This was not merely a matter of a bad tempered God who would kill him if he didn't get it just right. He was coming into the presence of enormous power. You don't wander in among high tension lines without taking safety precautions. If you want an idea of how this works, see the movie *Raiders of the Lost Ark* for an idea. The scene at the end of the movie where they open up the Ark will give you an idea of what it might have been like.

In this case, Aaron had to be prepared with certain offerings for purification, and he had to be properly attired. He had to take a bath and dress properly. Then he had to make certain offerings for himself and his family. Aaron, the High Priest, had to be ceremonially perfect, because in this ceremony he would represent Jesus Christ and his work.

Once he finished all of his preparation, he took two kids of the goats and presented them before the Lord at door of the Tabernacle. He then cast lots upon the two goats; one lot for Jehovah, and the other lot for the "scapegoat." Each of these two little goats had a role to play.

First, though, he took incense and put it on hot coals inside the Holy of Holies to generate plenty of smoke. God said he would appear there, and the smoke would screen Aaron from the intense light of God's presence. Then he took the blood of a bullock and offered it for himself and for his family, making an atonement for them, sprinkling the blood of the bullock on the *cover* of the ark.

It is worth noting a play on words here. Yom Kippur means literally a day of covering. The making of an atonement, in Hebrew is to make a covering. And the word translated "Mercy seat" in the Bible is actually "Cover" and specifies the lid on the Ark of the Covenant.

Then the priest came back outside and killed the goat that was "for the Lord" as a sin offering. He took that blood into the Holy of Holies and made an atonement for the sins of the Children of Israel. For a Christian reader, this falls easily into place. The High Priest has to first make an atonement for himself, so he can represent Christ. Then, representing Christ, he takes the blood of the goat into the Holy of Holies and makes an atonement for everyone.

In Christian typology, that would be Christ, presenting his blood before the Father's throne as an atonement for mankind. The actual event, not the ceremonial event, took place on the Sunday morning after the resurrection of Jesus which was explained in chapter seven of this book.

When the High Priest, representing Christ, finished that atonement, he returned to the people, perhaps representing Christ returning to earth.

And he shall go out to the altar that is before the LORD, and make atonement for it, and shall take some of the blood of the bull and some of the blood of the goat, and put it on the horns of the altar all around. Then he shall sprinkle some of the blood on it with his finger seven times, cleanse it, and consecrate it from the uncleanness of the children of Israel. And when he has made an end of atoning for the Holy Place, the tabernacle of meeting, and the altar, he shall bring the live goat (Leviticus 16:18-20).

All this seems strange in that the Altar of God is holy, and it should not need cleansing. What may explain this is that throughout the year as sin offerings were made, the blood of those offerings is sprinkled again and again on this altar. The altar in itself becomes, in a way, polluted. So once a year, the priest must make an atonement for the altar, the Holy Place, and the Holy of Holies. The implication is that once, in the passage of all time, all this has to be reconciled to God.

Now this live goat is of particular interest. He is called the "scapegoat." In the Hebrew, he is the *Azazel*, which means the goat of departure or the goat that escapes.

Aaron shall lay both his hands on the head of the live goat, confess over it all the iniquities of the children of Israel, and all their transgressions, concerning all their sins, putting them on the head of the goat, and shall send it away into the wilderness by the hand of a suitable man. The goat shall bear on itself all their iniquities to an uninhabited land; and he shall release the goat in the wilderness (Leviticus 16:21-22).

This goat is not killed. The first goat was the one that shed blood, this goat lives on in the wilderness. And you might well ask why, since an atonement has been made for sin, is there any sin left to confess? If the sin has been forgiven, why is there yet another ceremony regarding sin? This is an important question from a Christian perspective.

Justification, as a Christian concept, is the forgiveness of sins past. But all of us know that even though we are forgiven, we still commit sin. We are forgiven but sin still dogs our steps. Sin seems to take on a life of its own, and mere forgiveness does not solve all the problems. We know this as a practical matter of fact.

If you stood outside the Temple and watched the High Priest lay both his hands on the head of the scapegoat, and heard him confess all the sins of the house of Israel on this goat, what would you have thought and felt as you watched the goat depart? Perhaps you would recall the Psalm, "As far as the east is from the west, so far hath he removed our transgressions from us" (Psalms 103:12).

And so we come to realize that we must not only be forgiven of our sins, but the effect of the sins, the continuing burden of the sin must be sent away from us to free us of the lingering consequences. The Jews call the days leading up to Yom Kippur "The Days of Awe." They are days in which they examine themselves before coming to God for reconciliation. A Jewish sage spoke about this concept and cited an ancient prayer:

> How can we complain, what can we say, how can we speak, and how can we justify ourselves? We will examine our ways and scrutinize them, and we will return to You, for Your Hand is outstretched to accept returnees. Not with abundance and *not with deeds* have we come before You; like paupers and mendicants we knock on Your door. Throughout the year, we try to present ourselves before others (and before our own selves) as the proud owners of spiritual wealth, as capable and accomplished individuals. Only upon the arrival of *the moment of truth* does it become clear that "like paupers and mendicants we knock on Your door." This does not mean that we are devoid of accomplishment; rather, any accomplishments we have attained cannot be attributed to us.[v]

This is a long way from salvation by works. You may have heard the ten days from Trumpets to Atonement are called "The Days of Awe." A better phrase in English is "The Days of Repentance." What the Jews are looking for on the Day of Atonement is *Grace*. This may come as a surprise to those who think that Judaism is a kind of salvation by works.

After the ceremony on Yom Kippur, Aaron had to change clothes and bathe again, and so did the man who let go the goat in the wilderness. There was a lot of washing going on. It is this ceremony that the writer of Hebrews is talking about in his 9th chapter.

> For if the blood of bulls and goats and the ashes of a heifer, sprinkling the unclean, sanctifies for the purifying of the flesh, how much more shall the blood of Christ, who through the eternal Spirit offered Himself without spot to God, cleanse your conscience from dead works to serve the living God? (Hebrews 9:13-14).

It is plain that Paul is drawing a strong connection between the blood of that little goat being taken into the Holy of Holies, and the blood of Christ offered, one time, to God for us.

> For when Moses had spoken every precept to all the people according to the law, he took the blood of calves and goats, with water, scarlet wool, and hyssop, and sprinkled both the book itself and all the people, saying, "This is the blood of the covenant which God has commanded you." Then likewise he sprinkled with blood both the tabernacle and all the vessels of the ministry. And according to the law almost all things are purified with blood, and *without shedding of blood there is no remission* (vv. 19-22).

This takes us back to Jesus and his disciples at the Last Supper when he gave them a little cup of wine and said, "Here, take, drink it all. This is my blood of the New Testament, shed for you."

> For Christ has not entered the holy places made with hands, which are copies of the true, but into heaven itself, now to appear in the presence of God for us; not that He should offer Himself often, as the high priest enters the Most Holy Place every year with

blood of another; He then would have had to suffer often since the foundation of the world; but now, once at the end of the ages, He has appeared to put away sin by the sacrifice of Himself. And as it is appointed for men to die once, but after this the judgment, so Christ was offered once to bear the sins of many. To those who eagerly wait for Him He will appear a second time, apart from sin, for salvation (vv. 24-28).

All this is compared to the High Priest who went once in the year into the Tabernacle with a sacrifice for sin. Now, once in the history of the world, Christ our High Priest, has offered his own blood for us.

We are left to wonder what Christ is going to do relative to that second goat when he returns the second time unto salvation. For there is no doubt that the writer of Hebrews is making this connection between the movements of the High Priest in this service and the ministry of Christ. And we are left to ponder the words "after this the judgment."

One may wonder why there are two "Sacrifices of Christ" along this thread. Our best chance to understand this question is to pick up the thread and follow it on.

---

i. There are no less than 46 direct citations from the Old Testament in the Epistle to the Romans alone.

ii. "Then I proclaimed a fast there, at the river of Ahava, that we might afflict ourselves before our God, to seek of him a right way for us, and for our little ones, and for all our substance" (Ezra 8:21).

iii. The Hebrew day began and ended at sunset, not at midnight as in later civilization.

iv. The verb tenses here, according to the NASB, suggest that this is written while the Temple is standing and the service continuing.

v. Raval Amital, from "The Selichot Prayers."

15

Reconciled to God

For if, when we were enemies,
we were reconciled to God by the death of his Son,
much more, being reconciled,
we shall be saved by his life (Romans 5:10).

If you have read much of the Bible, or if you have gone to church very long, you already know that somewhere, out there in the future, there is a day of judgment. Somehow, in my youth, in listening to various preachers, I got the impression of God, sitting behind a bench in a courtroom setting with a lot of books open before him, judging my life. One preacher I recall envisioned God playing our sins back for us on a giant movie screen for everyone to see. I groaned inside and figured I would want to crawl under my pew and find a place to hide.

Another preacher envisioned God having a big lever by his throne, and when we come there for judgment, some go to heaven but for others, he pulls the lever and a trapdoor opens and sends them screaming down to hell. That one left my hair standing on end.

Most of what you hear about Judgment Day owes more to the imagination of man than to the Bible. But we have already seen that there is a day of judgment. Even dying doesn't get us away from it. Sooner or later, we have to face up to judgment. As Paul said, "It is appointed for men to die once, but *after this* the judgment" (Hebrews 9:27).

But this Judgment Day is nothing like the traditional depictions, and there is one very surprising thing about it which I will come to later. But the first thing to know about it is that, in spite of the fact that the day of judgment is pictured on the Feast of Trumpets, the Day of Atonement is also tied to Judgment Day. This is not entirely surprising, because Jewish tradition also connects Rosh Hashana and Yom Kippur. The author of the book of Hebrews is a Hebrew himself, writing to Hebrews, who would have naturally made the connection. As noted, the days between Rosh Hashana and Yom Kippur, they call "The Days of Awe." They are days of self examination and repentance in preparation for the Atonement.

One can only wonder why something so meaningful in the plan of God, and so firmly connected to biblical holidays, is so consistently neglected across Christendom. Every one of these "Jewish" holidays is a festival showing forth the life, work, plan, and ministry of Jesus Christ. The fact that most Christians have forgotten them in favor of holidays that are not in the Bible notwithstanding, these days are crucial to understanding the plan of God.

So, what do we know about Judgment Day? Earlier, we looked at what Jesus had to say about it. On the first occasion where he sent his disciples out on their own, he told them where to go, where not to go, and what to do and say. On this journey, they were to take no money. They were to depend entirely on the hospitality of the people of the town. Then Jesus told them that whatever house or city they entered where the people would not listen, they were to leave and to shake the dust off their feet. "Assuredly, I say to you," Jesus said, "it will be more tolerable for the land of Sodom and Gomorrah in the day of judgment than for that city!" (Matthew 10:15).

Now it is hard to imagine any place more corrupt than Sodom and Gomorrah and yet we find the curious fact that there may be some greater level of *tolerance* for them in the day of judgment than for some other cities. There is a day of judgment, and there are distinctions to be made. And we should make no mistake. If there is reason why a person should have known better, there isn't going to be very much slack. Ignorance of the law is no excuse, but apparently it can be mitigating on the day of judgment. On yet another occasion, Jesus chastised his audience and warned, "But I say to you that for every idle word men may speak, they will give account of it in *the day of judgment*" (Matthew 12:36).

It sends a little chill down your spine, doesn't it? There is not a one of us who has not spilled out words that we later wish we hadn't said. But if every slip of the lip is going to be judged, what about some of our more serious crimes? Every idle word, not just the malicious words, will be judged.

I discussed earlier how the Temple elite were already consulting about how to dispose of Jesus. It is incredible that they would contemplate murdering such a man, especially in the face of all he had done. But the awful truth is that Jesus' message threatened their hold on power and that trumped every other consideration. Returning to that passage in John, Jesus, knowing all that was in their hearts and minds, told them this:

> Most assuredly, I say to you, the Son can do nothing of Himself, but what He sees the Father do; for whatever He does, the Son also does in like manner. For the Father loves the Son, and shows Him all things that He Himself does; and He will show Him greater works than these, that you may marvel (John 5:19-20).

The first step was to establish the foundation of Jesus' authority. He wasn't the harbinger of a new religion. He wasn't acting on his own. He was only carrying out the will and intent of the Father. How far could this reach? All the way to the resurrection of the dead:

> For as the Father raises the dead and gives life to them, even so the Son gives life to whom He will. For the Father judges no one, but has committed all judgment to the Son (vv. 21-22).

This is stunning. It isn't the remote God who sits in judgment of sinful man, it is the *Son*. There is a reason for this which he develops as he goes forward:

> That all should honor the Son just as they honor the
> Father. He who does not honor the Son does not
> honor the Father who sent Him. Most assuredly, I say
> to you, he who hears My word and believes in Him
> who sent Me has everlasting life, and shall not come
> into judgment [Gr. "condemnation"], but has passed
> from death into life. Most assuredly, I say to you, the
> hour is coming, and now is, when the dead will hear
> the voice of the Son of God; and those who hear will
> live. For as the Father has life in Himself, so He has
> granted the Son to have life in Himself, and has given
> Him authority to execute judgment also, because He
> is the Son of Man (vv. 23-27).

So now we know who the Judge is. It is not the Father, it is
the Son. And he is given judgment *because he is the son of man.* I
take that to mean that authority to judge was given because he had
been human. He had lived in the flesh. He had been tempted in every
way that we are,[i] and yet had never yielded. He had the authority and
the right to judge.

> Do not marvel at this; for the hour is coming in which
> all who are in the graves will hear His voice and come
> forth; those who have done good, to the resurrection
> of life, and those who have done evil, to the
> resurrection of condemnation. I can of Myself do
> nothing. As I hear, I judge; and My judgment is
> righteous, because I do not seek My own will but the
> will of the Father who sent Me (vv. 28-30).

Jesus is not acting unilaterally. He does nothing of himself,
and judgment is once again connected to the resurrection. His
judgment is right and is fair. We now know who the Judge is and we
know why.

Something very important follows on the heels of this piece of
information. I said before that the statement in Hebrews about the
Judgment Day, "it is appointed unto men once to die, but after this
the judgment," came in the middle of a commentary on the Day of

Atonement ceremony. That ceremony, which is described in some detail in Leviticus 16, is interesting for a number of reasons. One is the clear connection between the duties of the High Priest on that day and the ministry of Jesus. On this day, the priest made certain offerings, went into the Holy of Holies for the one and only time of the year, sprinkled blood there, made an atonement for the people, put all the sins of Israel on the head of a goat and sent him away.

But what did the people do on the Day of Atonement? Nothing. Absolutely nothing. But didn't they have to fast? Well, yes, but fasting is doing nothing – not even eating. They did have to come before God in a repentant spirit. The ten days from the Feast of Trumpets to the Day of Atonement are called the days of repentance. They take time for self examination and repentance at this season.

But on the Day of Atonement, they do nothing. The High Priest does everything for them. The whole ceremony, the animals that had to be killed, all the washings, all the sprinkling of blood, all the sanctifying of vessels, altars and Tabernacle, were all done by the priests. The people stood there in assembly and did absolutely nothing. The corollary with the ministry of Jesus is clear. There is nothing we can do to justify ourselves. We cannot earn the forgiveness of sin. We cannot accomplish it with sacrifices and *never could have*. And so when we come to stand before God in judgment, there is nothing we can do. Everything has to be done for us, by our High Priest, Jesus Christ.

Even Israel of old could not achieve forgiveness by their own efforts. There was nothing they could do. They had to assemble on the Day of Atonement in humility and fasting and do nothing, while the High Priest made an atonement for them and reconciled them to God. It is odd how many people seem to believe there was a different way of salvation for people in the Old Testament from the way in the New Testament. In the Old Testament, they think, the Jews were saved by works, but in the New Testament, men are saved by grace. Not so. *Salvation has never been by works.* It was never possible that it could have been done by works. The Day of Atonement makes that clear enough.

> For Christ has not entered the holy places made with hands, which are copies of the true, but into heaven itself, now to appear in the presence of God for us; not that He should offer Himself often, as the high priest enters the Most Holy Place every year with blood of another (Hebrews 9:24-25).

This is a plain reference to the ceremony on the Day of Atonement in the Temple, where the priest symbolically went into the presence of God, into the Holy of Holies and sprinkled blood there to make an atonement for the people. Jesus is now at the right hand of the Father, appearing in the presence of God on our behalf.

> He then would have had to suffer often since the foundation of the world; but now, *once* at the end of the ages, He has appeared to put away sin by the sacrifice of Himself. And as it is appointed for men to die once, but after this the judgment, so Christ was offered once to bear the sins of many. To those who eagerly wait for Him He will appear a second time, apart from sin, for salvation (Hebrews 9:26-28).

It is a lot like the ceremony of the Day of Atonement in that he appears before God once to make an atonement for us. And then for those of us who look for him, he will appear the second time, like the High Priest returning to the people from the Holy of Holies, this time without sin, this time for salvation. Judgment Day is actually, for those in Christ, a day of salvation, not condemnation. If you are in Christ, when you stand before him at the last day, it is not to be condemned, it is to be saved. And there is nothing for you to do when you get there. You don't have to bring in a list of good works. You don't have to bring in your good deeds, your accomplishments, your righteousness. None of that will help. What you need, and all that you will need, is Christ.

Paul continues his letter along this theme, comparing Christian salvation to the Day of Atonement.

For the law, having a shadow of the good things to come, and not the very image of the things, can never with these same sacrifices, which they offer continually year by year, make those who approach perfect (Hebrews 10:1).

There was no consideration that all the sacrifices in the world would somehow make you right with God. If that had been the case, then there would have been no further need for them.

For then would they not have ceased to be offered? For the worshipers, once purified, would have had no more consciousness of sins. But in those sacrifices there is a *reminder* of sins every year (vv. 2-3).

The continual round of sacrifices seems to have been for the purpose of keeping a man mindful of the fact that he is a sinner, something we find all too easy to forget. Paul then underlines this in the plainest of words: "For *it is not possible* that the blood of bulls and goats could take away sins." It never was. This should be obvious, but it may take a mental adjustment on our part, and perhaps a reevaluation of some favorite Scriptures to get this straight.

But if the blood of animals didn't affect salvation, how did those people get their sins forgiven? The only way this could possibly have been efficacious was by looking forward to Christ in those sacrifices they made.

Therefore, when He came into the world, He said: "Sacrifice and offering You did not desire, But a body You have prepared for Me. In burnt offerings and sacrifices for sin You had no pleasure" (vv. 5-6).

That last is an Old Testament citation.[ii] It is not some new idea. Then why were animal sacrifices offered? And if they didn't forgive sins, how were people in the Old Testament forgiven their sins? One can only conclude that they were forgiven the same way we are. By the sacrifice of Christ. I can only see animal sacrifices in the Old Testament as living icons. They were reminders of sin, a presentation on the stage of the Temple that told us how God was going to forgive our sins by the shedding of blood. They were all images, verbal icons, of the work of Jesus Christ.

> Then I said, "Behold, I have come; In the volume of the book it is written of Me; To do Your will, O God." Previously saying, "Sacrifice and offering, burnt offerings, and offerings for sin You did not desire, nor had pleasure in them" (which are offered according to the law), then He said, "Behold, I have come to do Your will, O God." He takes away the first that He may establish the second. By that will we have been sanctified through the offering of the body of Jesus Christ once for all (vv. 7-10).

He takes away sacrifices and burnt offerings for sin, that he may establish the will of God. The idea of "once" is repeated again and again to connect to the one time in the year when the priest did this, signifying the *one time in history* when Christ would do it.

> And every priest stands ministering daily and offering repeatedly the same sacrifices, which can never take away sins. But this Man, after He had offered one sacrifice for sins forever, sat down at the right hand of God, from that time waiting till His enemies are made His footstool. For by one offering He has perfected forever those who are being sanctified. But the Holy Spirit also witnesses to us; for after He had said before, "This is the covenant that I will make with them after those days, says the LORD: I will put My laws into their hearts, and in their minds I will write them" Then He adds, "Their sins and their lawless deeds I will remember no more." (vv. 11-17).

This is a surprising statement. He doesn't say he is going to do away with the law, but rather that he will write the law in their hearts and minds. It is not a matter of whether the law exists, but where it resides. It is no longer external, it is internal. "Now where there is remission of these," Paul continued, "there is no longer an offering for sin." Once you have repented, been baptized, and been forgiven, there is no further need for any sin offering.

As Paul continues, remember the parallel with the priestly ceremony of the Day of Atonement.

> Therefore, brethren, having boldness to enter the Holiest by the blood of Jesus, by a new and living way which He consecrated for us, through the veil, that is, His flesh, and having a High Priest over the house of God, let us draw near with a true heart in full assurance of faith, having our hearts sprinkled from an evil conscience and our bodies washed with pure water (vv. 19-22).

All of these icons are well recognized as elements of the ceremony of the Day of Atonement: The entering into the holiest of all, a new and living way, drawing near to the very throne of God, the full assurance of faith, the sprinkling of our hearts, our bodies washed with pure water like the priests also had to do. Any Hebrew reader would hear the echoes of the ceremony of the Day of Atonement.

> Let us hold fast the confession of our hope without wavering, for He who promised is faithful. And let us consider one another in order to stir up love and good works, not forsaking the assembling of ourselves together, as is the manner of some, but exhorting one another, and so much the more as you see the Day approaching. For if we sin willfully after we have received the knowledge of the truth, there no longer remains a sacrifice for sins, but a certain fearful expectation of judgment, and fiery indignation which will devour the adversaries (vv. 23-27).

Here is where some people become frightened. We don't want to hear about the unpardonable sin. But recall that on the Day of Atonement, we only have to come before God in a repentant spirit. Remember that the law requires that we fast as a sign of repentance and there is nothing for us to do. I think this is the way we have to understand the admonition in Hebrews. Any sin that can be repented of can be forgiven. But you do have to take that step. There is no need to be afraid of judgment if you come to God repentant. The act of atonement is accomplished entirely by Christ. All this would be immediately clear to his Hebrew readers.

In his letter to the Romans, Paul returns again to the theme of the Day of Atonement. It seems the ceremony played very large in his thoughts.

> Therefore, having been justified by faith, we have peace with God through our Lord Jesus Christ, through whom also we have access by faith into this grace in which we stand, and rejoice in hope of the glory of God. And not only that, but we also glory in tribulations, knowing that tribulation produces perseverance; and perseverance, character; and character, hope. Now hope does not disappoint, because the love of God has been poured out in our hearts by the Holy Spirit who was given to us. For when we were still without strength, in due time Christ died for the ungodly (Romans 5:1-6).

And those who could be described as ungodly will be able to stand before God, justified, in the day of judgment.

> For scarcely for a righteous man will one die: yet peradventure for a good man some would even dare to die. But God commendeth his love toward us, in that, while we were yet sinners, Christ died for us. Much more then, being now justified by his blood, we shall be saved from wrath through him. For if, when we were enemies, we were reconciled to God by the death of his Son, much more, being reconciled, we shall be saved by his life. And not only so, but we also joy in God through our Lord Jesus Christ, by whom we have now received *the atonement* (vv. 7-11 KJV).

The whole idea of atonement is the reconciliation of man to God. It is a pity that more Christian people do not take notice of this day, because this day pictures what their faith is all about.

---

i. "For we do not have a High Priest who cannot sympathize with our weaknesses, but was in all points tempted as we are, yet without sin (Hebrews 4:15).

ii. Psalm 40:6 ff.

16

The Feast of Tabernacles

On Jordan's stormy banks I stand and cast a wistful eye,
To Canaan's fair and happy land where my possessions lie.
I am bound for the promised land, yes I am
I am bound for the promised land.
Oh who will come and go with me,
I am bound for the promised land.

It seems to me that we in the Christian faith have lost touch with our roots in important ways. We are so comfortable in the modern world, so at home in it, so in touch with it, that some of our old hymns really don't mean much to us any longer. Take the fine old hymn above. We may cast a wistful eye, but it is as likely to be toward next year's Mercedes sitting in the showroom as it is to be toward "Canaan's fair and happy land where our possessions lie." Our possessions are in the garage. What do Jordan and Canaan have to do with the Christian faith, anyhow? Then there is this old gospel song:

> This world is not my home,
> I'm just a passin' through
> If heaven's not my home,
> O Lord what shall I do?
> The angels beckon me

From heaven's open door,
And I can't feel at home in this world any more.

One of the most fundamental Christian beliefs is that we are not at home here. We are strangers, we are pilgrims, and we look for a better world to come. As strangers in a foreign land, we are not supposed to be comfortable in this world. But in this modern world, comfort is the game.

Christianity is a faith for the hard times. It doesn't flourish amid wealth and easy times and easy going. One reason the Christian faith took such firm root among black slaves was that there was so little hope for them in this world. They identified with Moses because Moses was the great leader who led the slaves out of Egypt. They sang the old spiritual: "Go down, Moses, way down to Egypt land. Tell ole Pharaoh: Let my people go." They identified with Jesus:

Poor little Jesus boy
They laid you in a manger
Poor little holy chile
They didn't know who you was.

And the Negro Spiritual identified with the Jordan River and Canaan as well. One of the greatest, *Deep River*, groaned with longing for a better place and time.

Deep River, I long to cross over Jordan.
Deep River, I long to cross over into campground.

The Jordan River, in hymns and spirituals, became the symbol of passing from this life into the next life. I recall vividly a song my father used to sing with the Stamps Quartet. He was their bass singer, and one of his solo numbers was *I Won't Have to Cross Jordan Alone*.

When I come to to the river at the ending of day,
when the last winds of sorrow have blown.
There'll be somebody waiting to show me the way,
I won't have to cross Jordan alone."

The song presumed that this life is a hard, tough way to go, and that we look forward to a time when we can move forward into a better life and a better land. The River Jordan was the symbol of crossing over from this world to that better world, from this life into the next life.

The promised land was the Kingdom of Heaven, and the wilderness wanderings of Israel represented the temporary nature of life. We are only here for a while. "This world is not my home. If heaven's not my home, O Lord, what shall I do?"

It is hard to account for the shift that has taken place among Christians who no longer read the Old Testament, and who never think about the significance of the Old Testament to the Christian Faith. I can't help wondering how much of it has to do with prosperity.

The Apostle Paul wrote out of hard times. "If in this life only we have hope in Christ Jesus," he said, "we are of all men, most miserable." He also wrote about Israel of old: "Now all these things happened to them as examples, and they were written for our admonition, upon whom the ends of the ages have come" (1 Corinthians 10:11). In other words, all that happened to Israel, all that they did, all the suffering they endured, all the correction and chastisement, all of it had to do with us. It is written in the Word for our admonition.

Christians of an earlier generation found much in the history and practice of Israel that they could identify with. They saw themselves as "The Israel of God." [i] In this book, I have been talking about the holydays in the Bible that many assume are merely "Jewish" holidays. And I think many people are surprised to find how meaningful these days are to Christians.

There is one festival in particular that falls into line with these old hymns I have been talking about, hymns which form a great part of Christian tradition. In the 23rd chapter of Leviticus, where God lays out the entire scheme of his appointed festivals through the year, one of the greatest is the Feast of Tabernacles.

> Speak to the children of Israel, saying: The fifteenth day of this seventh month shall be the Feast of Tabernacles for seven days to the LORD. On the first

day there shall be a holy convocation. You shall do no customary work on it (Leviticus 23:34-35).

What do you do on these festivals? You take off work and go to church. It's a holiday. The qualifier, "customary" work leaves room for the preparation of the feast, because on these days, God's children were supposed to celebrate. There would be a lot of food available because of the offerings on these days. And the first and last days of this festival are Sabbaths when no ordinary work should be done.

> For seven days you shall offer an offering made by fire to the LORD. On the eighth day you shall have a holy convocation, and you shall offer an offering made by fire to the LORD. It is a sacred assembly, and you shall do no customary work on it. These are the feasts of the LORD which you shall proclaim to be holy convocations, to offer an offering made by fire to the LORD, a burnt offering and a grain offering, a sacrifice and drink offerings, everything on its day; besides the Sabbaths of the LORD, besides your gifts, besides all your vows, and besides all your freewill offerings which you give to the LORD. Also on the fifteenth day of the seventh month, when you have gathered in the fruit of the land, you shall keep the feast of the LORD for seven days; on the first day there shall be a Sabbath-rest, and on the eighth day a Sabbath-rest (vv. 36-39).

As long as Israel had a priesthood and a Tabernacle, they made certain offerings on these days. One primary aspect of sacrifices was that there was plenty of food for the festival. So how hard is this? We take off two days from work and we celebrate with a Texas style barbecue. People who call these observances a "yoke of bondage"[ii] give me a chuckle. Here are people who have been slaves all their lives, who worked every hour they could, seven days a week, from daylight until dark, every day of their lives. And here comes someone saying, "Let's put a yoke of bondage on these people. Let's give them the day off and make them eat a lot." These are holidays where we eat, we drink, we celebrate, we come together and we worship, all in God's presence. Oh yes, there was something else the Israelites had to do at this festival.

> And you shall take for yourselves on the first day the fruit of beautiful trees, branches of palm trees, the boughs of leafy trees, and willows of the brook; and you shall rejoice before the LORD your God for seven days. You shall keep it as a feast to the LORD for seven days in the year. It shall be a statute forever in your generations. You shall celebrate it in the seventh month (vv. 40-41).

What were they to do with these tree limbs? They were to make themselves a brush arbor, something that used to be done in the autumn among farm people in certain parts of the country. They built a brush arbor and had a seven day revival. I recall vividly going to one of these brush arbor meetings with my grandparents. They farmed 40 acres in Arkansas, and the brush arbor was a good two mile walk from the farm home where I was born. They sang hymns, prayed, and the preacher preached. But that was back in rural Arkansas in the 30s and 40s. Life was harder then. This idea for this brush arbor had to come from Leviticus, but people back then paid more attention to the Old Testament.

> You shall dwell in booths for seven days. All who are native Israelites shall dwell in booths, that your generations may know that I made the children of Israel dwell in booths when I brought them out of the land of Egypt: I am the LORD your God. So Moses declared to the children of Israel the feasts of the LORD (vv. 42-44).

Israel lived in booths, also called "tabernacles," for 40 years in the wilderness. During these years, their tabernacles were hardly brush arbors for there weren't that many trees in the desert. They were usually tents that they had to carry with them. There was plenty of time for them to develop a yearning for a better land, a better world. This idea is deeply rooted in the Bible, and it is not merely a Jewish thing. It was around before there ever was a Jew and it persisted all the way into Christianity. As in the earlier chapters, we have to take another look at Father Abraham.

> By faith Abraham, when he was called to go out into a place which he should after receive for an inheritance, obeyed; and he went out, not knowing whither he went. By faith he sojourned in the land of promise, as in a strange country, dwelling in *tabernacles* with Isaac and Jacob, the heirs with him of the same promise: For he looked for a city which hath foundations, whose builder and maker is God (Hebrews 11:8-10 KJV).

Among Christian people, the word "tabernacle" has taken on a wide variety of meanings. You will see some pretty elaborate churches called "tabernacles." The use of the word for a church building probably derives from the central "Tabernacle," also called the "tent of meeting." It was a place of worship. But it wasn't a building. It was a tent, and it persisted in Israel all the way through the reign of David. The Christian Tabernacle is usually a permanent home for the church.[iii]

But in Abraham's case, he was not at home, even in the promised land. He, his son and grandson lived out their lives in tabernacles, an old word for "tent." He looked for a city with some permanence, but he never saw it. He left a city at God's command, and spent the remainder of his life living in tents. And he, in a very real sense, is an icon down through all generations of what the life of a man of God in this world is supposed to be.

> By faith Sarah herself also received strength to conceive seed, and she bore a child when she was past the age, because she judged Him faithful who had promised. Therefore from one man, and him as good as dead, were born as many as the stars of the sky in multitude; innumerable as the sand which is by the seashore. *These all died in faith*, not having received the promises, but having seen them afar off were assured of them,

embraced them and confessed that they were strangers
and pilgrims on the earth (vv. 11-13).

There is nothing more fundamental to the Christian faith than
the awareness that we are strangers and pilgrims on the earth, that we
are not at home. And what is of special interest here is that the
promise was *never fulfilled* in this life. When God has given you a
promise, and you die never having received it, how on earth can you
die in faith? Well, only if you realize that this world, this life, is not
all there is, that this world is not your home. Your home is elsewhere
at another time.

For those who say such things declare plainly that they
seek a homeland. And truly if they had called to mind
that country from which they had come out, they
would have had opportunity to return. But now they
desire a better, that is, a heavenly country. Therefore
God is not ashamed to be called their God, for He has
prepared a city for them (vv. 14-16).

In an important way, the observance of the Feast of
Tabernacles is a *confession* that we are strangers and pilgrims, that
we are not at home here, that we look for something far better. And
the idea of a great city also passed into Christian hymns as a symbol
of our hope of a better and more enduring world. One old hymn
declares, "I'm bound for that city."

The very idea and role of the man Abraham is that he lived his
entire life in hope of something he never got. A permanent home.
And this, I guess, is the fundamental definition of faith. I fear
sometimes we think that having faith means we trust that God is
going to give us the promise now, in this life. But no, faith involves a
commitment to something beyond this life. Abraham confessed that
his home was not in this world. Something too many Christians seem
to have completely forgotten.

And what more shall I say? For the time would fail me
to tell of Gideon and Barak and Samson and Jephthah,
also of David and Samuel and the prophets: who

through faith subdued kingdoms, worked righteousness, obtained promises, stopped the mouths of lions, quenched the violence of fire, escaped the edge of the sword, out of weakness were made strong, became valiant in battle, turned to flight the armies of the aliens. Women received their dead raised to life again. And others were tortured, *not accepting deliverance*, that they might obtain a better resurrection (Hebrews 11:32-35).

A better resurrection. The icon for this is crossing Jordan and entering the promised land. People actually accepted torture, spurning deliverance, that they might achieve this resurrection.

Still others had trial of mockings and scourgings, yes, and of chains and imprisonment. They were stoned, they were sawn in two, were tempted, were slain with the sword. They wandered about in sheepskins and goatskins, being destitute, afflicted, tormented; of whom the world was not worthy. They wandered in deserts and mountains, in dens and caves of the earth (vv. 36-38).

Not one of them was ever at home. Not one of them had a comfortable recliner and table to sit up to and enjoy a warm meal. Not one of them had a Mercedes. They had to walk everywhere they went. It is fair to say that the world was not worthy of these men and women.

And all these, having obtained a good testimony through faith, did not receive the promise, God having provided something better for us, that they should not be made perfect apart from us (vv. 39-40).

There is only one conclusion you can draw from this. The promise is not in this world. It's "across Jordan," in the world to come. All this has everything to do with the Feast of Tabernacles as a *Christian* holiday.

Now I can already hear someone objecting: "Well, yes, but it was the people who were Israelite *born* who were to keep this feast. It was a part of their national history. You already cited the verse."

True, but I have two important things to say about this. One, it was the dwelling in booths in *particular* that was a lesson for Israelites. They did this as an example for us upon whom the ends of the world are come,[iv] for us to learn from their experience of 40 years in the wilderness. But the festival is also one of the "appointed times of Jehovah." It is not merely an Israelite festival. None of them are. They are the times at which God acted in history.

Then there is a fascinating passage of Scripture that casts an entirely different light on the subject. You find it, oddly enough, in a prophecy of the future, in Zechariah, chapter 14. It starts with a vision of the "Day of the Lord," a singular day in the history of the world, and a day yet in our future. It takes place at the very end time, and it is the day of God's wrath. The chapter starts with very bad news for the people of Jerusalem and some of the implications are truly stunning.

> Behold, the day of the LORD is coming, And your spoil will be divided in your midst. For I will gather all the nations to battle against Jerusalem; The city shall be taken, The houses rifled, And the women ravished. Half of the city shall go into captivity, But the remnant of the people shall not be cut off from the city (Zechariah 14:1-2).

These are terrible tidings, but they shouldn't be surprising for anyone living in the 21st century. Jerusalem has been the focal point for wars and killings for as long as we can remember. And not a few of the prophets, including Jesus himself, have seen major disaster for the city at the time of the end. But you don't have to be a prophet to recognize that the slow burn around Jerusalem is eventually going to boil over. Odd thing is, that this prophecy calls for half the city to be carried away and half to be left. And for a generation or more we sat looking at Jerusalem as a divided city. The good news is that when this finally takes place, God himself will take a hand.

Then the LORD will go forth And fight against those nations, As He fights in the day of battle. And in that day His feet will stand on the Mount of Olives, Which faces Jerusalem on the east. And the Mount of Olives shall be split in two, From east to west, Making a very large valley; Half of the mountain shall move toward the north And half of it toward the south (vv. 3-4).

The striking thing about this is that the Lord's feet have not stood on the Mount of Olives since Jesus ascended from that very spot nearly 2000 years ago. On that day, an angel spoke to the disciples as they stood gaping and looking up. "Men of Galilee," said the angel, "why do you stand gazing up into heaven? This same Jesus, who was taken up from you into heaven, will so come in like manner as you saw Him go into heaven."[v] Apparently, he will return back to the same place. And if you have ever been to Jerusalem you have seen with your own eyes that this prophecy is yet to be fulfilled, because the mountain is still whole.

"Thus the LORD my God will come," continues Zechariah, "And all the saints with You" (v. 5). This implies clearly the return of Christ, and one thing that happens when Christ returns is the resurrection of the saints. They rise to meet him in the air, and if we have Zechariah right, they come right back down with him to the Mount of Olives.

It shall come to pass in that day That there will be no light; The lights will diminish. It shall be one day Which is known to the LORD; Neither day nor night. But at evening time it shall happen That it will be light. And in that day it shall be that living waters shall flow from Jerusalem, Half of them toward the eastern sea And half of them toward the western sea; In both summer and winter it shall occur. And the LORD shall be King over all the earth. In that day it shall be; "The LORD is one," And His name one (vv. 6-9).

Well. This leaves the student of prophecy little room for error.

We have arrived at the Kingdom of God and the establishment of that kingdom over all the earth. All this is future. And there is some heavy going even here.

> And this shall be the plague with which the LORD will strike all the people who fought against Jerusalem: Their flesh shall dissolve while they stand on their feet, Their eyes shall dissolve in their sockets, And their tongues shall dissolve in their mouths (v. 12).

This may be the source for some of the special effects in *Raiders of the Lost Ark*. But it is in verse 16 where we suddenly find our thread again.

> And it shall come to pass that everyone who is left of all the nations which came against Jerusalem shall go up from year to year to worship the King, the LORD of hosts, and to keep *the Feast of Tabernacles* (v. 16).

There is no reason why the Gentile nations should dwell in booths to recall Israel's wilderness wanderings. Obviously, the booths are particular to Israel's history, but that is not all there is to the festival. And the Jews are not the only ones who are going to be keeping the Feast.

> And it shall be that whichever of the families of the earth do not come up to Jerusalem to worship the King, the LORD of hosts, on them there will be no rain. If the family of Egypt will not come up and enter in, they shall have no rain; they shall receive the plague with which the LORD strikes the nations who do not come up to keep the Feast of Tabernacles. This shall be the punishment of Egypt and the punishment of all the nations that do not come up to keep the Feast of Tabernacles (vv. 17-19).

Is it commanded? Oh yes, it is commanded. With sanctions. So the meaning of the festival clearly transcends Israel's wandering in the desert, living in tents, many thousands of years ago. The Israelite meaning of the feast does not apply to the Egyptians, and they have to keep the feast anyway. Why? The reason can't be physical. It has to be spiritual. They too need to confess that this world is not their home, their hope. They too must come to confess that they seek a city with foundations.

> In that day "HOLINESS TO THE LORD" shall be engraved on the bells of the horses. The pots in the Lord's house shall be like the bowls before the altar. Yes, every pot in Jerusalem and Judah shall be holiness to the LORD of hosts. Everyone who sacrifices shall come and take them and cook in them. In that day there shall no longer be a Canaanite in the house of the LORD of hosts (vv. 20-21).

We are no longer dealing with a situation where everything around is common except for a small island of holiness. Everything will be holy.[vi] I'm not sure how to take all that but one thing is clear. All mankind is going to come to Jerusalem and everything in the city is going to be holy.

The Feast of Tabernacles makes the confession that we are strangers, that we don't really belong here, that we seek a better country. It looks forward to the Kingdom of God and cries out with the slave, "Deep River, Lord, I want to cross over into camp ground."

---

i. Galatians 6:16.

ii. As per Galatians 5:1, "Stand fast therefore in the liberty by which Christ has made us free, and do not be entangled again with a yoke of bondage."

iii. The English word, "tabernacle" comes from the Latin, tabernaculum, which means, "tent."

iv. See 1 Corinthians 10:11

v. Acts 1:11.

vi. That people sacrifice does not necessarily imply a sacrificial system of worship as under the Levitical system. Any animal killed under the law was to be properly killed, and sacrifices were meat for people to eat.

17

Only Here a Little While

Then I saw an angel coming down from heaven,
having the key to the bottomless pit and a great chain in his hand.
He laid hold of the dragon, that serpent of old, who is the Devil
and Satan, and bound him for a thousand years
(Revelation 20:1-2).

I hesitate to tell you this, because when I do, you are liable to snap the book shut and find something else to read. But I have given this a lot of thought and study, and I have come to the conclusion that, sooner or later, one way or another, we are all going to die. See what I mean? No one wants to hear that. But if you are still reading, stay with me a little further and see what I am driving at.

I had my 72nd birthday not long ago and like most people my age, I have some minor health problems, some of which could become more serious with the passage of time. So I take my vitamins and supplements in hope of getting rid of some of the creaks and groans, and I follow my doctor's instructions on therapy. I read articles and books on health related issues, and a range of stuff comes in the mail that promises to cure nearly every ailment known to man. And every once in a while, I stop and laugh at myself, because I know I am looking for the fountain of youth. Maybe, I think, I can stop this process, maybe I can feel the way I did when I was 40. Now I know I am fighting a losing battle. The battle is worth fighting, because I have a lot of work I want to do and I would like to keep the old body going as long as it will go. But I know, and you know, that in the end, we all die.

Our old friend Paul faced up to the same question for different reasons. He faced death in more ways than we ever will. His problems were not altogether health-related. He had some people who wanted to kill him. From time to time, he got a little mellow when he wrote to his friends, and talked about his mortality. He had been through some hard going by the time he wrote his second letter to the Corinthians. "Therefore, since we have this ministry," he said, "as we have received mercy, we do not lose heart" (2 Corinthians 4:1).

It was not that he didn't have good reason to give up. The story he tells elsewhere of what he had to go through for the sake of the Gospel is almost heartbreaking. But it was the ministry that drove him on and wouldn't allow him to quit. He wrote further:

> But we have renounced the hidden things of shame, not walking in craftiness nor handling the word of God deceitfully, but by manifestation of the truth commending ourselves to every man's conscience in the sight of God (v. 2).

Paul's language, coming as it does from the Greek, is somewhat cumbersome, but the point comes through. There were no marketing strategies in Paul's ministries. There was no manipulation of the audience, no spin. The expression "by manifestation of the truth," means that Paul tells it like it is. It is an open statement. No craftiness, no tricks. Paul's approach was to speak the truth and let the chips fall where they may. In doing so, he placed himself before each man's sense of right and wrong, his conscience. In a way, he originated the idea of "we report, you decide."

> But even if our gospel is veiled, it is veiled to those who are perishing, whose minds the god of this age has blinded, who do not believe, lest the light of the gospel of the glory of Christ, who is the image of God, should shine on them. For we do not preach

> ourselves, but Christ Jesus the Lord, and ourselves
> your bondservants for Jesus' sake. For it is the God
> who commanded light to shine out of darkness, who
> has shone in our hearts to give the light of the
> knowledge of the glory of God in the face of Jesus
> Christ. But we have this treasure in earthen vessels,
> that the excellence of the power may be of God and
> not of us (vv. 3-7).

For just a moment, Paul becomes something of a poet, something he doesn't often do. He draws an image of an earthenware crock filled with diamonds, pearls and rubies. He and his companions are the earthenware crocks, something easily broken, cheaply replaced, and not particularly attractive. The treasure is the Gospel.

> We are hard pressed on every side, yet not crushed;
> we are perplexed, but not in despair; persecuted, but
> not forsaken; struck down, but not destroyed; always
> carrying about in the body the dying of the Lord
> Jesus, that the life of Jesus also may be manifested in
> our body. For we who live are always delivered to
> death for Jesus' sake, that the life of Jesus also may be
> manifested in our mortal flesh (vv. 8-11).

It seems counterintuitive, but Paul is saying that you will only come to appreciate the value of life when you come face to face with your own mortality, when you understand that you are going to die. Only then, does the life held out to us by God really mean very much.

> So then death is working in us, but life in you. And
> since we have the same spirit of faith, according to
> what is written, "I believed and therefore I spoke," we
> also believe and therefore speak, knowing that He
> who raised up the Lord Jesus will also raise us up
> with Jesus, and will present us with you (vv. 12-14).

Paul vividly sees that this earthly life, this perishable existence is not the end. It is a means to an end, a vehicle that carries Paul forward to a goal. And for Paul, everything he went through was, as with Christ, for the sake of his people.

> For all things are for your sakes, that grace, having spread through the many, may cause thanksgiving to abound to the glory of God. Therefore we do not lose heart. Even though our outward man is perishing, yet the inward man is being renewed day by day (vv. 15-16).

This is what I started out to say. The outward man will, indeed must, perish. It isn't possible to take flesh and blood into the Kingdom of God.[i] So when you look in the mirror and see the wrinkles begin to show, and the flesh begin to sag, you have to face up to it. You can't take this body with you into the Kingdom of God. This is one of the most fundamental of Christian teachings and it ties directly into the thread we have been following. You and I are going to die, and unless we "put on immortality," to use Paul's words, it's all over.

> For our light affliction, which is but for a moment, is working for us a far more exceeding and eternal weight of glory, while we do not look at the things which are seen, but at the things which are not seen. For the things which are seen are temporary, but the things which are not seen are eternal (vv. 17-18).

The body with which you and I walk through this life, is *temporary*. I have brought you all the way through this chapter to help us get used to this idea because it is fundamental to the Feast of Tabernacles. Paul will make that connection next.

"For we know," he said, "that if our earthly house of this tabernacle were dissolved, we have a building of God, an house not made with hands, eternal in the heavens" (2 Corinthians 5:1). Now it is plain that Paul, in speaking of his earthly "tabernacle" is talking about the physical body. He has already said that he bears in his body the dying of the Lord Jesus. And whether we like it or not, we bear about in our bodies every day, the dying, the decay, the rot. He realizes that the physical human body was never intended to be permanent. It is temporary – a tabernacle. We sometimes have to remind one another, "We are just not going to get out of this alive." The body is a tabernacle, a tent.

> For in this we groan, earnestly desiring to be clothed with our habitation which is from heaven, if indeed, having been clothed, we shall not be found naked. For we who are in this tent [this tabernacle] groan, being burdened, not because we want to be unclothed, but further clothed, that mortality may be swallowed up by life (2 Corinthians 5:2-4).

I think I understand what Paul is saying. Now that I am getting a little older, I catch myself groaning more often. There is a grunt when I bend over to tie my shoes. A groan when I get out of a chair where I have sat too long. The human body is like an old tent you keep using year after year on your vacation. The poles get bent, it starts to leak, it has holes in it, and it never kept you very warm anyway. Then, one hunting season, you find that your ridge pole is missing, so you substitute a rope between two trees. It's not very pretty but it keeps off the night air. In some ways, our bodies are a lot like that old tent, and it isn't hard to imagine why Paul might have selected a tent as a metaphor for the human body.

But all his life up to this day, he had observed the Feast of Tabernacles, so the simile of comparing his body to a tabernacle or tent followed easily. He had probably pitched the same tent year after year. His trade was making tents, so the idea came naturally to mind.

> You shall dwell in booths for seven days. All who are native Israelites shall dwell in booths, that your generations may know that I made the children of Israel dwell in booths when I brought them out of the land of Egypt: I am the LORD your God (Leviticus 23:42-43).

It may be from this that many make the assumption that the Feast of Tabernacles was merely a Jewish feast. As it happens, that is a mistaken assumption. It is a strange one for Christians to make when you look back over all the old hymns we sing. We compare ourselves to Israel, wandering in the wilderness, looking for a homeland, wanting to cross Jordan into the promised land. All the imagery is of a church that is "the Israel of God." [ii] And all that time of living in tabernacles is compared to this life, here and now, the temporary nature of this life. Crossing over Jordan is crossing over into the Kingdom of God, which flesh and blood cannot inherit.

Even in the Old Testament, one can see that it is a mistake to think that the Feast of Tabernacles is only for Israelites. In the last chapter, we read what the Prophet Zechariah saw happening after the return of Christ. He saw all the kingdoms of the world, even Egypt, coming up to Jerusalem to keep the Feast of Tabernacles, and suffering sanctions if they didn't come. It was *mandatory*. [iii]

This is an end time prophecy, but it should be plain enough that the Egyptians don't keep the Feast of Tabernacles with the same meaning as the children of Israel. They didn't dwell in booths for 40 years in the wilderness. Israel did. Yet it is mandatory for Egypt to keep the Feast of Tabernacles. Is it possible that people have been too quick to dismiss the holidays of the Bible as being merely Jewish? After all, they are the appointed times of Jehovah.

The Tabernacle was a natural metaphor for Paul to use in his letter, because he was *still* observing this festival many years after his conversion. We learn this from incidental references, but they are illuminating. For example, Paul came to Ephesus on his way back to Jerusalem and went to the synagogue as was his long standing custom:

> And he came to Ephesus, and left them there; but he himself entered the synagogue and reasoned with the Jews. When they asked him to stay a longer time with them, he did not consent, but took leave of them, saying, "I must by all means keep this coming feast in Jerusalem; but I will return again to you, God willing." And he sailed from Ephesus (Acts 18:19-21).

Most commentators note that the feast in question was certainly the Feast of Tabernacles. Paul didn't merely say he wanted to be there at the feast. He said he wanted to *keep* the feast in Jerusalem. The Feast of Tabernacles is not merely a Jewish holiday. The earliest Christians kept the feast at the same time as the Jews, though doubtless with a modified sense of meaning that translated over into Christian symbolism.

But what are those meanings? The idea of the temporary nature of life is the meaning of one of them. Camping out in the wilderness is another. That this world is not our home is yet another. The fact that we look for a city that is permanent becomes part of the meaning. The Feast of Tabernacles is a confession, a reminder, that we are strangers and pilgrims here below, that we don't belong here, that we belong to a higher kingdom. We encounter all these things as we follow the thread year by year.

But there may be even more than that. We have already connected, in earlier chapters, the Feast of Trumpets to the return of Christ. That placed us in the book of Revelation among the prophecies of the last days.

> Now I saw heaven opened, and behold, a white horse. And He who sat on him was called Faithful and True, and in righteousness He judges and makes war. His eyes were like a flame of fire, and on His head were many crowns. He had a name written that no one knew except Himself. He was clothed with a robe dipped in blood, and His name is called The Word of God (Revelation 19:11-13).

There is no mistaking who this is. This is the returning Christ, at the head of all the armies of heaven. He comes this time to fight, and "He treads the winepress of the fierceness and wrath of Almighty God." He now carries the title: King of Kings and Lord of lords. Then comes the great battle with all the nations who have gathered to fight against Jerusalem – the battle that ensues, we call Armageddon. It is a grisly scene that the prophet sees. It is really "apocalyptic."

But then the scene changes. Since the Feast of Tabernacles follows the Feast of Trumpets with the return of Christ, and the Day of Atonement with the Last Judgement, what would naturally follow in the course of events?

> Then I saw an angel coming down from heaven, having the key to the bottomless pit and a great chain in his hand. He laid hold of the dragon, that serpent of old, who is the Devil and Satan, and bound him for a thousand years; and he cast him into the bottomless pit, and shut him up, and set a seal on him, so that he should deceive the nations no more till the thousand years were finished. But after these things he must be released for a little while (Revelation 20:1-3).

This is that time that some people call "The Millennium." If you read much about prophecy, you have probably heard people speak of premillennial, amillennial, or postmillennial approaches to the interpretation of these events. A millennium is simply a thousand years. During this thousand year epoch, Satan is bound. In Revelation, it appears that Christ returns before that thousand years begins. The work that has to be done starts with the binding of Satan, an event that some compare to the second goat of the ceremony on the Day of Atonement. That goat is not killed as a sacrifice, but is led away and left in the desert, alive.

> And I saw thrones, and they sat on them, and judgment was committed to them. Then I saw the souls of those who had been beheaded for their witness to Jesus and for the word of God, who had not worshiped the beast or his image, and had not received his mark on their foreheads or on their hands. And they lived and reigned with Christ for a thousand years. But the rest of the dead did not live again until the thousand years were finished. This is the first resurrection (vv. 4-5).

Since this follows the Feast of Trumpets and the return of Christ, and it follows the Day of Atonement when according to one belief, Satan is bound, it is only natural to think that the Feast of Tabernacles may picture the Millennium, the time when the Kingdom of God is established.

So every year in the autumn, thousands of people descend on Jerusalem to keep the Feast of Tabernacles. Many who live in the city create little booths, or tabernacles on their roofs or balconies and actually sleep in them during the Feast. And you might be surprised to learn that a rather large number of Christian people travel to Jerusalem to observe the Feast of Tabernacles every year. As a percentage of Christianity, that number is small, but they must have come to see, somewhere along the way, what the Feast of Tabernacles means from a Christian perspective, or they wouldn't be doing that.

I don't think one has to go to Jerusalem to keep the Feast. Jews all around the world keep the Feast, even though they cannot go to Jerusalem. So do a surprising number of Christian folk. You can find some of them, if you make the effort.

Now there is a curious thing about the Feast of Tabernacles. It is said to be a seven day festival, and then there is an eighth day. No one knows for sure the chronology of the world from Adam to this day, but as it is presented to us in the Bible, it forms what appears to be a seven thousand year plan. We have just about finished six thousand years of human thrashing around trying to find our own way. The seventh thousand year period is the rule of Christ, and not only his rule, but that rule shared with those who have trusted him and served him in this life. It is these who come up in "the First Resurrection."

> Blessed and holy is he who has part in the first resurrection. Over such the second death has no power, but they shall be priests of God and of Christ, and shall reign with Him a thousand years (v. 6).

Where? Well, right here on the earth, where there is work to be done. Do you recall what Jesus said about the meek? "Blessed are the meek: for they shall inherit the earth" (Matthew 5:5). It is odd that we think those who are blessed by God are going to heaven, when Jesus says they will inherit the planet. This is not to say that they will not *eventually* go to heaven, but apparently, not quite yet. The Kingdom of God, the Kingdom of Heaven, is *here*. On the earth. Because it is here that Christ comes to rule, and where he rules is the Kingdom of Heaven.

But did you notice that sentence above: "The rest of the dead lived not again until the thousand years were finished"? The passage doesn't say a word about a second resurrection, but in saying this and adding, "This is the first resurrection," it certainly implies it. The First Resurrection is said to be all the dead in Christ. Then the rest of the dead who don't live again until the thousand years are finished, must of necessity be the dead who are *not* "in Christ." It would seem that there is a resurrection at the beginning of the thousand years, and a resurrection at the end of it.

"Blessed and holy is he who has part in the first resurrection," the messenger said, "over such, the second death has no power." This statement does not necessarily extend to those in the second resurrection.

> Now when the thousand years have expired, Satan will be released from his prison and will go out to deceive the nations which are in the four corners of the earth, Gog and Magog, to gather them together to battle, whose number is as the sand of the sea. They went up on the breadth of the earth and surrounded the camp of the saints and the beloved city. And fire came down from God out of heaven and devoured them (vv. 7-9).

There are still people down here, this late, who are ready to fight with God. This is hard to understand. I'll confess that quickly. How, at the end of a thousand years of Christ's rule, could there still be people who could be deceived and who could turn on God? Yet there is a part of me that recognizes how true it is. That no matter how clear the evidence, some people still have an antipathy toward God which is almost impossible to explain. The final destruction of these people is almost like a cutting off of all the loose ends. And at this moment, Satan is finally disposed of.

This is followed by one of the really great events in the plan of God.

---

i. "Now this I say, brethren, that flesh and blood cannot inherit the kingdom of God; nor does corruption inherit incorruption. Behold, I tell you a mystery: We shall not all sleep, but we shall all be changed; in a moment, in the twinkling of an eye, at the last trumpet. For the trumpet will sound, and the dead will be raised incorruptible, and we shall be changed. For this corruptible must put on incorruption, and this mortal must put on immortality (1 Corinthians 15:50-53).

ii. Galatians 6:16.

iii. See Zechariah 14:17 ff.

18

The Dilemma

*Brethren, my heart's desire and prayer to God for Israel
is that they may be saved (Romans 10:1).*

Many years ago, before I learned better than to argue religion,
I was engaged in a discussion with a chap about heaven and hell and
salvation. I had a problem with his beliefs and he had a problem with
mine. He believed that everyone goes to heaven or hell immediately
at death. There were no intermediate categories of people, and no
stops along the way. Not only that, but he believed that only those
who had accepted Jesus Christ as personal Savior would go to heaven
and the rest would go immediately to hell.

Hell, in his belief system, is a tough proposition. In hell, one
is tormented by fire, not for a few hours until he dies, not for a few
days, not even a few years. Hell is forever. I once heard a preacher
explain how long that is. He asked us to imagine a mountain of
granite one mile high and one mile in diameter at the base. Once a
year a little sparrow flies to the top of that mountain and proceeds to
sharpen his beak. When that little sparrow, sharpening his beak once
a year, will finally have worn that mountain of granite down to a little
pebble he could carry away, *one day* of eternity will have passed. If
you happen to be one of those souls in hell, that is rather a long day.
And the torment by fire goes on forever.

My granddad was a salty old fellow. I don't know if he ever

went to church in his life. He was known to use bad language when provoked. But overall, he was a pretty good sort. He was good to his family and his friends. He took me fishing many times, and we camped out together on the banks of a river, ran trot lines all night, fished all day.

Now if you want to tell me old J.D., my maternal grandfather, can't go to heaven because he didn't meet some standard of religious actions, I might be able to live with that. But there is no system of human logic that can see any justice in tormenting him with fire and brimstone for all eternity. There is something wrong with that picture.

But at least old J.D. knew who Jesus Christ was, he just didn't think Jesus made much difference to him. My discussion with the gentleman in question focused on people who had never heard the name of Jesus at anytime. How could it be right for God to torture these people forever? Tell me he is just going to leave them dead and we have one picture. Tell me he has arranged for their eternal torment and we have another altogether. Mind you, hell, as presented, isn't something that is just there. It has been created, because there is nothing that exists that God did not create. So we are presented with a God who created a place of torture and torment and planned for the torment of people who never even heard of him.

And then, there are the children. I asked him if all these people, including countless children, who had never had a chance to be saved, would burn for all eternity. I think I must have backed him into a corner, because he then said something completely off the wall, "Well, if they never had a chance to be saved, then they are saved."

I was flabbergasted, but I couldn't let that stand. "So, why then," I pressed, "does your church send missionaries to these people? To give them a chance to be lost?"

This came at the end of a rather long discussion about the whys and wherefores of churches who send missionaries into the far flung corners of the world because they believe that people out there in India, Africa, and Asia, are going to hell and burn for eternity. How is it, I wondered, that we spend all this time in our business meetings discussing whether we should install an air conditioner, stained glass windows, or taller steeples? If we really believe, as one television evangelist said in a letter, people are going to burn in hell for all eternity if we don't get the Gospel to them, why aren't we moving heaven and earth and spending every spare dime to keep missionaries in the field? There is an inconsistency here, and I hope every reader can see that.

That ended my discussion with the gentleman, but I had another not so long ago with my sister-in-law. We made our way through the discussion to the point where one has to deal with the question of salvation for people who never had a chance to be saved in this life. She knew as well as I did that you can't postulate a God who will torment forever people who never had a chance to be saved. Any thinking person is going to have a problem with that. She thought about it for a moment and then concluded, "Well, I believe that God will make a way."

We finally found agreement at that point, because I too believe that God will make a way. But I think it would be strange indeed if, in all the pages of the Bible, we couldn't find so much as a hint as to what that way is.

I am not so sure I would have seen this if it had not been for the thread we have been following. Many years ago, I began observing the holydays of the Bible and it was in one of these festivals that I found my hint as to what God's way of handling this dilemma might be.

I found that this is not a new question. It has been around for a long time. I know that a lot of people have shed many tears, and lain awake long nights worrying about loved ones who have died without accepting Jesus Christ as their personal Savior. They worry about hell, but they also fret about losing any chance of ever seeing their loved ones again. Apart from any concern about torment, the mere loss of the loved one forever is excruciating.

The Apostle Paul struggled with this same question for slightly different reasons. Paul traveled all over the Roman Empire, and everywhere he went, he went first to the synagogue and preached the Gospel of Christ. He preached with all the fervor of his being. He had seen Christ alive after his death and burial. Moreover, he had thoroughly investigated all the claims about Jesus, and he was absolutely convinced. He preached and argued the resurrection of Jesus in the synagogues, mostly to blank faces. Once, he got himself stoned for preaching this Gospel. But everywhere, most of the Jews rejected the message. This troubled Paul greatly. There was something profoundly wrong with the picture he was seeing, and he struggled through this question in his important letter to the Christians in Rome.

I have asked myself several times why Paul addresses this question in this particular letter. It is a long discussion, running three chapters. I have looked at the context and can't find any reason why the discussion arises here. The only thing I can conclude is that it was bothering Paul and he was able to find some resolution only by talking it out with someone.

Paul's style is elliptical. That is, he leaves a lot unsaid that he expects will be understood by his readers. Unfortunately, not many modern readers of the New Testament have the background in the Old Testament to quickly grasp what Paul is talking about. In the letter to the Romans alone, there are 46 direct citations from the Old Testament, and still more indirect references. They are taken in their original form, but without context. Unless you know the original point of the citation, you can easily miss what Paul is driving at. He is a difficult study at all times, and nowhere more so than in this passage.

It was at this point in Romans that I suddenly realized that the question that troubled me was not new. It had bothered Paul as well. What on earth, he wondered, is going to happen to the Jews? These are God's people. They know who God is, they have kept his laws, they have tried their best to be faithful to God, and for reasons Paul couldn't grasp, they were rejecting the Gospel wholesale. When you read these chapters in the book, consider that you have gotten this letter from an old friend (Paul knew many Roman Christians personally) who is pouring out his frustrations to you and working his way through a troubling issue. He begins with an unusual, threefold affirmation, which means he thinks you won't believe what he is about to tell you.

> I tell the truth in Christ, I am not lying, my conscience also bearing me witness in the Holy Spirit, that I have great sorrow and continual grief in my heart. For I could wish that I myself were accursed from Christ for my brethren, my countrymen according to the flesh, who are Israelites, to whom pertain the adoption, the

glory, the covenants, the giving of the law, the service of God, and the promises; of whom are the fathers and from whom, according to the flesh, Christ came, who is over all, the eternally blessed God. Amen (Romans 9:1-5).

It was that bad. I know you won't believe this, said Paul, but if it would help, if there were any way it could make a difference, I would even be willing to be cut off from Christ. It was a great heaviness for Paul, a constant sorrow to him, that all these people, God's people, such a talented, accomplished people, were continually turning their backs on the one they had been waiting for all their lives. So what's going on here?

But it is not that the word of God has taken no effect. For they are not all Israel who are of Israel, nor are they all children because they are the seed of Abraham; but, "In Isaac your seed shall be called." That is, those who are the children of the flesh, these are not the children of God; but the children of the promise are counted as the seed (vv. 6-8).

This is a long, hard sentence. But what Paul is driving at is that the word of God *has* taken effect, because those who are counted as Israel were not necessarily those who were ethnic Israelites, but those who believed, of whatever race or land. There is an Israel of God, there are children of Abraham, and it is the *believers* who are counted as such.

For this is the word of promise: "At this time I will come and Sarah shall have a son." And not only this, but when Rebecca also had conceived by one man, even by our father Isaac (for the children not yet being born, nor having done any good or evil, that the purpose of God according to election might stand, not of works but of Him who calls), it was said to her, "The older shall serve the younger." As it is written, "Jacob I have loved, but Esau I have hated" (vv. 9-13).

Many find this statement troubling, but it is crucial to the point Paul is making. Only someone familiar with the story from Genesis will fully grasp what Paul is driving at. Many generations before, God looked down upon a woman bearing twin boys inside her womb. Before either of the boys was born, so that he could establish one principle that was important for all men to understand in all ages, God said that what was to follow was not a matter of merit. It was a matter of his choice. The elder shall serve the younger. I will love Jacob. I will not love Esau. And so it was, as history played out.

While we are all prepared to accept that God is sovereign, and he can do whatever he wills, it doesn't make sense that Esau was rejected without so much as a chance to do the right thing. Paul recognized that, and went on to address it.

> What shall we say then? Is there unrighteousness with God? Certainly not! For He says to Moses, "I will have mercy on whomever I will have mercy, and I will have compassion on whomever I will have compassion" (vv. 14-15).

I know that God is sovereign. I know I can't lift up my voice and argue with him about things like this, but I have to be honest. If we are talking about forever, I don't get it. If the acceptance of one and the rejection of another is final, for all eternity, this seems unfair and wrong. But if it is for this life only that this decision holds, and if there is more beyond this life, then maybe there is something more to understand.

> So then it is not of him who wills, nor of him who runs, but of God who shows mercy. For the Scripture says to Pharaoh, "For this very purpose I have raised you up, that I may show My power in you, and that My name may be declared in all the earth." Therefore He has mercy on whom He wills, and whom He wills He hardens (vv. 16-18).

I don't mind telling you, I have struggled with this all my life. As a very young man, I read this and wondered, "What if I am one whom God has hardened?" How would I know, and what hope is there for me if he has hardened me? Obviously, he had not, but instead of being grateful that he had mercy on me, I was struggling with the other side of the equation.

Then there are those of us who have fathers, mothers, sisters, brothers, sons and daughters we love dearly and who might seem to have been hardened. At least, they show all the signs of it, and in many cases have departed this world in that condition. Does that mean they are lost to you forever based on an arbitrary decision made by God, a decision made, not on the merits of the person, but as it were, on the flip of a coin? Or is there something that we don't yet understand?

I suspect Paul had wrestled with this himself, and so he lays out his thought processes. I feel that he, to borrow his phrase, only saw this "through a glass, darkly." He had an idea of what God was doing, but it had to grow on him as he followed his knowledge of God and the Scriptures, linking them to what was actually happening on the ground. He seems only now to be putting it all together.

> You will say to me then, "Why does He still find fault? For who has resisted His will?" But indeed, O man, who are you to reply against God? Will the thing formed say to him who formed it, "Why have you made me like this?" Does not the potter have power over the clay, from the same lump to make one vessel for honor and another for dishonor? (vv. 19-21).

One can hardly argue with God, but I sit here wondering, "What's the point?" What is there that I can do, and does it make any difference what I do? I can accept what Paul is saying here, but it isn't very comforting. And what if I am one of those made for dishonor? This last idea once made me sweat.

> What if God, wanting to show His wrath and to make His power known, endured with much longsuffering the vessels of wrath prepared for destruction, and that He might make known the riches of His glory on the vessels of mercy, which He had prepared beforehand

for glory, even us whom He called, not of the Jews only, but also of the Gentiles? (vv. 22-24).

This is all well and good, but one can only hope he is "a vessel of mercy," and not "a vessel of wrath." It wasn't that I was worried so much about myself, but about all those people I have loved and lost, people who are *not* "vessels of mercy."

As He says also in Hosea: "I will call them My people, who were not My people, And her beloved, who was not beloved." And it shall come to pass in the place where it was said to them, "You are not My people," There they shall be called sons of the living God. Isaiah also cries out concerning Israel: "Though the number of the children of Israel be as the sand of the sea, The remnant will be saved. For He will finish the work and cut it short in righteousness, Because the LORD will make a short work upon the earth" (vv. 25-28).

And so the theme emerges. Out of all these people who have lived and died, only a remnant shall be saved. But what about the rest? What is to happen to them, are they just lost? This had been bothering Paul for months and he is only now beginning to make sense of it. He is working his way through this question in the full realization that, as far as this life is concerned, some are saved, most are lost, and there is not very much we can do to change that.

And as Isaiah said before: "Unless the LORD of Sabaoth had left us a seed, We would have become like Sodom, And we would have been made like Gomorrah." What shall we say then? That Gentiles, who did not pursue righteousness, have attained to righteousness, even the righteousness of faith; but Israel, pursuing the law of righteousness, has not attained to the law of righteousness. Why? Because they did not seek it by faith, but as it were, by the works of the law. For they stumbled at that stumbling stone. As it is written: "Behold, I lay in Zion a stumbling stone and rock of offense, And whoever believes on Him will not be put to shame" (vv. 29-33).

But what about the rest of them? You have to say of many of these people that they did their best. Why didn't they make it? Paul continues his argument by stating, in the firmest and most heartfelt terms, what it was he wanted to come out of this.

> Brethren, my heart's desire and prayer to God for Israel is that they may be saved. For I bear them witness that they have a zeal for God, but not according to knowledge. For they being ignorant of God's righteousness, and seeking to establish their own righteousness, have not submitted to the righteousness of God (Romans 10:1-3).

The first thing to take away from this is that these are not all bad people. Many are good people who, in their ignorance, have gone about this the wrong way. They have tried to establish their own righteousness, but have not understood the righteousness of God. Are we going to punish these people forever for what they did in ignorance, for doing the best they knew given their circumstances? Paul goes on in this tenth chapter to establish clearly the principle of salvation by grace, and then sets it opposite salvation by works. This, at least, is something well understood throughout the Christian faith. Having made and elaborated this point, he goes on to ask and answer the core question.

> I say then, has God cast away His people? Certainly not! For I also am an Israelite, of the seed of Abraham, of the tribe of Benjamin. God has not cast away His people whom He foreknew (Romans 11:1-2).

What are we to make of all this? He has told us that it was the Gentiles who had found God even though they had not looked for him. He was made manifest to those who did not ask after him. He said of Israel, "All day long I have stretched out My hands to a disobedient and contrary people" (Romans 10:21).

Which is it? Are they disobedient and contentious, or are they ignorant and without understanding? What is going to happen to them? Paul asks the key question. Has God cast them away? No, there is more to come.

> Or do you not know what the Scripture says of Elijah, how he pleads with God against Israel, saying, "LORD, they have killed Your prophets and torn down Your altars, and I alone am left, and they seek my life"? But what does the divine response say to him? "I have reserved for Myself seven thousand men who have not bowed the knee to Baal." Even so then, at this present time there is a remnant according to the election of grace (Romans 11: 2-5).

So there is a remnant, but that is not the question. What about the rest of them? The answer to that is cold comfort.

> What then? Israel has not obtained what it seeks; but the elect have obtained it, and the rest were blinded. Just as it is written: "God has given them a spirit of stupor, Eyes that they should not see, And ears that they should not hear, To this very day" (vv. 7-8).

Here we sit struggling with the question, "Is this fair?" Is it right for God to blind them, to give them a spirit of stupor so they *could* not see, and then to destroy them forever? He could, of course, just not ever raise them from the dead. Or he could raise them, judge them and then burn them up in a lake of fire. Or still worse, he could torment them in fire for eternity. Paul struggles alongside us.

> I say then, have they stumbled that they should fall? Certainly not! But through their fall, to provoke them to jealousy, salvation has come to the Gentiles. Now if the fall of them be the riches of the world, and the diminishing of them the riches of the Gentiles; how much more their fullness? (vv. 11-12).

How does that work? Down through all the ages, the religion of the Jews had been just that – a Jewish religion with a Jewish God. In many ways, the Jews had made Jehovah their own national property. "He is our God," they said, "not yours." This jealousy, this holding on to God, this xenophobia by the Jews had prevented the truth of God from going to the world. The answer is, they have to fall. It is only through their fall that salvation can go to the Gentiles.

What Paul is coming to is an acceptance of the fact of Judah's fall, and a recognition that this is not the end. What is going to happen so the other half of this, their fullness, can come to pass? It is right here that we get our hint of what God has in store. "For if their being cast away is the reconciling of the world," Paul wrote, "what will their acceptance be *but life from the dead?*" (v. 15).

The problem is not merely that we put these Israelites aside for a while so the Gentiles could come in, and then we'll go back and get them later. What about those who have died while we were getting this done? For there would have been many. Paul's answer? The receiving of them is "life from the dead."

In the nature of the problem we are wrestling with, Paul has sent up a small signal flag. The answer, Paul suggests, may be in the resurrection from the dead.

> For I do not desire, brethren, that you should be ignorant of this mystery, lest you should be wise in your own opinion, that blindness in part has happened to Israel until the fullness of the Gentiles has come in. And so all Israel will be saved (vv. 25-26).

That is a relief to hear, but how can it be? We follow the thread onward.

19

The Last Great Day

Thus says the Lord GOD: Behold, O My people,
I will open your graves and cause you to come up from your
graves, and bring you into the land of Israel (Ezekiel 37:12).

I had a friend once who allowed that human beings were like fish eggs. He and I were sitting in the sun on a bass boat trying unsuccessfully to catch something and he was trying to make sense of the world. A fishing boat is a great place for philosophizing. "I know," he said, "that there is only one way of salvation, and that is by the name of Jesus Christ. But I also know that the vast majority of the people who have ever lived have never so much as heard that name."

So he proceeded to draw an analogy to the life cycle of the largemouth bass who lays millions of eggs. Many of her eggs will be eaten by the male that fertilizes them. Most of her eggs will be eaten by bream and other small fish and will never hatch. Of those that do hatch, most of those tiny fish will be eaten by minnows and bream. As they mature to minnow size, most of those will be eaten by adult bass. And in the end, only a tiny fraction of the eggs originally laid will become mature bass. She has to lay millions of eggs in order to get a very few mature fish.

My friend speculated that God, in order to bring a very few sons to his kingdom, had to put billions of us here on the earth to allow for wastage. I had to admit that the idea had a perverse logic to it. But what did it say about the kind of being who would create a system like that for man? For we are not fish, we are human. We suffer. We hope, we love, we create.

Is the God we read about in the Bible the sort of being who would waste real people in their billions to achieve his objectives? It is one thing for God to give man the freedom to accept or reject life with God, but another thing altogether to subject man to the kind of suffering we see in this world without giving him hope of something better. And the picture is even more bleak if you think God is going to take all those billions who were never saved, and torment them in hell for billions of years.

We know what Paul thought about this: "For this," he said, "is good and acceptable in the sight of God our Savior, who desires all men to be saved and to come to the knowledge of the truth" (1 Timothy 2:3-4).

So we know what God's intent is. That doesn't mean that every last person will finally be saved, because we can push God away if we wish. But we know the salvation of all is in his plan.

The Apostle Paul couldn't bring himself to think otherwise. It was unlike God, he thought, to just throw people away, to cast them to the wolves. We would like to think that a man like Paul had all the answers, but it is apparent that he didn't, at least not all at once. Paul struggled with this, thinking out loud in his letter to the Christians in Rome. He tried to take what he knew about God and his plan, to develop an explanation for what was happening as he took the Gospel to the Jews. In city after city where Paul went, the Jews rejected the Gospel while Gentiles flocked to it. It didn't make sense to Paul, and it is easy to see why it didn't. Here was a people who lived in hope of the Messiah. They looked for the Messiah, they prayed for the Messiah, they expected the Messiah. Some expected him in their own lifetime. The very idea of a Messiah is a Jewish idea.

And now, a man walks into their synagogue and announces that the Messiah has come. Paul might have expected them to be excited at the news, but they brushed it off. The Gentiles, who knew nothing of a Messiah apart from the Jews, flocked to Christ in droves. This is the problem Paul has been debating at length in his letter to the Roman Christians.

Now he begins to see the answer and explains, using an olive tree as his chosen analogy. Having come to the conclusion that a resurrection must, somehow, be a factor, he goes further. "If the root is holy," he said, speaking of an olive tree, "so are the branches. And if some of the branches were broken off, and you, being a wild olive tree, were grafted in among them, and with them became a partaker of the root and fatness of the olive tree . . ." (Romans 11:16-17).

Consider what he is driving at. We have a natural olive tree. We have broken out some of the branches to make room for branches from another species of olive. The new branches are Gentile, and having been grafted in, they are as holy as the natural branches were. But, Paul continued, "do not boast against the branches. But if you do boast, remember that you do not support the root, but the root supports you" (v. 18).

> You will say then, "Branches were broken off that I might be grafted in." Well said. Because of unbelief they were broken off, and you stand by faith. Do not be haughty, but fear. For if God did not spare the natural branches, He may not spare you either (vv. 19-21).

Now the logical question is this. Why does it help to remove the Jewish branches from the tree in order to graft in Gentiles? Why wasn't there room for everyone? The picture Paul draws is of an olive tree that has a limited capacity for branches, both for room and for sustenance. If we are going to make the graft, we have to make room for it. It is a fact, that most Jews were simply not ready to make room for Gentiles in the community of God's people. The battle to make room for Gentiles is the big story of the book of Acts. The first line of defense was, "Well, if they are going to come in, they all have to be circumcised." [i]

The early church decided against that, but the struggle didn't go away. And the truth is, if all the synagogues where Paul preached had accepted the Gospel, then Christianity would have been seen by most as a purely Jewish faith, and that's where it would have ended. But it didn't. As the Jews rejected the Gospel, Paul was forced to turn to the Gentiles who, marvel of marvels, accepted it wholeheartedly and in growing numbers.

Paul cautioned his readers to "consider the goodness and severity of God: on those who fell, severity; but toward you, goodness, if you continue in His goodness. Otherwise you also will be cut off" (v. 22). And this is what my friend cited to support his idea. "Behold the severity of God." For the tiny bass that get eaten, it is just tough luck, he theorized. But Paul isn't quite ready to allow that. Speaking of the Jews, he continued:

> And they also, if they do not continue in unbelief, will be grafted in, for God is able to graft them in again. For if you were cut out of the olive tree which is wild by nature, and were grafted contrary to nature into a cultivated olive tree, how much more will these, who are natural branches, be grafted into their own olive tree? For I do not desire, brethren, that you should be ignorant of this mystery, lest you should be wise in your own opinion, that blindness in part has happened to Israel until the fullness of the Gentiles has come in. And *so all Israel will be saved,* as it is written: "The Deliverer will come out of Zion, And He will turn away ungodliness from Jacob" (vv. 23-26).

In calling this a mystery, Paul admits that this is not something that is easily grasped, but ignorance is not acceptable. Now I dare say we could ask more questions than Paul himself could answer, but he understood the basics. He understood that the cutting off of the Jews was a temporary expedient. It was being driven by the plan of God. He understood that it was God's intent to save all of Israel, not just a few. We naturally wonder how, but Paul doesn't help us a lot here.

> For this is My covenant with them, When I take away their sins. Concerning the gospel they are enemies for your sake, but concerning the election they are beloved for the sake of the fathers. For the gifts and the calling of God are irrevocable. For as you were once disobedient to God, yet have now obtained mercy through their disobedience, even so these also

have now been disobedient, that through the mercy shown you they also may obtain mercy (vv. 27-31).

Paul is simply saying that the unbelieving Jews were in the same boat with unbelieving Gentiles, and could receive mercy the same way. But there is this to consider: "For God hath concluded them all in unbelief, that he might have mercy upon all" (v. 32).

How on earth does it make sense to shut a people up in *unbelief* that he might have mercy on them? I would think giving them belief would be the merciful thing to do. Well, there is a short statement in the book of Hebrews that might help, even though it is disquieting.

> For if we sin willfully after we have received the knowledge of the truth, there no longer remains a sacrifice for sins, but a certain fearful expectation of judgment, and fiery indignation which will devour the adversaries. Anyone who has rejected Moses' law dies without mercy on the testimony of two or three witnesses. Of how much worse punishment, do you suppose, will he be thought worthy who has trampled the Son of God underfoot, counted the blood of the covenant by which he was sanctified a common thing, and insulted the Spirit of grace? For we know Him who said, "Vengeance is Mine, I will repay," says the Lord. And again, "The LORD will judge His people" (Hebrews 10:26-30).

Disturbing though it may be, it is clear enough. Willful sin, with the knowledge of the truth is, quite simply, the end. But if God concludes that people sinned ignorantly, in unbelief, or in weakness, then there is room for mercy. So if God senses that the Jews will reject the knowledge of the truth, perhaps He concludes that it is safer not to show them the truth for the time being. Paul concludes his argument to the Romans:

> Oh, the depth of the riches both of the wisdom and knowledge of God! How unsearchable are His

judgments and His ways past finding out! For who has known the mind of the LORD? Or who has become His counselor? Or who has first given to Him And it shall be repaid to him? For of Him and through Him and to Him are all things, to whom be glory forever. Amen (Romans 11:33-36).

Paul does not do us the grace of explaining his conclusions, but perhaps he has given us something to go on. Some have said they don't know what God is going to do with all those who never had a chance to be saved. They just believe that God will "make a way." Paul seems to feel the same way but, Old Testament scholar that he was, he was still looking for hints. He has already hinted that it might be life from the dead. What was he driving at?

Well, there is an obscure prophecy from Ezekiel that I have found fascinating, ever since I first heard it in a Negro spiritual. Now you have to understand that this prophecy is set way out into the future. It is obscure in its own way as many prophecies are. But it may provide a glimpse into the mind of God on this very important question. Also, it is not real. It is a vision of something that has not yet come to pass. And it is highly symbolic.

Poor Ezekiel. In the course of receiving and getting to the end of a long series of visions, he must have been thoroughly wrung out. But now, he is carried out and set down in the middle of a valley full of broken skeletons. Everywhere he looked, he saw rib cages, spines, skulls, femurs, obviously the bones of human beings. Ezekiel walked around, following instructions and took note of how dry and old the bones were. I have been out hunting and have come across the bones of animals long dead, bleached white, dry, porous and easily broken.

God then spoke. "Son of man," he asked, "can these bones live?" Ezekiel is noncommital, "O Lord GOD, You know" (Ezekiel 37:3).

Again He said to me, "Prophesy to these bones, and say to them, 'O dry bones, hear the word of the LORD!' Thus says the Lord GOD to these bones: "Surely I will cause breath to enter into you, and you shall live. I will put sinews on you and bring flesh upon you, cover you with skin and put breath in you; and you shall live. Then you shall know that I am the LORD" (vv. 4-6).

How strange it must have seemed, to have chosen an elevated spot and then to have begun preaching to a huge bone yard. And the message was just as strange. I would have felt thoroughly silly standing there preaching with no one around, but Ezekiel was a man who did as he was told.

So I prophesied as I was commanded; and as I prophesied, there was a noise, and suddenly a rattling; and the bones came together, bone to bone. Indeed, as I looked, the sinews and the flesh came upon them, and the skin covered them over; but there was no breath in them (vv. 7-8).

I expect some of the shaking going about this time was Ezekiel himself. What a thing to watch. There is a scene in the movie, *The Fifth Element*, where a human being is reconstructed from nothing but her hand. It is eerie to watch, but no more than what Ezekiel saw. When the shaking was finished, he was surrounded by complete, restored bodies. But they were not yet alive.

Also He said to me, "Prophesy to the breath, prophesy, son of man, and say to the breath, Thus says the Lord GOD: 'Come from the four winds, O breath, and breathe on these slain, that they may live.'" So I prophesied as He commanded me, and breath came into them, and they lived, and stood upon their feet, an exceedingly great army (vv. 9-10).

But an army of what, of whom? Who are these people, and what is this vision all about? The answer follows apace.

Then He said to me, "Son of man, these bones are the whole house of Israel. They indeed say, 'Our bones are dry, our hope is lost, and we ourselves are cut off!' Therefore prophesy and say to them, 'Thus says the Lord GOD: Behold, O My people, I will open your graves and cause you to come up from your graves, and bring you into the land of Israel'" (vv. 11-12).

You can almost hear Paul reciting the same Scripture as he made his point. "And so, all Israel shall be saved." Now it is clear that this is a vision, not a reality that Ezekiel sees. It is just as clear that it is symbolic. But the allusions to a resurrection of physical bodies and a restoration to the land is clear enough. Normally, when Christians think of the resurrection, they think of a resurrection with a spiritual body and a rising up into the air. This is a resurrection to physical life and a restoration to the land of Israel. This resurrection involves bone, sinew, muscles, flesh, and breath.

> Then you shall know that I am the LORD, when I have opened your graves, O My people, and brought you up from your graves. *I will put My Spirit in you,* and you shall live, and I will place you in your own land. Then you shall know that I, the LORD, have spoken it and performed it, says the LORD (vv. 13-14).

Take special note. The Lord says, "I will put my Spirit in you." Whatever this may finally mean, it holds out a possibility of a resurrection, bone to bone, skin to skin, flesh to flesh, breath to breath, and an opportunity for receiving the Holy Spirit, to those who are raised in this cohort. Can God do that? Is that fair? Is it right?

Well, God is sovereign. He can do whatever he wants to do. Putting it another way, whatever he does *is* right.

> Again the word of the LORD came to me, saying, "As for you, son of man, take a stick for yourself and write on it: For Judah and for the children of Israel, his companions. Then take another stick and write on it, For Joseph, the stick of Ephraim, and for all the house of Israel, his companions. Then join them one to another for yourself into one stick, and they will

become one in your hand. And when the children of your people speak to you, saying, 'Will you not show us what you mean by these?;'" say to them, "Thus says the Lord GOD: Surely I will take the stick of Joseph, which is in the hand of Ephraim, and the tribes of Israel, his companions; and I will join them with it, with the stick of Judah, and make them one stick, and they will be one in My hand. And the sticks on which you write will be in your hand before their eyes" (vv. 15-20).

If you didn't know the history of Israel, how after the death of Solomon the kingdom was divided into two, the House of Israel and the House of Judah, you might not understand the import of this. The House of Israel had gone into captivity in Assyria many years before Judah went captive into Babylon, and was lost to history and never heard from again. But at the very end time, the time of the resurrection and the time of a restoration to the land of Israel, the House of Judah and the House of Israel will be reunited. But that suggests that the House of Israel, though seemingly lost, is a political entity at the time of the end. Nearly everyone knows where the House of Judah is. But where is the House of Israel as a separate political entity?

---

i. See Acts 15:1 ff.

20

Saving the World

On the last day, that great day of the feast,
Jesus stood and cried out, saying,
"If anyone thirsts, let him come to Me and drink.
He who believes in Me, as the Scripture has said,
out of his heart will flow rivers of living water" (John 7:37-38).

What in the world is God doing? I suspect there are those who would say, "Not very much." The world looks like God wound it up, started it spinning, and then walked away from it. That is, more or less, the deist view. And if you should ask, "How is the Gospel doing in the world?" someone might reply, "Not very well." After all, most of the world is not Christian, and never has been. All those dead people who never heard of Jesus in their lifetime, where are they?

Now I realize I am making some people uncomfortable with these questions, but they are honest questions that deserve an honest answer. Paul told Timothy that it was God's will that all men be saved and come to the knowledge of the truth.[i] So we know it is God's will that all men be saved. Yes, there may be some who reject this in the end, but surely not half the world.

Most people who have ever lived on this planet never got a chance to reject salvation. Let me show you a paradox. One day, after Jesus had unloaded a rather elaborate parable on the crowd, the disciples came to Jesus and wanted to know what he was doing.

"Why," they asked, "do You speak to them in parables?" (Matthew 13:10).

Conventional wisdom is that Jesus' parables are illustrations, literary devices he used to make his meaning clear. If that is so, then why did the disciples ask this question? The answer is that a parable is more like an allegory than an illustration. An allegory is "the representation of spiritual, moral, or other abstract meanings through the actions of fictional characters that serve as symbols." [ii] And it is in the nature of an allegory that the reader or listener has to find the meanings by himself. What that means is that different people are apt to find different meanings in an allegory. Hence the disciples question, "Why do you speak to them in allegories?"

Jesus' answer is nothing short of astonishing. He said: "Because it has been given to you, to know the mysteries of the kingdom of heaven, but to them *it has not been given*" (v.11).

So here is our paradox. On the one hand, it is God's will that all men should be saved. On the other hand, Jesus spoke in allegories so that some would understand the Gospel and others would not. In fact, to this day, people understand Jesus differently and by anyone's definition of salvation, many people who claim to be Christian, aren't.

You might think that God isn't really trying very hard to save the world, and you would be right. For if God is God, if he is all powerful, all knowing, and nothing can be withheld from him (and he is all these things), then if he were trying hard to save the world right now, he would do it. So maybe our answer is that God is not trying to save the whole world *right now*. Maybe that is just a little bit further on in God's plan. Years ago, I learned that the holydays in the Bible actually picture his plan. Virtually the entire Christian world dismisses these holydays as merely Jewish. They think these days picture things out of Jewish history and have no relevance to the Christian faith. They see it much as Americans see the 4th of July. It is a celebration of American independence, and nothing else.

But anyone who looks at the holydays of the Bible that way is mistaken. Every single one of those biblical holydays also pictures part of the plan of God and is entirely relevant to the Christian faith. In this book, we have walked through each of these seven seasons in the year and have found Christ and his work in every one of them.

The questions I am asking you right now arise from the last of these holydays, and from the great question of the Christian faith – what happens to all the rest of the millions of people who never heard of Jesus? What of the Gentiles, the nations, who were to all intents and purposes down through history, cut off from God and shut out from the promises?

Well, something new is about to come on the scene, and if we keep following the thread, we are bound to run into it. Jesus had begun to stay in Galilee because it was becoming too dangerous for him to travel in Judea. The Jews around Jerusalem had already begun looking for ways to do away with him. But, the Feast of Tabernacles was a hitch in his plans, because the law called upon him to go.

Jesus had brothers (I know that gives some people the vapors, but never mind) and they were real brothers, because they gave him a hard time about his ministry. They said, "You need to go to Judea so your disciples there can see the work you are doing" (John 7:3). There was probably some irony in their remarks, because John notes that at that time, even his brothers did not believe in him. But Jesus didn't respond in kind.

> Then Jesus said to them, "My time has not yet come, but your time is always ready. The world cannot hate you, but it hates Me because I testify of it that its works are evil. You go up to this feast. I am not yet going up to this feast, for My time has not yet fully come." When He had said these things to them, He remained in Galilee. But when His brothers had gone up, then He also went up to the feast, not openly, but as it were in secret (vv. 6-10).

Jesus wanted to avoid going into Jerusalem with his brothers. He would have been spotted immediately. It was better and safer to go alone. The truth is, there was nothing remarkable about Jesus' appearance, and he could easily enter Jerusalem as a solitary pilgrim and be lost in the crowds.

The Jews knew he had to be there and they had men out looking for him. There were arguments among the people about him, some thinking he was a good man, others arguing the contrary. "No," they said, "He deceives the people." But no one spoke openly of him for fear of the Jewish leadership.

Jesus was a rabbi, though, and about mid feast, he was up in the Temple teaching. The most common question about Jesus the teacher was, "How does this Man know letters, having never studied?" (v. 15).

> Jesus answered them and said, "My doctrine is not Mine, but His who sent Me. If anyone wants to do His will, he shall know concerning the doctrine, whether it is from God or whether I speak on My own authority. He who speaks from himself seeks his own glory; but He who seeks the glory of the One who sent Him is true, and no unrighteousness is in Him. Did not Moses give you the law, yet none of you keeps the law? Why do you seek to kill Me?" (vv. 16-19).

"You're crazy," the people said. "Who goes about to kill you?" They knew, but they didn't know that Jesus knew.

"I have done one work," Jesus replied, "and you all marvel." He had read their minds, but it didn't require that much discernment to see the murderous intent on some of their faces. So Jesus went straight to the issue that had triggered all this in the first place, his Sabbath day healings:

> Moses therefore gave you circumcision (not that it is from Moses, but from the fathers), and you circumcise a man on the Sabbath. If a man receives circumcision on the Sabbath, so that the law of Moses should not be broken, are you angry with Me because I made a man completely well on the Sabbath? Do not judge according to appearance, but judge with righteous judgment" (vv. 22-24).

The logic was irrefutable. They would allow circumcision on the Sabbath, because that had to be done on the eighth day, regardless. But they were angry with Jesus because he healed on the Sabbath. Of course, that wasn't the real reason they wanted him dead.

He was a threat to the existing power structure. And the events of that festival did nothing to allay their concerns.

> Now some of them from Jerusalem said, "Is this not He whom they seek to kill? But look! He speaks boldly, and they say nothing to Him. Do the rulers know indeed that this is truly the Christ? However, we know where this Man is from; but when the Christ comes, no one knows where He is from" (vv. 25-27).

Jesus didn't let that stand. "You both know me," he said, " and you know where I come from. You know I come not of myself, but that he that sent me is true. The problem is, you don't know him." That was too much for the leadership, and they tried to have him arrested. But no one would lay hands on him because his time had not come.

> And many of the people believed in Him, and said, "When the Christ comes, will He do more signs than these which this Man has done?" The Pharisees heard the crowd murmuring these things concerning Him, and the Pharisees and the chief priests sent officers to take Him. Then Jesus said to them, "I shall be with you a little while longer, and then I go to Him who sent Me. You will seek Me and not find Me, and where I am you cannot come" (vv. 31-34).

This was a moment of great danger for the Pharisees. Jesus was gaining ground with the people and he was, to them, openly defiant. They wondered among themselves, "Where does He intend to go that we shall not find Him? Does He intend to go to the Dispersion among the Greeks and teach the Greeks?"

What was behind that response? It is generally not realized that the truth of God, the promises, the covenants, all the great gifts of God, were given to the Jews who were in turn supposed to share them with the world. They had done precious little of that.

There are many references to Gentiles in both Testaments, along with instructions to take the truth to the Gentiles. Those listening to Jesus on this occasion knew all this, and they wondered when and how Jesus might do that. All this went on through the last half of the feast, and finally Jesus made a proclamation.

> On the last day, that great day of the feast, Jesus stood and cried out, saying, "If anyone thirsts, let him come to Me and drink. He who believes in Me, as the Scripture has said, out of his heart will flow rivers of living water." But this He spoke concerning the Spirit, whom those believing in Him would receive; for the Holy Spirit was not yet given, because Jesus was not yet glorified (vv. 37-39).

We have once again found the thread we have been following. This is one of the great days in the Hebrew calendar, the Last Great Day of the Feast. It does not seem to be distinct from the Feast of Tabernacles. The Jews are well enough aware of it, but most Christians will not have heard of it beyond this passage. Nor will they realize that on this occasion, Jesus is engaging in some very important symbolism. It is on this particular day that Jesus issues a call, not just to some, but to all men to come to him.

The first mention of this day in the Bible lies far back along our thread, and we have been there before. It is that chapter of Leviticus where all the festivals, the holydays, are laid out in order. In that part of the chapter dealing with the Feast of Tabernacles, there are instructions for this day as well.

> Speak to the children of Israel, saying: "The fifteenth day of this seventh month shall be the Feast of Tabernacles for seven days to the LORD. On the first day there shall be a holy convocation. You shall do no customary work on it. For seven days you shall offer an offering made by fire to the *LORD. On the eighth day you shall have a holy convocation*, and you shall offer an offering made by fire to the LORD. It is a sacred assembly, and you shall do no customary work on it (Leviticus 23:34-36).

The first day and the eighth day are Sabbaths where a "holy convocation," an assembly, was required. You take off work, and you go to church.

Now there is some question about whether this eighth day is a separate festival or the last day of the Feast of Tabernacles.[iii] We will leave that aside for the time being and consider the special significance of the day for Christian people. The last day of the feast was characterized by a pouring of water. It was a great water festival. One source says that the Temple Mount was awash in water on this day. Hence Jesus' statement: "If anyone thirsts, let him come to Me and drink. He who believes in Me, as the Scripture has said, out of his heart will flow rivers of living water" (John 7:38).

And the greatest meaning of the day is found in the words, "any man." Not just some, not just the Jews, not just those in the western world. For to this day, the Gospel has not been extended to *every man*. And so Jesus, somehow, on this Last Great Day of the Feast, stands and cries in the Temple that the time has come for the Gospel to go to *every* man.

There is a parallel between the Feast of Tabernacles and human history. The pattern in the Bible appears to be that man has six thousand years of human rule to do his best. And oddly, even though archaeologists and other scientists have found evidence of civilization existing some ten thousand years ago, the Bible appears to lay out the ideal six thousand years. This doesn't mean the Bible is wrong, only that we don't have all the data.

The seventh thousand years period, the Millennium, is the time of the Kingdom of God. But if you have been following this carefully, you may wonder, "Hey, then, what about that eighth day? That's outside the seven thousand year plan"

Yes, it is, isn't it? What comes at the end of the plan? You don't have to be a scholar to know where to look in the Bible for the end of the plan. You just go to the back of the Book. And here it is:

> Then I saw an angel coming down from heaven, having the key to the bottomless pit and a great chain in his hand. He laid hold of the dragon, that serpent of old, who is the Devil and Satan, and bound him for a thousand years; and he cast him into the bottomless pit,

and shut him up, and set a seal on him, so that he should deceive the nations no more till the thousand years were finished. But after these things he must be released for a little while (Revelation 20:1-3).

This certainly has not yet happened. The Devil is still on the loose in our world. But this thousand year period when Satan is bound and out of the picture, is what people are talking about when they speak of the Millennium. It is the ideal seventh period of biblical history. It is symbolic, and it connects to the Feast of Tabernacles. It lies right along our thread.

And I saw thrones, and they sat on them, and judgment was committed to them. Then I saw the souls of those who had been beheaded for their witness to Jesus and for the word of God, who had not worshiped the beast or his image, and had not received his mark on their foreheads or on their hands. And they lived and reigned with Christ for a thousand years (v. 4).

You won't find the word, "Millennium" in the Bible, but this is where the idea of the Millennium arises. It is odd in some Christian circles that it is commonly called "the Millennium" rather than "The Kingdom of God," because that is what it really is. But there is something else here that we don't want to overlook:

But the rest of the dead did not live again until the thousand years were finished. This is the first resurrection. Blessed and holy is he who has part in the first resurrection. Over such the second death has no power, but they shall be priests of God and of Christ, and shall reign with Him a thousand years (vv. 5-6).

When John said, "the first resurrection," he implies at least one more. In fact, what we have is a first and second resurrection a thousand years apart. I realize that there are many ways to interpret a vision like this, but one way is to take the most obvious intent, which is what I have done here.

> When the thousand years are over, Satan will be
> released from his prison and will go out to deceive the
> nations in the four corners of the earth--Gog and
> Magog--to gather them for battle. In number they are
> like the sand on the seashore. They marched across
> the breadth of the earth and surrounded the camp of
> God's people, the city he loves. But fire came down
> from heaven and devoured them. And the devil, who
> deceived them, was thrown into the lake of burning
> sulfur, where the beast and the false prophet had been
> thrown. They will be tormented day and night for ever
> and ever (vv. 7-10 NIV)

Mind you, this comes at the end of a thousand years of peace,
of God's reign. Now the Devil is loose again, and this is what
happens. But finally, he has a very unpleasant future thrust upon him.
One might suppose that this terrible sequence is to cut off all the
loose ends of those people who, no matter what, will not accept
God's way. And there are a lot of them.

> Then I saw a great white throne and Him who sat on it,
> from whose face the earth and the heaven fled away.
> And there was found no place for them. And I saw the
> dead, small and great, standing before God, and books
> were opened. And another book was opened, which is
> the Book of Life (vv. 11-12).

Consider where we are in time. This is a vision, of course, but
we have been following a sequence in time. We are at the end of the
Millennium. And earlier we read that there was a first resurrection
and then that the rest of the dead did not live again until the thousand
years were finished. The first resurrection is all those in Christ. So
here we are, with the rest of the dead standing before God in
judgment. What is it when the dead stand up? A resurrection? Yes,
and this one is the second general resurrection.

But there is an anomaly here. One of the books that was
opened was the book of life. If we think this through, there are some
questions we need to answer. The Book of Life is the book in which

all the names of the saints, of all those in Christ, are written. Your name should already be there.

Here is the problem. Since everyone whose name was in the Book of Life was raised in the first resurrection, why are we opening the Book of Life again in this second resurrection? It can't be to see who is written in it, because they have already been given life. The only sensible reason why the Book of Life is opened at this late date, is to make new entries.

> And the dead were judged according to their works, by the things which were written in the books. The sea gave up the dead who were in it, and Death and Hades delivered up the dead who were in them. And they were judged, each one according to his works. Then Death and Hades were cast into the lake of fire. This is the second death. And anyone not found written in the Book of Life was cast into the lake of fire (vv. 12-15).

I don't know all the details of God's plan or how he will work out every aspect of it. But it is fairly clear when you follow this thread all the way through the plan, that when all is said and done, God is going to revisit a lot of those who have lived and died in this world, because he is a merciful God and he isn't finished with them yet.

All those who never knew him will come up out of their graves, and they will be judged. We might assume that they are standing before the bar being judged only on the basis of what they have done in the past. But take the judging of a prizefight as an illustration. A fight is being judged while it is being waged. These people may well be right back in the land, being judged by the way they live their lives, the second time around.

So it may be that your old Uncle Bob, who never found time for religion in this life, will in the second resurrection, find time for God.

Still have questions? So do I. But what we have seen is that God does indeed intend to "make a way" to solve our problem. In the festivals of the Bible, we find a promise of a future beyond our imagination. In that future, we will meet those lost loved ones one more time. And this time, it will be different. Having followed the thread this far, I find new meaning in an old Gospel song:

I will meet you in the morning
I will meet you in the morning on the bright riverside,
When all sorrows have drifted away.
I'll be standing at the portal with the gates open wide
At the close of life's long, dreary day.

Chorus: I'll meet you in the morning with a "How do you do?"
And we'll sit down by the river, and with rapture, old acquaintance renew.
You'll know me in the morning by the smile that I wear.
When I meet you in the morning in that city that is built foursquare.[iv]

---

i. 1 Timothy 2:3-4.

ii. Merriam-Webster's Collegiate Dictionary.

iii. As to whether the eighth day is a separate festival, there was a standard offering to be made on each of the holydays through the year. The details are laid out in Numbers 28 and 29, starting with the daily sacrifice, the sacrifice for the Sabbath and the for the new moons. The standard holyday offering was two bulls, one ram, seven yearling lambs and a goat for a sin offering (Numbers 28:17-22). This is true for the first day of the Feast of Unleavened Bread and Pentecost. Once we come to the autumn festivals, there is a change. On the Feast of Trumpets and the Day of Atonement, everything is the same except there is one bull instead of two. There is an anomaly when it comes to the Feast of Tabernacles. The first day of the Feast, 13 bulls are offered, plus two rams, 14 yearling lambs and the usual one goat. But that is not the curious thing. Each day of the Feast, everything remains the same except that one less bull is offered each day until seven bulls are offered on the seventh day of the feast. If the eighth day was part of the Feast of Tabernacles, one would expect there to be six bulls for the offerings. But on that day, the pattern reverts to the same as it is on the Feast of Trumpets and the Day of Atonement. This suggests that the eighth day is a distinct festival even though it has no name beyond "The Eighth Day."

iv. *I Will Meet You in the Morning*, by Albert Brumley.

21

The New Testament Sabbath Day

Remember the Sabbath day, to keep it holy.
Six days you shall labor and do all your work,
but the seventh day is the Sabbath of the LORD your God.
In it you shall do no work . . . (Exodus 20:8-10 NKJV).

Would it surprise you to learn that during the entire time when the New Testament was being written, the entire Christian Church throughout the known world observed the Sabbath day? No, I don't mean Sunday. I mean what most people would call "The Jewish Sabbath," Saturday. As late as the 80s and 90s of the first century, when the last words of the New Testament were being written, the New Testament church *universally* observed the Sabbath. This is beyond dispute. It is not a matter of a few proof texts and technical arguments. It is something that is woven into the very fabric of the New Testament.

What may be the first subtle clue is found in Luke's account of one of Jesus' earliest sermons. It was not long after his baptism when Jesus, "came to Nazareth, where he had been brought up: and, *as his custom* was, he went into the synagogue on the Sabbath day, and stood up for to read." [i]

No one can doubt for a moment that the seventh day Sabbath was the universally recognized day of rest and worship among all Jews when Christ came on the scene. So it was Jesus' custom, his *ethos*, to attend synagogue on the Jewish Sabbath and that Sabbath was, week by week, on the day we call Saturday. Jesus was a member of this synagogue and had been accepted there ever since he was a boy. This was surely not the first time he had stood to read in this synagogue.

Now here is my question: How did the Jews in that synagogue think about the Sabbath? What was the *status and meaning* of the Sabbath day in their faith and practice? How important was it? Bear in mind also that all Jesus' disciples were Jews. They had all grown up attending synagogue and had learned to read the Scriptures in synagogue schools. How did Jesus' disciples look at the Sabbath day? These are questions we can answer with clarity.

First and foremost, the Sabbath was the fourth of the Ten Commandments. It was the heart and core of their covenant with God.[ii] But for the Jew of those days, the Sabbath was more than that. The Sabbath lay at the very heart of the *identity of their God*. They all knew well the significance of this passage from the book of Exodus:

> And the LORD spoke to Moses, saying, "Speak also to the children of Israel, saying: 'Surely My Sabbaths you shall keep, for it is a sign between Me and you throughout your generations, that you may know that I am the LORD who sanctifies you'" (Exodus 31:12-13).

Due to a curious convention in most Bibles, there is something here that is easily overlooked. Whenever you see the small caps LORD in your Bible, that means that the Hebrew word there is YHWH (written Hebrew has no vowels). It is pronounced "Yahweh," or more familiarly, "Jehovah" (with the J pronounced as Y). It all depends on the vowels inserted.

The Sabbath, then, was not merely a sign of who the Jews were, but the sign that identified who their God was – *by name*. "Verily my Sabbaths ye shall keep: for it is a sign between me and you throughout your generations; that ye may know that I am *Jehovah*." For a Jew in that time and place, changing the Sabbath was unthinkable. *It would be tantamount to changing his God.* Now consider the rest of that passage in Exodus.

> You shall keep the Sabbath, therefore, for it is holy to you. Everyone who profanes it shall surely be put to death; for whoever does any work on it, that person shall be cut off from among his people. Work shall be done for six days, but the seventh is the Sabbath of rest, holy to the LORD. Whoever does any work on the Sabbath day, he shall surely be put to death. Therefore the children of Israel shall keep the Sabbath, to observe the Sabbath throughout their generations as a perpetual covenant. It is a sign between Me and the children of Israel forever; for in six days the LORD made the heavens and the earth, and on the seventh day He rested and was refreshed (vv. 14-17).

For a Jew in the synagogue on that day when Jesus stood up to read, the Sabbath was the sign that identified his God. The Sabbath was not going away. It was a *perpetual* covenant to last forever. It even carried the penalty of death for a presumptuous violation. For a Jew of the first century, the Sabbath could not be taken lightly. They all knew from Ezekiel's prophecies that the failure to keep the sign of the Sabbath was a direct reason why they had spent 70 years in Babylonian exile.

Ezekiel was already a well recognized prophet when the Jews found themselves in Babylon. Some of the elders came to him to inquire of God, but God was having none of it. "Speak to these elders," God said to Ezekiel, "and say to them, 'Thus says the Lord GOD: Have you come to inquire of Me? As I live, says the Lord GOD, I will not be inquired of by you'" (Ezekiel 20:3).

These are strong words, and strongly put. "Will you judge them?" God asked Ezekiel, "Will you judge them, son of man? Then confront them with the detestable practices of their fathers" (v. 4). What follows is a litany of the sins that ultimately led to the Jews downfall as a nation. Included prominently in this list is the Sabbath day:

> And I gave them My statutes and showed them My judgments, which, if a man does, he shall live by them. Moreover I also gave them My Sabbaths, to be a sign between them and Me, that they might know that I am the LORD who sanctifies them (Ezekiel 20:11-12).

Note that well. God gave them the Sabbaths as a sign so they might know who their God was. They were just coming out of Egypt where there was one set of gods and they were headed for Canaan where there was yet another set of gods. The Sabbath was more than just another law. *It was the law that identified their God.* It told them whose laws and rites they were to practice.

> Yet the house of Israel rebelled against Me in the wilderness; they did not walk in My statutes; they despised My judgments, which, if a man does, he shall live by them; and they greatly defiled My Sabbaths. Then I said I would pour out My fury on them in the wilderness, to consume them. But I acted for My name's sake, that it should not be profaned before the Gentiles, in whose sight I had brought them out (vv. 13-14).

It seems strange that the children of Israel were already corrupting the Sabbath while they were still in the wilderness. One would have thought it would have taken longer. But God isn't finished. Since they had failed, God went on to warn their children not to make the same mistake.

> But I said to their children in the wilderness, "Do not walk in the statutes of your fathers, nor observe their judgments, nor defile yourselves with their idols. I am the LORD your God: Walk in My statutes, keep My judgments, and do them; hallow My Sabbaths, and they will be a sign between Me and you, that you may know that I am the LORD your God" (vv. 18-20).

This is extremely important in understanding the mind set of all the Jews of the first century. They knew that Ezekiel proclaimed the same formula they had read in Exodus. The Sabbath identifies, not the children of Israel, but their God – *by name*. God warned them of the consequence of corrupting the Sabbath right from the start. It was the harbinger of a nation that would finally turn away from God completely. In the end, the Jews went into captivity in Babylon for a broad variety of transgressions, but the number one reason that led to all the others was that they corrupted the Sabbath day.

So by the time Jesus showed up in the synagogue to read the Scriptures that day, the Sabbath had been drilled into the conscience of every Jew assembled there. It was woven into the warp and woof of their faith. It was not a mere "doctrine" that could be abandoned if it became inconvenient. Changing the Sabbath was tantamount to changing their religion. And there was no question among Jews about which day it was. They learned this when the Sabbath became the test commandment.

It happened when God gave them manna to eat. He said to Moses: "Behold, I will rain bread from heaven for you. And the people shall go out and gather a certain quota every day, that I may test them, whether they will walk in My law or not." [iii] Thus, the Sabbath became the test commandment. If they won't do this, God said, there is hardly any point in going further.

The test was a simple one. They would get manna every morning for six days. Each day, they were to gather just enough for one day. If they kept it over to the second day, it would become wormy and start to stink. On the sixth day, though, they were to gather twice as much and prepare it for the seventh day, the Sabbath. That way, they would not have to do the work of cooking on the Sabbath day. On the Sabbath day, it would not breed worms and stink.

And so everyone had to observe the Sabbath, and they all had to observe it on the same day. No one was allowed to choose a Sabbath for himself. After all, it was God's Sabbath and His identifying sign, *not theirs*.

So the Jews of the first century had no questions about the Sabbath or when it was. It was perhaps the most crucial of all their laws and customs. My point in all this is simple. *When Jesus walked onto the scene, the seventh day Sabbath was an established and honored tradition in every sect of Judaism.* There were Pharisees, Sadducees, Essenes, and more. They may have been divided on many issues, but they were not divided on the importance of the Sabbath day. The observance of the Sabbath on the day appointed by God himself, was the identifying sign that they were worshiping Jehovah and not someone else.[iv]

Now we insert Jesus into the picture. After his baptism, his 40 day fast, and his temptation by the Devil, Jesus was ready to begin his ministry. What was the first thing he did, where did he do it, and on what day did he do it? That brings me back to where I started:

> Then Jesus returned in the power of the Spirit to Galilee, and news of Him went out through all the surrounding region. And He taught in their synagogues, being glorified by all. So He came to Nazareth, where He had been brought up. And as His custom was, He went into the synagogue on the Sabbath day, and stood up to read. And He was handed the book of the prophet Isaiah. And when He had opened the book, He found the place where it was written: "The Spirit of the LORD is upon Me, Because He has anointed Me To preach the gospel to the poor; He has sent Me to heal the brokenhearted, To proclaim liberty to the captives And recovery of sight to the blind, To set at liberty those who are oppressed; To proclaim the acceptable year of the LORD." Then He closed the book, and gave it back to the attendant and sat down. And the eyes of all who were in the synagogue were fixed on Him. And He began to say to them, "Today this Scripture is fulfilled in your hearing" (Luke 4:14-21).

And what day was that? The Sabbath day, of course. It was a part of Jesus' *ethos*, his customary practice, to attend synagogue on the Sabbath day. And it was on the Sabbath day that Isaiah's prophecy was fulfilled.

Okay, so Jesus kept the Sabbath at this point. But was it his intent to later change the day of worship for his disciples? This kind of change could not have been an afterthought. If it was part of the plan, Jesus knew that from the beginning. He knew it when he read Isaiah in the synagogue on that Sabbath. So was it his intent to change the Fourth Commandment or even to abolish it? If so, how would that intent have finally been expressed or carried out? And what would have been the consequences of that change?

First, it would have been necessary for Jesus at some point to clearly and definitively announce the change, and to give the reason for it. Remember that to any Jew, changing the Sabbath was tantamount to changing Gods. This is no mere doctrinal issue. All of Jesus' disciples were Jews. Like Jesus himself, they had been brought up in the synagogue and the Sabbath was a part of their *ethos*. They would never imagine that they had the authority to change the Sabbath without Jesus' *explicit authorization*.

Furthermore, if it was Jesus' intent to change the Sabbath to Sunday, there would have to be a point in time for the changeover. There would have to be a recognition that the change had been made and why it had been made. This isn't the sort of thing you slip into gradually.

Bear in mind, that for some 20 years after the ascension of Christ, the Church was composed entirely of Jews and proselytes. There was no wholesale conversion of Gentiles until Paul and Barnabas went on their first missionary journey in Acts 13. Now you can search through the four Gospels and up through Acts 12 and you will not find a word about a controversy over the Sabbath. You will find no instructions for a change in the day of worship, nor even any bread crumbs you can follow to indicate that such a change might have been made.

This is important, because a change in the day of worship would not merely have implied a change in custom. For every Jew and every proselyte, it would have implied *a change of God*. And this change would have to be dealt with in depth. Now you tell me. Could such a change have been made up to Acts 13 without a ripple of it showing up in the Bible?

I recognize that this is an argument from silence, but an argument from silence is decisive if it can be shown that the silence is significant. This silence could not be more significant.

---

i. Luke 4:16

ii. Exodus 20:8-11.

iii. Exodus 16:4.

iv. This is important because of a common belief that it doesn't matter which day you keep, as long as you keep a Sabbath. Obviously, it does matter. In truth, when you modify the law to suit your convenience, soon the law itself may become inconvenient.

22

The Sabbath and the Gentiles

*So when the Jews went out of the synagogue,
the Gentiles begged that these words might be preached to them
the next Sabbath (Acts 13:42).*

By the time Paul ends up in Antioch, everything has begun to change. Peter was sent down to the coast to baptize an uncircumcised Gentile named Cornelius. No one had baptized a Gentile before, because the Jews kept themselves apart from even God Fearers[i] like Cornelius. Meanwhile Christ called Saul of Tarsus into his service completely apart from the Jerusalem establishment. His commission included rather more than most of the Apostles had grasped up to now.

While Saul lay blind at Damascus, the Lord sent a disciple named Ananias to lay hands on him. Ananias, knowing Paul's reputation, was hesitant. But the Lord said, "Go thy way: for he is a chosen vessel unto me, to bear my name before the Gentiles, and kings, and the children of Israel" (Acts 9:15). So the Gentiles were about to surge into the future of the church. Paul hits the evangelism trail along with Barnabas. Did a change in the Sabbath take place at this time? What would the Sabbath mean to the new converts?

Paul and Barnabas sail out into the Mediterranean and eventually arrive in Antioch in Asia Minor. When they arrived, they did what they always did when arriving in a new city.

> [They] went into the synagogue on the Sabbath day and sat down. And after the reading of the Law and the Prophets, the rulers of the synagogue sent to them, saying, "Men and brethren, if you have any word of exhortation for the people, say on." Then Paul stood up, and motioning with his hand said, "Men of Israel, and you who fear God, listen" (Acts 13:16).

There were two categories of people there on this day, Jews and God fearing Gentiles. It was, of course, the Sabbath day. What follows is Paul's gospel to the Jews. You can read it for yourself, and you will find not a word about a change of Sabbath. Naturally. What would have been the response to such a suggestion? That is not hard to imagine. But when the Jews left that Sabbath day, something strange happened.

> So when the Jews went out of the synagogue, the Gentiles begged that these words might be preached to them the next Sabbath. Now when the congregation had broken up, many of the Jews and devout proselytes followed Paul and Barnabas, who, speaking to them, persuaded them to continue in the grace of God. On the next Sabbath almost the whole city came together to hear the Word of God. But when the Jews saw the multitudes, they were filled with envy; and contradicting and blaspheming, they opposed the things spoken by Paul (Acts 13:42-45).

Note well, this uproar was not because of a change in the day of assembly and worship. This was on the Sabbath day. *There had been no change.* The uproar was about sheer envy. Take another example from much later. A lot of water has gone under the bridge, the Jerusalem conference has taken place, and certain decrees established for the Gentiles. Paul crosses finally from Asia Minor to Greece on his second Journey, and came to Thessalonica "where there was a synagogue of the Jews."

> Then Paul, as his custom was, went in to them, and for three Sabbaths reasoned with them from the Scriptures, explaining and demonstrating that the Christ had to suffer and rise again from the dead, and saying, "This Jesus whom I preach to you is the Christ" (Acts 17:2-3).

Note that at this late date, it was still Paul's "manner," his *ethos,* to go to the synagogue *on the Sabbath.* The word is the same as the word used for Jesus' custom. Yes, Paul went to the synagogue, because that was where the Jews were, so he could preach to them. But that is not why Luke says he went there. Luke says that going to synagogue on the Sabbath was still Paul's *ethos*, his custom.

In the early years of the Christian faith, in all the years that are recorded in the pages of the New Testament, the Christian Church looked, to the outside world, to be nothing more than another Jewish sect. They not only observed the same Sabbath as the Jews, they observed the same holidays. They planned their travel according to the Jewish calendar. On one occasion, Luke makes this calendar notation: "But we sailed away from Philippi after the Days of Unleavened Bread, and in five days joined them at Troas, where we stayed seven days" (Acts 20:6).

Writing to the Corinthians, Paul makes reference to the practices of the Passover and the Days of Unleavened Bread saying, "For indeed Christ, our Passover, was sacrificed for us. Therefore let us keep the feast, not with old leaven, nor with the leaven of malice and wickedness, but with the unleavened bread of sincerity and truth" (1 Corinthians 5:7-8).

I know this will be shocking to some people, but it is right there on the page. Paul is exhorting a Gentile church to observe the Feast of Passover, and the Feast of Unleavened Bread. But there is still more. Paul wrote to the Colossians:

> Therefore do not let anyone condemn you in matters of food and drink or of observing festivals, new moons, or sabbaths. These are only a shadow of what is to come, but the substance belongs to Christ. Do not let anyone disqualify you, insisting on self-abasement and worship of angels, dwelling on visions, puffed up without cause

by a human way of thinking (Colossians 2:16-18).

Parse this passage carefully, and what you see is a church that is observing the festivals and Sabbaths but is being condemned for feasting on food and drink by Gentile ascetics.

So far, so good. There is not a word about a change in the day of worship for Jews or Gentile believers and, if a change was contemplated, something surely would have been said about it by someone, somewhere. But no, nothing like that is found.

I know someone reading this is thinking, "Wait a minute. Didn't John speak of Sunday as the Lord's Day in Revelation?" Well, no, he didn't. Here is exactly what John said:

> I, John, both your brother and companion in the tribulation and kingdom and patience of Jesus Christ, was on the island that is called Patmos for the word of God and for the testimony of Jesus Christ. I was in the Spirit on the Lord's Day, and I heard behind me a loud voice, as of a trumpet (Revelation 1:9-10).

There is not a word here to suggest that the Lord's Day is Sunday. If John is indeed referring to a day of the week, and if we are to use the Bible as our best historical source, the *Sabbath* is the Lord's Day. Consider an instance from Jesus' ministry. Jesus and his disciples were walking through a field of grain on the Sabbath day. His disciples plucked some ears of grain to eat (harvesting, according to Jewish law) and rubbed them between their hands (threshing). Here is the exchange that grew out of that incident.

> And some of the Pharisees said to them, "Why are you doing what is not lawful to do on the Sabbath?" But Jesus answering them said, "Have you not even read this, what David did when he was hungry, he and those who were with him: how he went into the house of God, took and ate the showbread, and also gave some to those with him, which is not lawful for any but the priests to eat?" And He said to them, "The Son of Man is also Lord of the Sabbath" (Luke 6:2-5).

Why would one, then, assume that Sunday is the Lord's day? I think it is clear enough that in the Apostolic era of the church, there were two Sundays in the year that were observed. One was the day the firstfruits were offered, the day Christ first appeared to His disciples and was presented to God as the first of the firstfruits. It is that singular day in the year called "The first day of the Weeks, " which was discussed at length in an earlier chapter. The other observed Sunday is the Feast of Pentecost.

Try to put yourself for a moment in the mind of one of the original disciples of Jesus. How would you have been different from what you are today? In the first place, you would have been a Jew. Like Jesus himself, you would have been a regular in synagogue attendance, and you would have been a Sabbath keeper.

The Sabbath, you must remember, was more than just another commandment, more than a mere doctrine. It was a matter of religious *identity*. The Sabbath was the identifying sign that answered the question, "Who is your God?" To change the Sabbath to another day would not merely have been a change in doctrine. It would have been tantamount to *changing their God*.

So if you had been one of the original disciples of Jesus, the Sabbath would not merely have been another doctrine to believe or not believe. It would have been the irrevocable sign of the identity of your God.

Now how and when did all that get changed? Why would you, at some later time, abandon the observance of the Sabbath in favor of Sunday? And what would have been the consequences of that change? Would you have expected Jesus to say something about it, to explain the change? For there would have had to have been a moment when the change came into effect, right? And being good Jews, you or some of your close friends would have wondered at the change.

It is very hard to imagine that one week the entire body of the disciples of Jesus (who were all Jews at the time) kept the Sabbath and the next week observed Sunday instead, with no explanation, no comment, not a ripple. So what did happen?

The conventional wisdom is that the crucifixion and resurrection changed everything. However, we must face up to the fact that there is *nothing* in the New Testament that says so. You would really expect that a change of this magnitude would be explained somewhere; that there would be a passage that gives us, not merely the change, but the reason for the change. The Sabbath had a theology that went with it. It identified who your God was. You were a worshiper of Jehovah, not Baal, and it was the Sabbath that established that identity.

So there should be a statement just as strong as the original statements about the Sabbath to explain who our new God is. No such passage exists. And, of course, there was no change in their God. And no change in their Sabbath.

There is a general presumption among Christians who do not keep the Sabbath, that the church began meeting on Sunday immediately after the resurrection of Jesus, and they did it because Jesus rose from the dead on Sunday morning. This is based in its entirety on eight New Testament texts that appear to mention the first day of the week. The superficial impression is that the Church was meeting regularly on Sunday, the first day of the week. But this is entirely misleading. Six of these scriptures refer to the same events on the same day – the day of Jesus first appearances to his disciples after his resurrection. So that only leaves two other passages that might lead one to this conclusion.

And there is something else you should know about these passages. There is no Greek word for "week" in any of them. In fact, there is no Greek word for "week" found in the New Testament *at all*. In every case where the word "week" is found, the word for it in Greek is *Sabbaton*, a transliteration of the Hebrew word, Sabbath. Take this instance for example; it is in the parable of the Pharisee and the publican:

> Two men went up to the temple to pray, one a Pharisee and the other a tax collector. The Pharisee stood and prayed thus with himself, "God, I thank You that I am not like other men; extortioners, unjust, adulterers, or even as this tax collector. I fast twice a week; I give tithes of all that I possess" (Luke 18:10-12).

Literally, the Pharisee says, "I fast twice of a Sabbath." It is genitive *singular* and an idiom that refers to the period between the Sabbaths, for no Pharisee would fast on any Sabbath apart from the

Day of Atonement. The very idea of "week," to a Jew, was based on the Sabbath.

Now, about the eight instances where the expression, "the first day of the week" is found. First, you should know that the Hebrews (and all Jesus' disciples at this time were Hebrews) did not identify days of the week in that manner. The Hebrew manner of designating Sunday would have been to call it "the morrow after the Sabbath." Second, you should know that in every case, the word for "week" is "Sabbaths" in the *plural*, and the word "day" is missing altogether – *in every one of these eight instances.*

Here is how the first instance reads: "Now after the Sabbath, as the first day of the week began to dawn, Mary Magdalene and the other Mary came to see the tomb" (Matthew 28:1). And here is how it reads *literally*: "Now after the Sabbath, as the first of the Sabbaths [plural] began to dawn, Mary Magdalene and the other Mary came to see the tomb." That is an odd expression since we know it was not a Sabbath that was dawning, but a Sunday morning. What does it mean?

First, it is probably correct to insert the word "day" as virtually all translations do in this passage. And if we understand the *plural* of the word "Sabbath" as used here to refer to "weeks" (not the singular "week"), then what we are looking at is "the first day of the *weeks*." How does that help? Well, there are seven weeks, seven Sabbaths, between this day and the Feast of Firstfruits, Pentecost. The day that is being referenced here is the first day of the 50 day countdown leading to Pentecost. It was the day when the first of the firstfruits were offered to God.[ii] It was also the day of Jesus' presentation to the Father as the first of the firstfruits from the dead.[iii] So this was not merely a day of the week. It was a special day of the year – the day that began the spring harvest.

But I said there are eight of these references to "the first day of the week." Maybe one of the others will clarify matters. Here are the next five, each of them using exactly the same idiom for the first day of the *weeks* leading up to Pentecost:

Now when the Sabbath was past, Mary Magdalene, Mary the mother of James, and Salome bought spices, that they might come and anoint Him. Very early in the morning, on the first day of the week(s), they came to the tomb when the sun had risen (Mark 16:1-2).

Now when He rose early on the first day of the week(s), He appeared first to Mary Magdalene, out of whom He had cast seven demons (Mark 16:9).

Now on the first day of the week(s), very early in the morning, they, and certain other women with them, came to the tomb bringing the spices which they had prepared (Luke 24:1).

Now on the first day of the week(s) Mary Magdalene went to the tomb early, while it was still dark, and saw that the stone had been taken away from the tomb (John 20:1).

Then, the same day at evening, being the first day of the week(s), when the doors were shut where the disciples were assembled, for fear of the Jews, Jesus came and stood in the midst, and said to them, "Peace be with you" (John 20:19).

As to the last of these being a meeting, there is nothing here to suggest that anything new was going on. They were frightened and confused and did the natural thing. They huddled together trying to make sense of what had happened.

So we have found nothing here about a new custom of meeting on Sunday vs. Sabbath, have we? If I were one of the disciples of Jesus, I would have found nothing here to change anything concerning the Sabbath day. Would you?

These are six of the eight occasions where the New Testament refers to "the first day of the week." But these all refer to the events of *the same day*. That thins out considerably the argument that a new custom had started in the Church. There are only two references left with which to establish a new day of worship on the first day of every week. Perhaps the most familiar of the two is the following, appearing on offering envelopes at a lot of churches:

> Now concerning the collection for the saints, as I have
> given orders to the churches of Galatia, so you must do
> also: On the first day of the week(s) let each one of you
> lay something aside, storing up as he may prosper, that
> there be no collections when I come (1 Corinthians
> 16:1-2).

There are a couple of important things to notice here. First,
this is precisely the same idiom we saw in the previous six instances.
It is a reference to the first day of the seven weeks of harvest, and
therefore is the first opportunity they will have to store up grain for
the "collection for the saints." This was famine relief for the saints in
Jerusalem. Paul discusses it again at length in the second letter, and it
is evident that there is a major effort involving the churches in
Macedonia and Galatia, to put together grain for Paul and his men to
take to Jerusalem. Something similar is described in Acts, where a
prophet arrives in Antioch with a message of impending famine. The
church put together food and sent relief to the saints in Jerusalem by
the hand of Barnabas and Paul (see Acts 11:27-30).

Notice the instruction that each of them was to "lay something
aside" for his offering of grain so it would be ready to go when Paul
got there. Further, that means that "the first day of the weeks" was
not a day of worship – it was a *work day* for gathering the harvested
grain for shipment to Palestine. The use of this passage as an excuse
for taking up an offering every Sunday is ludicrous to anyone who
understands what was actually going on. The NIV renders the verse
thus: "On the first day of every week, each one of you should set
aside a sum of money in keeping with his income, saving it up, so
that when I come no collections will have to be made.

And there is not a thing here about a church meeting." This in
spite of the fact that there is no Greek word for money in the passage.
Moreover, money is of little use when there is no food to buy. They
were sending grain not shekels.

That leaves us with only one more instance of "The first day
of the week" in the New Testament:

> Now on the first day of the week(s), when the disciples
> came together to break bread, Paul, ready to depart the

next day, spoke to them and continued his message until midnight (Acts 20:7).

This is the only passage in the New Testament that suggests that the Church met on 'the first day of the week," and even here it is Saturday night, not Sunday, per se. It is also precisely the same idiom we have seen previously.[iv]

Now here is our problem. We have the flimsiest of circumstantial evidence that the Church met on the first day of the week, except for Pentecost. What we have is incidental, that is to say that it is an isolated *incident*, not a custom of the Church. At no point is it said to be the *ethos*, the custom of the Church to meet on Sunday.

We have to explain how the earliest Jewish Christians abandoned the observance of the Sabbath and substituted Sunday. We have to explain when they did it, why they did it, and how they dealt with the certain fact that the Sabbath day was the identifying sign of their God. And we have to find all this in the New Testament.

The idea is that it was *the Sunday resurrection of Jesus* that prompted the change. But we have an even greater problem with that. Are you ready for this? No one in the New Testament bears witness to the *time* of Jesus' resurrection for the simple reason that no one witnessed it. We have an abundance of witnesses that he was alive from Sunday morning on, but no witnesses as to the actual time he opened his eyes and left the tomb. See chapter seven of this book for a complete analysis of what happened.

Jesus Was a Jew

One of the strangest things about the Christian faith is that somewhere in history Christians forgot that Jesus was a Jew. Not only that, but that all His original disciples were Jews. Moreover, during the entire time covered by the New Testament writings, the Christian Church looked very much like another Jewish sect.

Everywhere, especially in the East of the Roman Empire, there would be Jewish Christians whose outward way of life would not be markedly different from that of the Jews. They took for granted that the Gospel was continuous with the faith of Abraham; for them the Christian Covenant, which Jesus had established at the

Last Supper with his disciples and sealed by his death, did not mean that the covenant made between God and Israel was no longer in force. They still observed the Feasts of Passover, Pentecost, and Tabernacles; they also continued to be circumcised, to keep the weekly Sabbath and the Mosaic regulations concerning food. According to some scholars, they must have been so strong, that right up to the fall of Jerusalem in A.D. 70 these observant Jews were the dominant element in the Christian movement.

From the beginning of the New Testament all the way through the 12th chapter of Acts, the Church was composed entirely of Jews and circumcised proselytes. And there is not a word of any major change in practice during this entire time. For example, when Saul went hunting for Christians to arrest, where did he look?

> Then Saul, still breathing threats and murder against the disciples of the Lord, went to the high priest and asked letters from him to the synagogues of Damascus, so that if he found any who were of the Way, whether men or women, he might bring them bound to Jerusalem (Acts 9:1-2).

It is probably surprising to the modern reader to realize that the Christians in Damascus didn't have a church of their own. Why were they still in the synagogues? And if they were still attending synagogue, they were still keeping the Sabbath. When Paul was arrested, he made a revealing remark to his fellow Jews:

> Now it happened, when I returned to Jerusalem and was praying in the temple, that I was in a trance and saw Him saying to me, "Make haste and get out of Jerusalem quickly, for they will not receive your testimony concerning Me." So I said, "Lord, they know that in every synagogue I imprisoned and beat those who believe on You" (Acts 22:17-19).

My job is to report and let you decide, but I find it impossible to believe that in these early years the Church had made any change in its days of worship. There is not a hint about Christmas or Easter and no suggestion that the Church had ceased observing the Seventh Day Sabbath. So if it didn't take place within the time frame while the New Testament was being written, when did it happen?

Circumcision

Before I talk about that, there was one major change that was made by the early Church and even that one is not very well understood. There were two Jewish practices that particularly identified the Jews in the first century: The Sabbath and circumcision. And circumcision became a major bone of contention while the Sabbath did not. This is what makes the silence regarding the Sabbath so significant. When a major change was contemplated, it made waves.

As I remarked earlier, up through Acts 12, the Church is entirely Jewish and none of these questions had been raised. But God had no intention of being the sole property of the Jews, and in Acts 13, a momentous beginning is recorded. For the first time, a serious effort was made toward unbelieving Gentiles. Paul and Barnabas launched their first "Missionary Journey."

Wherever they traveled, they went first to the synagogue in every city, and when the Gospel was rejected by most in the synagogues, they turned to the Gentiles. And the Gentiles began to be baptized in droves. With this great success in hand, Paul and Barnabas returned to Antioch. They rehearsed all that God had done with them and how God had opened the door of faith to the Gentiles.[v]

But as word spread, there appeared a fly in the ointment. "And certain men came down from Judea and taught the brethren, 'Unless you are circumcised according to the custom of Moses, you cannot be saved'" (Acts 15:1).

There was a fundamental difference in world view of those involved in this dispute. Those who were making this argument, we learn later, were Pharisees who had come to believe that Jesus was the Messiah. Now can you imagine this group of people not being Sabbath keepers? It is inconceivable. Why, then, was the Sabbath not an issue while circumcision was? The answer is simple enough. There was nothing in Paul's work with the Gentiles to change anything regarding the Sabbath.

217

The Pharisees rightly saw circumcision as a matter of national identity. But they assumed that God was only the God of the nation of Israel. To serve God, you had to join the tribe by being circumcised.

But there was a fundamental difference between circumcision and Sabbath observance. Circumcision identified the Jews. *The Sabbath identified God.* This is a major point of confusion among many people to this day.

So how did this conflict play out? "When therefore Paul and Barnabas had no small dissension and disputation with them, they determined that Paul and Barnabas, and certain other of them, should go up to Jerusalem unto the apostles and elders about this question." And thus was convened the great Jerusalem conference described in Acts 15.

After Paul and the others had declared all that God had done with them, "there rose up certain of the sect of the Pharisees which believed, saying, That it was needful to circumcise them, and to command them to keep the law of Moses" (Acts 15:5). This was pretty hard for Paul to take, since God had been giving the Holy Spirit to uncircumcised Gentiles right and left. Even Peter stood to take exception to this idea since he had been the very first to take the Gospel to a Gentile and to see with his own eyes that God had done the very same thing that Paul was describing:

> And when there had been much dispute, Peter rose up and said to them: "Men and brethren, you know that a good while ago God chose among us, that by my mouth the Gentiles should hear the word of the gospel and believe. So God, who knows the heart, acknowledged them by giving them the Holy Spirit, just as He did to us, and made no distinction between us and them, purifying their hearts by faith. Now therefore, why do you test God by putting a yoke on the neck of the disciples which neither our fathers nor we were able to bear? (vv. 7-10).

Now this is an odd thing to say, for the Jews had borne circumcision easily enough for generations. Peter is implying that believing Pharisees were raising the bar higher for Gentiles than they had for Jews. We have to recall at this point, that the Pharisees were demanding circumcision and obedience to the law *to be saved*. Peter makes it clear enough that these had never been the condition for salvation. The conference finally reached a conclusion:

> They wrote this letter by them: The apostles, the elders, and the brethren, To the brethren who are of the Gentiles in Antioch, Syria, and Cilicia: Greetings. Since we have heard that some who went out from us have troubled you with words, unsettling your souls, saying, "You must be circumcised and keep the law"; to whom we gave no such commandment (vv. 23-24).

Now there is an absurdity beckoning in this passage. The temptation is to say, "See there, the Gentiles did not need to keep the law." The absurdity is that this would suggest that the Gentiles were free to kill, lie, cheat, steal, and commit adultery. The issue was not mere obedience to the law, but the law as an instrument of salvation. The issue is stated in the first verse of Acts 15: "And certain men which came down from Judaea taught the brethren, and said, Except ye be circumcised after the manner of Moses, *ye cannot be saved.*"

What is important to know about this section is that circumcision was not abolished. Nothing was changed, in fact. Circumcision was a matter of national identity, not of spiritual identity. It always had been and *continued* to be. There is not a hint here that the Apostles stopped circumcision for *Jewish Christians*. Paul identifies the core issue in his letter to the Galatians when he addresses the issue of this conference:

> Then after fourteen years I went up again to Jerusalem with Barnabas, and also took Titus with me. And I went up by revelation, and communicated to them that gospel which I preach among the Gentiles, but privately to those who were of reputation, lest by any means I might run, or had run, in vain. Yet not even Titus who was with me, being a Greek, was compelled to be circumcised. And this occurred because of false

> brethren secretly brought in (who came in by stealth to spy out our liberty which we have in Christ Jesus, that they might bring us into bondage), to whom we did not yield submission even for an hour, that the truth of the gospel might continue with you (Galatians 2:1-5).

The issue was not merely circumcision and law keeping. It was a question of whether the Gentiles might receive the Gospel or not. According to the believers who were Pharisees, circumcision and full participation in the Jewish community was required for salvation. Otherwise, salvation wasn't available to Gentiles.

In any case, circumcision was not abolished for Jews. There is another remarkable instance related to this.

> Then he came to Derbe and Lystra. And behold, a certain disciple was there, named Timothy, the son of a certain Jewish woman who believed, but his father was Greek. He was well spoken of by the brethren who were at Lystra and Iconium. Paul wanted to have him go with him. And he took him and circumcised him because of the Jews who were in that region, for they all knew that his father was Greek (Acts 16:1-3).

This is truly remarkable. The Jewish mother of Timothy made him a Jew. And it was necessary for him to be circumcised. Why am I telling you this? Because it all takes place in utter silence on the other major issue – the Sabbath.

As I mentioned previously, for an argument from silence to carry any weight, the silence must be shown to be significant. In this case, we have met that requirement. The silence speaks louder than words. The fact is that all through this time, the entirety of the Christian Church observed the Sabbath day, the same Sabbath as the Jews. Jewish and Gentile Christians all observed it and felt no need to comment on it. The Sabbath was taken for granted in the New Testament.

The Change

So if the change from Sabbath to Sunday didn't take place in Apostolic times, when did it take place, and why? There is an interesting little aside in Acts 18: "After these things Paul departed from Athens, and came to Corinth; And found a certain Jew named Aquila, born in Pontus, lately come from Italy, with his wife Priscilla; (because that Claudius had commanded all Jews to depart from Rome:) and came unto them." The story is told remarkably well in Samuelle Bacchiocchi's seminal work, *From Sabbath to Sunday.*

> In the year A.D. 49 the Emperor Claudius . . . expelled the Jews from Rome since they rioted constantly at the instigation of Chrestus (a probable erroneous transcription of the name of Christ). The fact that on this occasion converted Jews like Aquila and Priscilla were expelled from the city together with the Jews (Acts 18:2) proves, as Pierre Batiffol observes, "that the Roman police had not yet come to distinguish the Christians from the Jews. Fourteen years later, however, Nero identified the Christians as being a separate entity, well distinguished from the Jews.[vi]

By this time, Christianity in Rome was taking on a rather different cast from Christianity in the east, particularly in Palestine. The political structure of Rome gave both Jews and Gentiles good reason to separate themselves from one another, something that had not happened elsewhere. This suggests the possibility that the abandonment of the Sabbath and adoption of Sunday as a new day of worship may have occurred first in Rome as a part of this process of differentiation from Judaism. [vii]

Toward the end of the first century, relations between the Jews and the Roman Empire had deteriorated drastically. The Romans had previously recognized Judaism as a legitimate religion and had even shown a level of respect and even admiration for the religious principles of the Jews. But the Jewish wars that began about A.D. 66 changed all that.

Militarily, the statistic of bloodshed as provided by contemporary historians, even allowing for possible exaggerations, is a most impressive evidence of the Romans's angry vengeance upon the Jews. Tacitus (ca. A.D. 33-120), for instance, gives an estimate of 600,000 Jewish fatalities for the A.D. 70 war. . . Besides military measures, Rome at this time adopted new political and fiscal policies against the Jews. Under Vespasian (A.D. 69-79) both the Sanhedrin and the office of the High Priest were abolished and worship at the temple was forbidden. Hadrian (A.D. 117-138). . . outlawed the practice of the Jewish religion and particularly the observance of the Sabbath.[viii]

Such circumstances invited Christians to develop a new identity, not only characterized by a negative attitude toward the Jews, but also by the substitution of characteristic Jewish religious customs for new ones. These would serve to make the Roman authorities aware that the Christians, as Marcel Simon emphasizes, "liberated from any tie with the religion of Israel and the land of Palestine, represented for the empire irreproachable subjects." This internal need of the Christian community to develop what may be called an "anti-Judaism of differentiation" found expression particularly in the development of unwarranted criteria of Scriptural hermeneutic through which Jewish history and observances could be made *void of meaning and function.*[ix]

As you might suspect, the change took place over a rather long period of time. Pope Innocent I, about 417 A.D., wrote a decretal which became canon law that the church should absolutely not observe the sacraments on Friday or Saturday. Which reveals, of course, that up until this time, a lot of people did. Two contemporary historians, Sozomen (about 440 A.D.) and Socrates (about 439 A.D.) confirm this.[x]

So as late as the fifth century, those who did *not* keep the

Sabbath were in the minority of Christian Churches. It is not saying too much to say that the Roman Church was determined to inhibit Sabbath observance. They ordered fasting on the Sabbath and this practice continued among some until after 1000 A.D.[xi]

Conclusion

There is really no question that the entire New Testament Church, through the period in which our New Testament was being written, observed the Sabbath on the day we call Saturday. And there is no question that most of the visible church changed their day of worship to Sunday after the last of the Apostles were dead. The question we must answer is whether that change was somehow authorized or whether it was unjustified and unwarranted.

The next question is what modern man must do about the Sabbath once he realizes what it is all about. I can make this suggestion. Take your Bible in hand and read the fourth commandment in Exodus 20:8-11. Pray and ask God to help you incorporate the Sabbath into your life. As much as lies within you, step aside from your ordinary work and *require* no one else to work on your behalf. In other words, give all the people for whom you are responsible the day off.

Use the Sabbath day for rest and recuperation. Sleep late Saturday morning. Spend some time in Bible study. Spend extra time with your family. Take some time to think about life and about what God might have in mind for you. Don't allow yourself to feel restricted by the Sabbath. But do hold this day apart for God. After all, it is His day, *the day that reminds us who our God really is.*

---

i. "God Fearers" was the term applied to Gentiles who had accepted the Jewish faith, but had stopped short of circumcision.

ii. Leviticus 23:10 f.

iii. John 20:17.

iv. It is worth noting that this occasion falls about a week after the Days of Unleavened Bread. This is at variance with the custom in Jerusalem where the "first day of the weeks" usually occurred within the festival. The reason for this is probably because the harvest had to begin later in Asia Minor due to their being in a more northerly latitude. They had to wait for the harvest in order to have the shipment of grain for the saints in Judaea.

v. Acts 14:27.

vi. Samuelle Bacchiocchi, *From Sabbath to Sunday*, pp. 167 f.

vii. Ibid. page 169.

viii. Ibid. Page 173.

ix. Ibid. Page 183.

x. Ibid. Page 196.

xi. Ibid. Page 193

23

Epilogue

LORD, You have been our dwelling place in all generations.
Before the mountains were brought forth,
Or ever You had formed the earth and the world,
Even from everlasting to everlasting, You are God
(Psalm 90:1-2).

We have come to the last chapter of the book. Have we reached the end of the thread? Surely not. The word for "everlasting" in the Psalm above is *owlam*. Literally, the word means "concealed," but it implies the vanishing point, the place where a line seen stretching into the distance vanishes. Either way we look, we can't see the end of a thread that has no beginning and no end.

When we talk about those things that, for want of a better term, are mysteries, someone is bound to ask, "Why hide all this stuff? Why doesn't God just come right out and say so?" The truth is, he does. There is nothing obscure about the Ten Commandments, nor is the Gospel hard to understand. But, there are two big problems that have to be overcome. One is that man often doesn't want to know. The truth will run against the grain of the way he wants to live his life. On the other hand, it is no easy task for a finite mind to grasp the infinite. Some things are just beyond our reach. Naturally, that doesn't keep us from trying.

Meanwhile, the essentials are fairly simple. "He has shown

you, O man, what is good; And what does the LORD require of you But to do justly, To love mercy, And to walk humbly with your God?" (Micah 6:8).

How hard is this? God does not ask us to "Climb every mountain, ford every stream." He doesn't require heroic efforts. He just requires a good life lived well. Okay then, you want to know, what is all the rest of this stuff about? "Why all the laws, the ceremonies, the rules, these holidays you keep talking about?"

I can think of a couple of reasons. First, the laws, commandments, rules, and stuff are all given to *define* justice and mercy, right and wrong. Otherwise, how would we know? Yes, I know, when the Holy Spirit reveals these things to us. But when you think about it, would you expect the Holy Spirit to tell you something entirely new and different from what has been revealed to men before? And how are you to try the spirits if not from what is already written? The Holy Spirit is not going to lead you in some new direction from where God has led man through history. And how is our conscience going to be educated if not from the Bible? And why should the Holy Spirit tell you something you should have known already from reading the Book?

Then, if you are going to walk humbly with God, you have to know where He is going. Otherwise it may not be God you are walking with. It may be someone entirely different.

The problem is that we human beings are never satisfied. We were made with a restless spirit. We can walk the simplest way with God, but something inside us tells us that there is more. And there is. It is in the observance of the holydays of the Bible that we learn more about the plan of God, where He is going, and how we can walk more closely with Him.

In this book, I have said that these are *Christian* holydays, not merely Jewish holidays. I have pointed out the obvious, that they are the only holidays found in the Bible. I can recall my own surprise when someone pointed out two important things about the traditional Christian holidays, Christmas and Easter. One, neither of them is found in the Bible, either in instruction or observance. Second, almost everything about these days is of non-Christian origin. Everything about Christmas, from the date of the observance to the tree, is of pagan origin – with one exception: the nativity of Jesus.

Everything about Easter, from the date to the colored eggs to the rabbits, is of pagan origin, with one exception: the resurrection of Jesus.

Then came the even bigger surprise. There were seven holidays commanded in the Bible that not only are not pagan, but have everything to do with the life, ministry and work of Jesus Christ. One of the greatest losses of the Christian faith is that so many have lost touch with these festivals and no longer see Christ in them, even though the early church certainly did keep them and saw Christ in every one of them.

In previous chapters, I told the story of how these changes came about. The tough question is how a Christian church that has lost touch with them could ever restore them. The resistance is strong and persistent and has hundreds of years of custom and habit built up. Jude provides the mandate for a church that is in danger of losing its way:

> Beloved, while I was very diligent to write to you concerning our common salvation, I found it necessary to write to you exhorting you *to contend earnestly for the faith which was once for all delivered to the saints*. For certain men have crept in unnoticed, who long ago were marked out for this condemnation, ungodly men, who turn the grace of our God into lewdness and deny the only Lord God and our Lord Jesus Christ (Jude 1:3-4).

That departure from the faith began in the first century and has continued to this day. Among some teachers, there is a rank hostility to the Law of God. In spite of all the statements in both testaments that the law is holy and just and good, there are some who persist in condemning the law at every turn.

But for those who respect the Law of God, it still serves as a lamp to their feet and a light to their path so they don't have to stumble in the dark. For me personally, the opening up of the festivals of the Bible in a *Christian* application was like turning on a light in a dark room.

These festivals are called "The appointed times of Jehovah," and around them flow the entire history of the people of God, from the Israelites, to the Jews, to the Christians of every race and nation. And not only the history of God's people, but their future as well.

I first began celebrating the festivals of the Bible nearly 50 years ago, but I can't say that I really understood them in the beginning. What I did was to follow the old rule: "When all else fails, do as you're told." So, since God said to do it, and all I had to do was take off work and go to church, I thought, "Let's do that." That was a simple first step. And because it was the custom to teach and study the meaning of the days in their seasons, year by year I learned the rich history of God's dealings with his people, especially at those pivotal points in their history, like the original Passover.

Once the groundwork was laid in the history, the analogies from that history became more and more obvious, and the connections to Christ became just as obvious. That could not be ignored. Paul warned the Corinthians about this:

> Moreover, brethren, I do not want you to be unaware that all our fathers were under the cloud, all passed through the sea, all were baptized into Moses in the cloud and in the sea, all ate the same spiritual food, and all drank the same spiritual drink. For they drank of that spiritual Rock that followed them, *and that Rock was Christ* (1 Corinthians 10:1-4).

This may be a surprise to you, as it was to me at one time, but most Christian churches believe that Jesus Christ preexisted his human birth, that He was with Israel in the wilderness. So did Paul. Notice it is spiritual food and drink Paul speaks of, drawing out the metaphor. The spiritual Rock, not to be confused with the hard rock that brought forth water, was none other than the one we know as Jesus Christ. Then Paul drives home the point of the analogy:

> Now these things became our examples, to the intent that we should not lust after evil things as they also lusted. And do not become idolaters as were some of them. As it is written, "The people sat down to eat and drink, and rose up to play." Nor let us commit

sexual immorality, as some of them did, and in one
day twenty-three thousand fell; nor let us tempt
Christ, as some of them also tempted, and were
destroyed by serpents; nor complain, as some of them
also complained, and were destroyed by the destroyer.
Now all these things happened to them as examples,
and they were written for our admonition, upon whom
the ends of the ages have come. Therefore let him
who thinks he stands take heed lest he fall (vv. 6-12).

I am appalled when I hear people say we don't need the Old
Testament any longer. Paul didn't see it that way, and neither do I.
Everything about the history of Israel was written down as an
admonition for those people upon whom the ends of the earth have
come. We are supposed to be admonished by these errors and what
came from them. That does not sound to me like something I don't
need any longer. We aren't there yet, and we need the road map to
tell us where we are and what we need to get it right.

So from the Old Testament, I began to learn what Paul meant
what he said, "Christ our Passover is sacrificed for us." It suddenly
became apparent that the Corinthians were even abstaining from
leaven during the Passover season and keeping the feast.[i]

As time went on, the metaphors that arise from these feasts
became increasingly obvious. I learned what John the Baptist meant
when he looked up, saw Jesus and said, "Behold the lamb of God."
We take that statement for granted, but it must have sounded very
strange indeed to John's disciples. I learned that, at the very moment
when the High Priest cut the throat of a lamb in the Temple, a Roman
soldier thrust a spear into the side of Jesus as he hung, nailed to a tree,
and blood and water came out of his side. The connection between the
Passover lamb and the Lamb of God that takes away the sin of the
world is there for all to see.

Oh sure, the original Passover was a historical institution for
Israel. But we have gone beyond that now. We have gone to the
world. Even in going to the world, we take to them the message of
the Passover Lamb.

I learned that I was supposed to eat unleavened bread for
seven days after Passover, because leaven is a type of sin, and as a

disciple of Jesus, I should live a holy life. At first, it seemed a strange thing to do, and yet, one Easter Sunday morning as I sat at brunch in a hotel dining room, there bounded into the room a six foot tall rabbit with big ears and a basket full of colored eggs. He went around giving eggs to all the kids. Now you tell me. Is that a strange custom or not? Why should I feel it is a strange custom to eat unleavened bread for seven days when the rest of the Christian world is doing this "normal" thing of dressing up like rabbits, giving out colored eggs to kids and claiming that rabbits lay eggs? Who is crazy?

And I learned it was not merely a matter of abstaining from leavened bread as a type of sin. I was to actually eat unleavened bread. The connection with the Last Supper is hard to miss. It is Paul again who reminds us that the Lord Jesus, in the night of his betrayal, took bread, broke it and handed it to his disciples saying, "Take, eat: this is my body, which is broken for you." [ii]

The eating of unleavened bread for seven days came to symbolize my need for the Bread of Life, every day of my life. And Jesus is that Bread of Life. It was in the observance of these days that I came to understand what happened the Sunday morning after Jesus' Resurrection. That at the very moment the priest in the Temple was presenting the firstfruits to God, Jesus was being presented to the Father in heaven as the firstfruits from the grave, the first human to be rescued from death and presented to the Father. And I learned that Jesus is the first of many to be so presented. I learned that the seven weeks of harvest between that day and Pentecost pictured the time of harvest in which we now live. I recalled that Jesus compared the field of harvest to a world of lost people, and urged his disciples to pray that God would send workers into that harvest.

I learned that the Feast of Pentecost pictured, not only the pouring out of the Holy Spirit upon all flesh, but the time of the presentation of the remainder of the firstfruits to God. I learned that the Feast of Trumpets in the autumn looks forward to the return of Christ and the Day of the Lord, when the last of the seven great trumpets is blown, and the saints are raised from the dead.

I learned that the Day of Atonement pictures the reconciliation of man to God and the final disposition of the age old problem of sin. I learned that the Feast of Tabernacles is a confession that we are strangers and pilgrims in the earth and that we look for the kingdom to come. I learned that this festival looks forward to the thousand year reign of Christ. And finally, I learned that there is this shadowy "eighth day" at the end of the festival that implies that all is not yet finished.

Once you embark on this road, all manner of new connections present themselves. For example, there is a man named Job who understood something that later generations seem to have lost. He has a soliloquy about man that should give us pause. "Man who is born of woman," he said, "is of few days and full of trouble."[iii] Truer words were never spoken. Man blossoms like a flower fades, and is gone almost as quickly. Job, who has been suffering terribly, wishes that God would just let him go, let him rest, even in the grave.

> Oh, that You would hide me in the grave, That You would conceal me until Your wrath is past, That You would appoint me a set time, and remember me! If a man dies, shall he live again? All the days of my hard service I will wait, Till my change comes. You shall call, and I will answer You; You shall desire the work of Your hands (Job 14:13-15).

It is profoundly encouraging to realize that Job, one of the very earliest of the patriarchs, knew about the resurrection. And he understood something very important that it takes some of us a long time to learn. God will not waste his work with us. He will not take us so far and then cast us away. Human beings are not biological waste to be incinerated. We are made in the image of God and destined to be like him.

It was in the observance of the Last Great Day of the feast that I came to understand that God will not waste anyone. Oh, I am not a universalist. I believe that there are some who will push God away in spite of everything and will ultimately be destroyed. But I believe, for those who are willing, that God will do whatever it takes to make us into glorious creatures who are just like him. Whatever pain and suffering we have to undergo in this life to get there, that is where he is taking us. Poor old Job suffered terribly to learn what that means. There is no way to understand why God allows us to suffer in this world unless we understand what God is trying to make of us.

In biblical terms everything is finished in seven days. Seven is the number of wholeness, of completion. So what lies beyond the finish line? Why is there an eighth day festival? Naturally, if you can't find the answer anywhere else, you look toward the end of the Bible – the logical place to put it. John saw, in vision, what lies out there. He saw a new heaven and a new earth, "for the first heaven and the first earth had passed away. Also there was no more sea" (Revelation 21:1).

When we go out into the night and look up at the sky, we see Polaris, the North Star, and all the familiar constellations. In John's vision, they are all gone, replaced by a new night sky entirely. It suggests that this "new earth" is in an entirely different location in space and time.

> Then I, John, saw the holy city, New Jerusalem, coming down out of heaven from God, prepared as a bride adorned for her husband. And I heard a loud voice from heaven saying, "Behold, the tabernacle of God is with men, and He will dwell with them, and they shall be His people. God Himself will be with them and be their God. And God will wipe away every tear from their eyes; there shall be no more death, nor sorrow, nor crying. There shall be no more pain, for the former things have passed away." Then He who sat on the throne said, "Behold, I make all things new." And He said to me, "Write, for these words are true and faithful." And He said to me, "It is done! I am the Alpha and the Omega, the Beginning and the End. I will give of the fountain of the water of life freely to him who thirsts. *He who overcomes* shall inherit all things, and I will be his God and he shall be My son (vv. 2-7).

It is absolutely breathtaking to consider. But this is not given to the man who drifts along. It is given to the man who overcomes. As we walk through life, we have battles we have to fight. We have to lay hold on our problems and fight to overcome them. We can't let these things just sweep us along. The Alpha and Omega says that it is the one who overcomes who shall inherit all things. "To the winner belongs the spoils."

Scientists tell us that, on a summer night, when we look out into space, we are looking out some 12 billion light years. And then, come winter when we look out in the opposite direction in space, we are looking 12 billion light years out that way (not that we can see the edge with the naked eye, but it is out there). Is there life out there? Someone replied, "If there isn't, it is a terrible waste of space."

What has God been doing for the past 12 billion or so years? Is Project Earth the first time he has done this? And will it be the last? I don't have the answer, but I can see the thread vanishing into the future. I can hardly wait to see where it goes from here.

---

i. 1 Corinthians 5:7-8.

ii. 1 Corinthians 11:24.

iii. Job 14:1.

Appendix 1

The Hebrew Calendar

And God said, Let there be lights
in the firmament of the heaven
to divide the day from the night;
and let them be for signs, and for seasons,
and for days, and years (Genesis 1:14 KJV).

Nothing God gave to man has been used so consistently for the purpose he intended. Every civilization of man has used the sun, the moon, or both for the demarcation of time. They had no choice. Even a hunting society had to take notice of the passage of seasons. When would the animals migrate to the north and when would they return? How soon would the antlered animals make their move down from the high country? No people dependent upon the land could fail to notice that there was a time to plant and a time to harvest. Their problem was the prediction of that time, and that required the observation of the sun. It required a calendar, and some form of calendar has always been a mark of civilization.

A calendar is more than a pretty picture with the days of the month laid out below. A calendar is a system of determining the beginning and ending of the year and dividing it up into seasons, months, weeks, and days. *To be of any use at all, it has to be done in advance.* A calendar from the past is no more than a diary. By its very nature, a calendar is predictive, and this is why the sun and the moon are so very useful – they are the most predictable elements in the environment of man.

We have no record of when man first noticed this, but it was a very long time ago. Even if he lost everything else God gave him, it is inconceivable that intelligent man – in the space of a lifetime living and working in the out of doors – would not come to know intimately the cycles of the sun, moon, and stars. He would be able to pass on to his children and grandchildren the exact location of sunset on the longest and shortest days of the year. Early on he would have figured out that the sun made that cycle regardless of what his priest said or did – his observations of the sun were not mere superstition.

This was quite a simple task for a man and his family. It became a bit more complicated with clans, communities, and ultimately, civilizations. Consider the problem. How would you go about setting up a calendar – a predictable calendar – for a small community? One of the simplest approaches is merely to count the moons. The American Indians did it this way.

But there is a problem with determining the year. The Islamic calendar is based solely on the moon with no corrections for the movement of the sun. It may not matter much in the desert that the seasons shift slowly forward through the calendar year, but it matters very much to a society dependent on grain and fruit crops. Most ancient calendars took account of the moon, but the problem they had to solve was the movement of the sun. It was not a particularly difficult problem, but it required some thought.

If we were to tackle this problem, we would first have to choose a place to make our observations. We would soon learn that moving about would lead to inaccurate observations. We could put a stick in the ground at the observation point, and then place another stick in the ground on a direct line with the sun when it rises. We could do this every day, and in the space of one year, we would have an arc of sticks that shows the exact point of sunrise on every day of the year. The northernmost stick would designate the day of the summer solstice, and the southernmost stick the winter solstice. The stick in the middle of the line would designate the equinox.

So far, this is a piece of cake. If someone asks, "What day is this?" all we have to do is run out to our line of sticks the next morning and check it out. Naturally, there are problems. What if an animal or a rainstorm dislodges some of our sticks? What if some prankster from a neighboring clan rearranges them? The people of the Salisbury Plain who built Stonehenge found a drastic, but effective solution to that problem.

No one knows who they were. Every vestige of the civilization around Stonehenge is gone except one – a circle of giant stones on a piece of level high ground in Southern England. It is plain that they took great pains to observe and predict the movement of the sun and moon. Stonehenge may or may not have been a place of worship, but it was certainly an observatory from which a calendar was devised and maintained.

It depends on which archaeologist you consult, but between the death of Noah (about 2,000 B.C.) And the death of Abraham (about 1,800 B.C.), a people moved into the Salisbury Plain in Southern England and proceeded to tackle the problem of constructing a calendar. We cannot be certain as to why they did some of the things they did, or even in what order; but there was a logic that we could follow today with the same results.

One of the first things they did was to dig 56 pits arranged in a circle some 240 feet in diameter. This might have resulted from going out at sunrise every 13 days and digging a pit on a line with sunrise and sunset. Having no doubt noticed the North Star never moved, they oriented the circle by building two mounds on the north and south axis of the circle.

By means of careful observation, they determined the point on the horizon where the sun rose at its northernmost point. This was the summer solstice – the longest day of the year. Outside their circle of stones, on a direct line with the sunrise, they placed a stone. This was not just any stone. Taking no chances on having animals, elements, or man alter the arrangement, they set up a 35 ton block of Sarsen sandstone – brought from 20 miles away. It is still in place nearly 4,000 years later.

Whoever these people were, they proceeded to mark other points of the compass – the winter solstice, the equinoxes – with stones, and to build earthworks around their observatory. It would have been a remarkable project in any age, but it is nothing short of astonishing for the time in which it was done. Plainly, the calendar was of great importance to these people.

Stonehenge was modified occasionally over succeeding generations. Bluestones weighing up to 50 tons were brought from Southwest Wales, and set up in concentric circles, once again aligned with the heavens. Two circles created in the earliest time contained 29 and 30 stones, respectively. The lunar month is about 29 ½ days, so it seems they made their months 29 and 30 days long.

There are two very important observations about Stonehenge. One is that a calendar based on the sun and the moon was one of the earliest achievements of civilized man. The other is the heroic efforts these people made to create and preserve their calendar. Of all the things that they might have done, all that is left is a circle of stones that has lasted for over 4,000 years – their calendar.

The people of Mesopotamia faced a different problem. Living in an alluvial plain, high ground was scarce and large stones nonexistent. They solved the problem by building their own "high ground." The land is dotted with the remains of ancient towers. From the tops of these towers, the horizon could be marked with the location of the winter and summer solstice.

The Bible describes a tower like this, including the building material and the reason for building it. The tower is the infamous Tower of Babel: "And they said, Go to, let us build us a city and a tower, whose top may reach unto heaven; and let us make us a name, lest we be scattered abroad upon the face of the whole earth" (Genesis 11:4 KJV).

The words "may reach" are not in the Hebrew text. They did not build the tower to reach heaven, but rather to observe the heavens. One source observed that there are frequent winter ground fogs along the Tigris and Euphrates rivers, and the towers enabled them to get above the fog for calendar observations.

We do know that the ancient Sumerians and Babylonians observed the heavens, and there is evidence that they oriented at least some of their towers to the heavens. We also know that they based their calendar systems on the movement of sun and moon. The people of Erech in Mesopotamia invented writing, and evidence of calendars was found in the ruins along with the earliest writings of man.

The Bible tells us that Noah settled in this region after the Great Flood, and we know that he brought a calendar with him. The years of Noah's calendar were reckoned from his birth: "In the six hundredth year of Noah's life, in the second month, the seventeenth day of the month, the same day were all the fountains of the great deep broken up, and the windows of heaven were opened" (Genesis 7:11 KJV). There are several calendar references in the account of the Flood, including a seventh month, a tenth month, and the first and second months of Noah's 601st year. There is one curious footnote – a period of five months is numbered at 150 days. It seems that Noah used 30 day months. A true lunar month would have alternated between 29 and 30 days, but there is probably no special significance in this. During this period of time, Noah may simply have been unable to observe the moon, and adopted a 30 day month. This would have required some adjustment once they left the ark and were once again able to see the moon, but then only Noah's family had reason to concern themselves with it. (There is no evidence to suggest that the lunar orbit was that different in Noah's day – rather the contrary.)

It was also from Mesopotamia that Abraham and his descendants came. There is no reason to doubt that Abraham, Isaac, and Jacob had a 12-month lunar calendar that was periodically adjusted for the movement of the seasons. They came from a civilization with a calendar like that.

So when God later spoke to the children of Israel and said, "This month shall be unto you the beginning of months" (Exodus 12:2), they did not have to ask, "Lord, what is a month?" Their people had used a calendar system from time immemorial.

But when God gave this instruction, He did not say "month," or even "moon." He used the Hebrew word for "new moon." Used throughout the Old Testament, it identifies the starting point for the Hebrew month. In fact, nearly all the ancient civilizations used the new moon rather than the full moon for the beginning of the month.

But in deciding to use the new moon, they still had questions to answer. What, for example, constituted the "new moon"? Logic falls out quickly in favor of the observation of the first sliver of the crescent moon, but what if we can't see it? It could be overcast, or there might be other conditions that prevent accurate observation. We usually think of seeing the new moon right after sunset, but it can occur at any time of the day. By one definition, the moon is "new" immediately after the conjunction, whether we can see it or not.

The ancients learned very early how to calculate the

conjunction (that is, the precise moment when the moon passes the sun as they both pass through the heavens). The Hebrews called this moment the *molad*. Having this piece of information, what were they to do about the "new moon"? Was it the day when the conjunction took place, or the day after? Sometimes they could see the first crescent of the moon on the day of the conjunction, and sometimes not – even in clear weather. It varied with the weather, the time of day of the conjunction, the time of sunset, the relative position of the sun and moon, and the location of the observer.

It would not be very difficult to design a system for determining the new moons. All we need is a set of rules. The first rule could be that the official day of the new moon is the first day that the new crescent is visible right after sunset. This has a lot of appeal. But we do have to allow for problems. What do we do if it is cloudy? That is not terribly difficult. Since lunar months can only be 29 or 30 days long, we can simply alternate when we can't see the moon. If last month was 30 days long, we'll just make this one 29. This will work fine most of the time – providing that we are all in the same location. If it is cloudy here and clear a thousand miles from here, we might often declare the new moon on different days. I suppose this could be acceptable if we don't all have to be together on everything.

If I could calculate the conjunction, and if it were up to me, I might simply declare that the day of the conjunction was the day of the new moon – no adjustments, no confusion. My problem is that I have no authority for one system over the other. The rules are easy to write – the problem is, who writes the rules?

Naturally, we would expect to turn to the Bible to see what the law told Israel to do. The problem is that the law didn't tell them. While there are plenty of indirect calendar references in the law, instructions about the calendar itself are almost nonexistent. In fact the only explicit instruction about the calendar is Exodus 12:2, "This month shall be your beginning of months; it shall be the first month of the year to you."

It may be hard to believe, but everything else we know about the calendar, we know from inference or from tradition. For example, how can you tell from the text just quoted which month was the first month? What time of year was it? Jewish tradition tells us it was in the spring, but the only help we get from the Bible is the name of the

239

month: "And Moses said unto the people, Remember this day, in which ye came out from Egypt, out of the house of bondage; for by strength of hand the LORD brought you out from this place: there shall no leavened bread be eaten. This day came ye out in the month Abib" (Exodus 13:3, 4).

And so we know the Hebrew name of the month – *Abib*. And we know that *Abib* means, "green ears." From other Scriptures we learn that the green ears in question were barley, so we infer that the month Abib is the month when there are green ears of barley in the field.

All this is very clever of us, but it is curious that something so important was left to inference instead of being stated. Instructions for sacrifices are laid out in excruciating detail. *Why were the instructions for the calendar not done the same way?* Naming a month after green ears of barley is better than nothing, but it leaves a lot of unanswered questions. What if the ears are not green until the last day of the month? How would you have known to make that month *Abib*? Okay, we can decide that the month following the onset of green ears is *Abib*. But what if the ears turn green on the second day of the new moon? Will they still be green the following month? The ears will often be green in two consecutive months. Which is *Abib*?

The Bible does not explain, and we seem to be left to figure out for ourselves how to do it. And yet this decision is critical, because the month of Abib is the beginning of the religious year (the civil year seems to have begun in the autumn).

The calendar of the Hebrews was not simply lunar, and it was not exactly lunisolar. The sun only indirectly affected their calendar. The Israelites did not merely observe the sun to calculate their calendar. They observed the crops and the weather.

The problem was that a 12 month lunar year falls some 11 days short of the solar year. So, when the lunar year had fallen about 30 days short, they simply added a 13th month to keep the Passover in the spring. Talmudic sources tell us that the calendar committee did not rely solely on calculation, but on observation as well. They added a 13th month "when the barley in the fields had not yet ripened, when the fruit on the trees had not grown properly, when the winter rains had not stopped, when the roads for Passover pilgrims had not dried up, and when the young pigeons had not become fledged." [i]

The leap years were reasonably predictable. If they had just added a 13th month, they could be sure they would not have to do that for the next two years. Early on, they noticed a 19 year cycle in which the leap years occurred on a repeating basis. Reasons suggest that they rarely had to fall back on observation to announce a leap year. Observation could confirm, but it came too late to predict. If they could not *predict*, how could pilgrims know when to leave home to arrive in time for the festival season. The determination of the calendar had serious practical considerations as well as religious implications.

Where did they find all this in the law? They didn't. In fact, they found nothing at all about calendar adjustments, leap years, 13th months, conjunctions and new crescents. *The children of Israel found in the law a presumption of a calendar and the sanctification of certain days in that calendar.* We do not know whether God revealed it to them, or whether they had to figure it out for themselves. All we have is the calendar tradition they have preserved for us along with the sacred Scriptures.

Paul may have been talking about this sort of thing when he spoke of the "oracles" of God. In writing about the Jews and their relationship with God, he asked, "What advantage then has the Jew, or what is the profit of circumcision? Much in every way! Chiefly because to them were committed the oracles of God" (Romans 3:1-2). The word for "oracles" is the Greek *logion* which means, literally, "sayings." The Jews retained an oral law besides the written law we find in the Bible, and that oral law included a complex calendar system into which God placed all the holy days of the sacred year.

The modern Hebrew calendar is sometimes challenged because the "new moon" may be postponed one or two days based on a complex set of rules. Actually, these rules are applied only once in the year – on the first day of the seventh month – the Feast of Trumpets. This particular moon (the beginning of the civil year) is determined and then all the others are established by it. Since a cycle of the moon is about 29½ days (plus 44 minutes), the first seven months of the religious year (in which all the holy days occur) simply alternate between 29 and 30 days. The extra 44 minutes creates an extra day at predictable intervals, and that is handled by having two consecutive 30 day months from time to time. In order to keep confusion to a minimum, those months are always in the second half of the year.

The objections to the Jewish custom come in two forms: one argues that any postponement from the conjunction is wrong, and the other argues that only the observed new crescent can start a month. But we recall at this point that the Bible does not define a new moon either way. If it did, I suppose there would be no argument.

In calculating the new moon of the Feast of Trumpets, the pivotal point of the Jewish year, the rules proclaim the new moon on the day of the conjunction with some exceptions. For example if the conjunction occurs after noon, the new moon is "postponed" to the following day. In fact, the first new crescent will almost certainly be observed the following day.

This rule generally satisfies those who want the month to begin with the observed new crescent. But there is another rule they find more troubling. When the conjunction occurs on a Sunday, Wednesday, or Friday, the official new moon (and the Feast of Trumpets) is postponed to the following day for religious reasons. The religious requirements are that the Day of Atonement (Yom Kippur) must not fall on the day before or after a Sabbath, and the day before the Last Great Day of the autumn feast cannot fall on a Sabbath. (There are other postponements required because of mathematical consequences of the first two.)

But can "religious requirements" take precedence over the law? In some cases, yes. When the Pharisees challenged Jesus and his disciples over Sabbath observance, he asked them, "Or have you not read in the law that on the Sabbath the priests in the temple profane the Sabbath, and are blameless?" (Matthew 12:5). In other words, the priest had to carry on the work of the sacrificial system even on the Sabbath day. This created a conflict between the sacrificial law (which required sacrifices every day) and the Sabbath (which required that no work be done).

We would normally assume that when laws come into conflict the lesser law would give way to the greater. There can be no greater law than the Ten Commandments, and yet the sacrificial law superseded even the Sabbath. The priesthood had special responsibilities on the holy days and the new moons, so it would not be surprising if they should take those duties into account when working out their calendar rules – *especially when the law gave them no specific instructions to the contrary.* They had a modest requirement to make a morning and evening sacrifice (each one a lamb) every day of the year. In addition, each Sabbath day they sacrificed two more lambs with meal, oil, and drink offerings (Numbers 28:9). All this work increased dramatically on the day of the new moon. On the first of every month, they were required to sacrifice ten animals – two young bullocks, one ram, and seven lambs – plus the other offerings. It is easy to see the importance of predictability when there is this much work to be done.

Each of the annual holy days also had special offerings. On the Day of Atonement, for example, the prescribed offering was one bullock, one ram, seven lambs, plus any prescribed meal, oil, and drink offerings, and a special goat for a sin offering. Since the Day of Atonement is a fast day, it should not be surprising if steps were taken to avoid it falling before or after a Sabbath day. One can, of course, argue to the contrary, but there is *no biblical authority that prevents the rules of the calendar from being written this way.*

We don't know with any precision when the rules for postponements came to be. They seem to have coalesced in their present form in the 10th century, but the principles underlying them are much older. There is evidence dating from much earlier that the authorities "adjusted" their observations to avoid having Yom Kippur fall just before or just after a Sabbath. It was no great trick. They just changed the observation point.[ii]

Does all this seem confusing to you? Never mind, it seems confusing to a lot of people. The reason most calendar calculations seem complex is because they are trying to give the illusion of precision. The truth is that the solar system is not precise. The moon is not always the same distance from the earth, and there are subtle variations in the time of its orbit. *In the nature of things, a calendar is only a rough measure of time.*

But suppose it was not God's intent to impose a new calendar system, but to reveal to Israel where, in their calendar system, his holy days were to fall? He does not tell them what constitutes a new moon, how many days there are in a month, how many months in a year, or how to adapt the lunar calendar to the solar year. Presumably, they already knew how to do that. Other peoples of the time knew, so there is no reason to suppose the Hebrews did not.

This may be a good place to deal with the concept of "holy time." The idea is that from creation there were certain segments of time set apart and designated as holy. The Sabbath day is said to be "holy time" as are all the annual holy days.

The problem with this lies in our concept of time. Suppose that just after sunset when the Sabbath has begun, you decide to telephone your mother, who lives a continent away from you. It is three hours earlier there, yet both still converse in the same moment in time. For you, it is the Sabbath, but not for her. She may be trying to get you off the phone so she can finish her housework *before* the Sabbath.

Since the Sabbath day begins at sunset, it does not begin at all places at the same time. How, then, can the Sabbath be "holy time"? In truth, the Sabbath is not holy time, it is a holy day. There is a difference. We in the United States keep the same Sabbath day as the Jews in Jerusalem, but we don't keep the same window of time.

Therefore the concept of "holy time" is probably misleading, especially pertaining to the annual holy days. The presumption is that the time when the earth reaches a certain point in its orbit around the sun is holy. The astronomer will see an immediate problem. The earth is not always at sunset when it reaches this special place. For the time to be holy, the rotation of the earth on its axis and the revolution of the earth around the sun would have to be synchronous. That is, the sun should always be setting as the earth comes to the place in its orbit that corresponds to the beginning of holy time. It is not.

What does it take to make a day holy? When Moses encountered the burning bush, God told him to take off his shoes for the ground he stood on was holy. The ground was not holy of itself; it was holy because God was there. The Tabernacle was not holy until God entered it and filled it with His presence. The spot where the Temple was built was only a threshing floor until Solomon built a temple on the spot and God entered it.

Both the Tabernacle and the Temple were built by human hands. True, God gave them specifications, but it was left to them to build. We know that God inspired the craftsmen, but we still have to

244

guess what certain parts of it looked like. As long as the Temple was a building built by craftsmen, it was only a building. It was when God entered it that it became holy.

In the same way, the rules of the calendar were written by men. The days of the year were not holy until selected by God. They are, in a sense, made holy by his presence. He told Israel what days in their calendar he would be present – what days he would meet with them. (The old expression "Tabernacle of the Congregation" actually means "Tent of Meeting.")

Did God give specifications for the calendar like he gave specifications for the Temple? We don't know. We do know that the Israelites got more from God than the book we call the Bible. The writer of the book of Hebrews opens his account by telling us that God spoke to the fathers in time past at "sundry times and in diverse manners." The Old Testament contains much, but not all of that communication. The leaders of God's people commonly consulted God about questions and judgments, and they got answers that are sometimes recorded for us – sometimes not.

We don't know whether Israel's calendar was an old calendar appropriated by God, or a new calendar revealed by God. What we do know is that the calendar became authoritative when God proclaimed certain days in it as his festivals. The days were not intrinsically holy – they were *made* holy.

We also know that God established an administration to go with the law. It may come as a surprise to learn that the law did not answer all questions pertaining to human relationships – not even of man's relationship with God. When Moses complained to God about the burden of leading the people of Israel, God gave him a solution:

> And the LORD said unto Moses, Gather unto me seventy men of the elders of Israel, whom thou knowest to be the elders of the people, and officers over them; and bring them unto the tabernacle of the congregation, that they may stand there with thee. And I will come down and talk with thee there: and I will take of the spirit which is upon thee, and will put it upon them; and they shall bear the burden of the people with thee, that thou bear it not thyself alone. . .

> And the LORD came down in a cloud, and spake unto
> him, and took of the spirit that was upon him, and gave
> it unto the seventy elders: and it came to pass, that,
> when the spirit rested upon them, they prophesied, and
> did not cease (Numbers 11:16-25 KJV).

This is the origin of the "seventy elders" of Israel – the basis
of the later Sanhedrin – charged with the responsibility of
administering the Law of God. We don't know what they did about
the calendar, but we do know that the rules and observations of the
calendar were, in the days of Jesus' ministry, in the hands of the
Sanhedrin. We also know that in spite of all the issues where Jesus
opposed the Jewish leadership, he never argued with them about the
calendar.

It is important for us to understand that, from the beginning,
there was an authoritative judiciary in Israel charged with the
responsibility of deciding points of law for the people. This system is
described in Deuteronomy 17:8-13. When one of these courts
rendered a decision, it was as binding as any law given by God
himself – even to the extent of exacting the death penalty. What they
bound on earth, was bound in heaven.

This is not to say that their authority extended into the
established church of Jesus Christ. That authority, Jesus explicitly
granted to the Apostles:

> Assuredly, I say to you, whatever you bind on earth
> will be bound in heaven, and whatever you loose on
> earth will be loosed in heaven. Again I say to you that
> if two of you agree on earth concerning anything that
> they ask, it will be done for them by My Father in
> heaven. For where two or three are gathered together
> in My name, I am there in the midst of them (Matthew
> 18:18-20).

Like the Sanhedrin, the apostles were granted the authority to
make decisions within the law. They did not have the authority to go
beyond the law. Like the Sanhedrin, they received the Holy Spirit to
guide them:

And when He had said this, He breathed on them, and
said to them, "Receive the Holy Spirit. If you forgive
the sins of any, they are forgiven them; if you retain
the sins of any, they are retained" (John 20:22, 23).

That spirit was poured out upon them at Pentecost that year,
and they prophesied, just as Moses' Sanhedrin had done (see
Numbers 11:24 ff.). From ancient times, the Sanhedrin had the
authority to make the rules and observations that sanctified the
Hebrew calendar. Jesus and the Apostles seem to have accepted their
authority in this area. While there is ample evidence that the early
Christians kept the holy days, there is no hint in the New Testament
that they ever attempted to sanctify a calendar apart from the
normative Hebrew calendar.

The Sanhedrin had always kept the rules for the calendar
secret – perhaps with some wisdom. There will always be someone
ready to argue with the rules, and the calendar could have been a
source of endless bickering. In the fourth century, the patriarch of the
Jewish religion published the hitherto secret rules and set up a system
whereby the calendar could be predicted far into the future.
Prediction, in the final analysis, is the work of the calendar. Most
Christian groups that observe the biblical festivals, with few
exceptions, have accepted that calendar as the basis for their religious
year.

Among those Christians who observe the annual holydays of
the Bible, the question is often raised as to whether they should, in
some way, observe the new moons. At present, there is nothing to do
on the new moons. The holy days are declared to be Sabbath days –
work is prohibited except for the preparation of food. There is also a
commanded assembly on each of the annual holy days. There are no
such requirements connected with the new moons.

There were, however, specific requirements *of the priests* on
these days. Trumpets were to be blown, and large numbers of
sacrifices were required (Numbers 10:10; 28:11 ff.). The killing of
sacrifices provided a lot of meat to be eaten, so the new moon was a
feast of sorts (see 1 Samuel 20). Beyond the work of the priests,
though, there were no statutory requirements of the people. We can
infer, nevertheless, that the new moons became an important part of

the system of festival and worship, and that they will be again. Looking ahead to the Kingdom of God, Isaiah says, "And it shall come to pass, that from one new moon to another, and from one sabbath to another, shall all flesh come to worship before me, saith the LORD" (Isaiah 66:23 KJV).

When the Temple was there, the new moons became days of special worship even though there was no command to do so. The activity of the priests, the special sacrifices, and the festive air made it so. Perhaps they will again when a temple is rebuilt.

The ministry of the vast majority of festival observing churches decided long ago to accept the published Hebrew calendar as the basis for the sacred year. The calendar is published by various Jewish sources, notably *The Comprehensive Hebrew Calendar*, by Spier. Methods of calculation are discussed there as well as in *The Jewish Encyclopedia*.

---

i. Arthur Spier, *The Comprehensive Hebrew Calendar*, p.1.

ii. See the *Encyclopedia Judaica*, article, "Calendar."

Appendix 2

In Defense of the Holydays

To those of us who have been keeping the holydays for years – in some cases, for all of our lives – the practice seems so natural, so right. The Scriptures supporting the practice seem so obvious. Why, we wonder, doesn't *everyone* observe the holydays?

Of course, the most obvious reason is that most Christians know little or nothing about the holydays, and the Old Testament is uncharted territory. For those who have more familiarity, the practice of religion in the Old Testament is viewed as essentially Jewish and irrelevant to the Christian.

There are Christians, however, who have studied the holydays carefully, and have arrived at a conscious decision *not* to observe them. Why? What is the rational, philosophic, theological or scriptural basis for this decision?

There are two broad categories of people who believe it is not necessary to keep the holydays: those who keep the Sabbath, and those who do not. Among those who do not keep the Sabbath, there are various other categories. There are some who believe that all the Old Testament was abolished and is irrelevant to Christians. There are others who believe the ceremonial law was abolished but the moral law was retained. Some believe none of the law was abolished, but it is the right of the church to interpret the law and even change the law if necessary.

This latter group recognizes that the early church kept the

Sabbath, and even the holydays, but they chronicle the change that took place in the church from Sabbath to Sunday and from the holydays to Easter and Christmas and conclude that the church had the right to make those changes.

The arguments on this subject fall into certain identifiable patterns, and it is quite instructive to examine them. A few basic premises advanced against the holydays may be listed as follows:

1. The holydays are essentially the national days of Israel. They apply only to Israel and not to other nations.
2. The holydays are essentially Levitical and ceremonial. All such laws passed away either at the cross or at the destruction of the Temple.
3. The holydays could only be observed at the Temple in Jerusalem and nowhere else.
4. All of the holydays are types which are fulfilled in Christ and are therefore no longer binding on Christians.

In the August, 1979, Bible Advocate, an article appeared titled, *Should We Keep Israel's Holydays?* by D.L. Prunkard. The Bible Advocate is a publication of the Seventh Day Church of God, a denomination that observes the seventh day Sabbath, but not the biblical festivals. The article is useful in that it includes an exhaustive collection of the arguments advanced against the observance of the biblical holydays. The author felt the need to deal with this in great detail, because there has been an ongoing discussion in his denomination over this very issue. It is a problem for them because of the difficulty in maintaining the weekly Sabbath while dismissing the annual Sabbaths. Shortly after the article appeared, I wrote and published a review. What follows is derived from that review. My apologies to D.L. Prunkard (hereinafter called "the author") for dredging up his work nearly 30 years later.

Logical Fallacies

Any debate is apt to place on display an array of logical fallacies, and religious debate is not immune. Most people do this without realizing it. *Should We Keep Israel's Holydays?* (Hereinafter called "the article") serves to illustrate.

The author asks, "Did Jesus command Christians to observe the national days of Israel?" This is called "begging the question."[i] If they are merely the national days of Israel, then why are we having this discussion? If you have read this book from the beginning, you will already know that the argument is on an entirely different plane. These days are not merely the "national days of Israel," but "Jehovah's appointed festivals." There is a difference.

The statement is also a "straw man" argument.[ii] I point this out, because you are almost certain to encounter it if you discuss very much theology. It sets up the issue in terms that those who argue for the observance of the holydays don't advance.

Also, the question, "Did Jesus command?" is misleading. Jesus did not attempt to create a new body of law, but he certainly validated an existing body of written law:

> Do not think that I have come to abolish the Law or the Prophets; I have not come to abolish them but to fulfill them. I tell you the truth, until heaven and earth disappear, not the smallest letter, not the least stroke of a pen, will by any means disappear from the Law until everything is accomplished. Anyone who breaks one of the least of these commandments and teaches others to do the same will be called least in the kingdom of heaven, but whoever practices and teaches these commands will be called great in the kingdom of heaven (Matthew 5:17-19 NIV).

What you need to know about this passage is that in speaking of letters and strokes of the pen, Jesus is affirming the written law as opposed to the oral law. He is emphasizing this, because he is about to reject many aspects of *Jewish* law, i.e., the traditions of the elders, also called the Oral Law.

When people set out to dispute the continuing observance of the festivals, they too often use loaded words to make their point. Words like "rituals," "obligatory," "ceremonial bondage," "rigorism," "legalistic religion," "Judaism," all serve to cloud the issue and all are used in the article. No one wants to be involved in rigorism or legalistic religion. And we surely want to avoid "ceremonial bondage," whatever that is.

But it's important to know how a person uses his terms. What, for example, does the author mean when he uses the term, "Judaism"? Judaism, as practiced in the 20th century, involves almost as much variety as Christianity. There are Orthodox, Reformed, and Conservative synagogues scattered all across the United States. There may be as many sects of Judaism extant today as there are Protestant churches in the United States.

So, when the article states that "Paul reacted in Galatians to infiltrating Judaism," we have to ask what the author means by that. Does he mean the religion of Israel as expressed in the law of Moses, or does he mean Judaism as expressed by the Pharisees, the Sadducees, or the Essenes? By "Judaism" does he mean the religion which God delivered to ancient Israel, or that Judaism which Jesus rejected while He still observed the law of Moses?

Whose Days Are They?

The article begins by outlining the holydays with their scriptural references and a brief sketch of the supposed meaning of each day. Unfortunately, scant attention is given to the *Christian* meaning so evident in all the festivals. It is, after all, an important question to ask. How do these holydays relate to Christians? Do they have any meaning for Christians? If they don't, then the rest of the discussion is mostly irrelevant and would then have to turn on purely legalistic arguments. If they do have meaning for Christians, then we are off into an entirely different discussion, and that discussion forms the basis for this book.

The author proceeds to develop a concept you may encounter elsewhere, so it is useful to study it here. It has to do with a critical theory of the structure of the Old Testament:

> The Pentateuch's third book was a manual of law for the priests, having to do with the cleansing, worship and service of the redeemed people. The manual contained priestly laws, *not transferable* to Gentiles.

They were administered only by the sons of Aaron. Much of the manual is mutely prophetic typifying Christ, and was, along with other aspects of Moses' economy, *operationally annulled* at Golgotha. (Emphasis his throughout.)

Thus is the book of Leviticus dismissed as having any application apart from Old Testament Israel. Now I am certain the author is familiar with the book of Leviticus and this argument is all the more puzzling. Consider, for example, the way Leviticus begins:

The LORD summoned Moses and spoke to him from the tent of meeting, saying: "Speak to *the people of Israel* and say to them . . ." (Leviticus 1:1-2 NRSV).

To be sure, the instructions had to do with sacrifices, but they were not exactly a "manual for the priests." The first three chapters of Leviticus continue with instructions *to the people* as to what they are to do about burnt offerings, meal offerings, and peace offerings.

Chapter 4 begins the same way: "Speak to the children of Israel, saying . . ." Yes, there are instructions to the sons of Aaron and the priests, but the book can hardly be called a "priestly manual." Those instructions are imbedded in a work addressed to all the people.

In chapter 11, Jehovah instructs both Moses and Aaron to "speak unto the children of Israel," concerning certain dietary laws. These are not priestly laws having to do with sacrifices, but laws for the people concerning what they should and should not eat. And, more to the point of the issue at hand, is the chapter about the festivals, where the Lord spoke unto Moses saying, "Speak to the people of Israel and say to them: These are the appointed festivals of the LORD that you shall proclaim as holy convocations, my appointed festivals" (Leviticus 23:2 NRSV). The instructions on the festivals were not merely given to the priesthood, but to the people.

One suspects the argument that Leviticus is a "priestly manual" has its origins in the higher critical schools and the theory that Moses did not write Leviticus at all. They place it much later. According to one school of literary criticism, Leviticus is a "legal fiction" and should be dated after the construction of Solomon's Temple. I don't think so, and there is no hint that the writers of the New Testament thought so either.

Misunderstanding "Gentiles"

Also misleading is the statement: "The manual contained priestly laws, *not transferable* to Gentiles". The author goes on to argue: "Gentiles were disallowed from the Israelite system and not permitted to enter the sanctuary of the Jerusalem Temple. Gentiles observing the days was illegal and unconscionable."

His overall approach to this question is legalistic, but here he climbs out on a limb. The limb he is on is one of the more widespread misconceptions about the Law of Moses. The first thing we have to do is to be sure what the words mean, and the word "Gentile" is a much abused example. The word comes from the Latin *gentillis*, which means "of the same clan or race." As used by the Jews, it means one of non-Jewish faith or race, and as used by Christians it means one *not a Jew*.

The Hebrew word translated "Gentile" in the Old Testament is *goy* and means nation or nations (as it is often translated). It is not used of a single individual, as in "He is a Gentile." Among the Hebrews the *individual* of a Gentile nation would be called "a stranger" (Hebrew, *ger*), one who is not an Israelite. If you have a concordance, you can answer this question for yourself. Just look up all the passages in the Old Testament where the word "stranger" is used. It will take a while to run through all of them, because the Bible has rather a lot to say about strangers. For example, was it illegal for a stranger, a *ger*, to observe the holydays of Israel? Interestingly enough, the matter is specified on one particular Holy Day – the Passover.

> And the Lord said unto Moses, and Aaron, this is the ordinance of the Passover: There shall no stranger eat thereof: but every manservant that is bought for money, when you have circumcised him, then shall he eat thereof. A foreigner and a hired servant shall not eat thereof. . . And when a stranger shall sojourn with

you, and will keep the Passover to the Lord, let all his males be circumcised, and then *let him come near and keep it*; and he shall be as one that is born in the land: For no uncircumcised person shall eat thereof. One law shall be to him that is homeborn, and unto the stranger that sojourns among you" (Exodus 12:43-49 KJV).

This passage of Scripture is of singular importance for several reasons. First, it is the only holyday where any restrictions at all are placed on "Gentile" observance. No such inhibition is expressed on any other festival. We can only presume that the stranger who sojourned among the Israelites was perfectly free to keep the other holydays, even without being circumcised. If, indeed, these festivals were God's expression to man of how, when and where he was to be worshiped, then no Gentile could worship God properly unless he did keep the holydays.

It is also important to note in this passage that the stranger could keep the Passover. Not only does the Bible fail to support the author's allegation that is was "illegal and unconscionable for Gentiles to observe the holydays," such observance is expressly permitted under certain circumstances.

But perhaps one of the most important statements made in this passage is the statement that there is to be one law for both the Israelite and the stranger that sojourned among them. There was only one way of worshiping God – one set of standards by which men would be measured. He did not have one religion for the Jews and yet another for strangers.

When you take a broader look at Leviticus you find a wide range of instructions for the stranger from a Gentile land.

This shall be a statute forever for you: In the seventh month, on the tenth day of the month, you shall afflict your souls, and do no work at all, whether a native of your own country or a stranger who dwells among you (Leviticus 16:29).

This is part of the instructions for observing the Day of Atonement. How can one argue, in the face of this clear statement, that the "Gentile" living in Israel who wished to worship the true God was not expected to fast and abstain from work on the Day of Atonement? There's more:

> Also you shall say to them: "Whatever man of the house of Israel, or of the strangers who dwell among you, who offers a burnt offering or sacrifice, and does not bring it to the door of the tabernacle of meeting, to offer it to the LORD, that man shall be cut off from among his people" (Leviticus 17:8).

This will come as a bolt from the blue for many readers of the New Testament, because in the time of the Second Temple, this could not happen. But the Law of Moses explicitly allows that strangers could offer a burnt offering or sacrifice. Here are two more examples.

> And whatsoever man there be of the house of Israel, or of the *stranger* that sojourn among you, that eateth any manner of blood; I will even set my face against that soul that eateth blood, and will cut him off from among his people (v. 10 KJV).

> Speak unto Aaron, and to his sons, and unto all the children of Israel, and say unto them, Whosoever he be of the house of Israel, or of the *strangers* in Israel, that will offer his oblation for all his vows, and for all his freewill offerings, which they will offer unto the Lord for a burnt offering; Ye shall offer at your own will a male without blemish . . ." (Leviticus 22:18-19 KJV).

If you do your own study, you may be in for still more surprises. You will find, for example, that the stranger was obligated by the law of blasphemy. The stranger was obligated by the laws of restoration and restitution. The stranger was included in the laws of usury – an Israelite could not take usury of a stranger who lived near him and had fallen into poverty. You will find that the laws of the book of Numbers include the stranger as well:

And if a stranger sojourn with you, or whosoever be among you in your generations, and will offer an offering made by fire, of a sweet savour unto the Lord; *as you do, so he shall do.* One ordinance shall be both for you of the congregation, and also for the stranger that sojourns with you, an ordinance forever in your generations: *as you are, so shall the stranger be before the Lord.* One law and one manner shall be for you, and for the stranger that sojourns with you (Numbers 15:14-16 KJV).

It would appear that God did not have one set of standards for the Jews and another for the Gentiles. The 15th chapter of Numbers continues with one law after another that applies to the stranger as well as to the children of Israel.

Later we even find that the matter of purification or separation made from the ashes of the red heifer was a law for the children of Israel and the stranger that sojourned among them (Numbers 19:10).

In Deuteronomy 5:14 the law of the *Sabbath* is applied to the alien. In Deuteronomy 14, the poor tithe is made available to the alien. Need we go on? I am puzzled as to why the article would declare that Gentiles were "disallowed" from the Israelite system, and that Gentiles observing the days was "illegal and unconscionable."

Actually, the statement is not entirely wrong if applied to the attitude of Jews toward Gentiles *in New Testament times.* The religion of the Jews in the first century bore some striking differences from the religion God delivered to Moses. The attitude of the Jews toward Gentiles in New Testament times can only be described as vile. They regarded Gentiles with extreme aversion, scorn, and even hatred:

They [the Gentiles] were regarded as unclean, with whom it was unlawful to have any friendly intercourse. They were the enemies of God and His people, to whom the knowledge of God was denied unless they became proselytes, and even then they could not, as in ancient times, be admitted to full fellowship. Jews were forbidden to counsel them, and if they asked about divine things they were to be cursed. All the children born of mixed marriages were bastards. That is what caused the Jews to be so hated by the Greeks and Romans, as we have abundant evidence in the writings of Cicero, Seneca and Tacitus. Something of this reflected in the New Testament (John 18:28, Acts 10:28; 11:3).[iii]

What misleads some superficial commentators on the New Testament is the assumption that this attitude is a reflection of the law of Moses. Nothing could be further from the truth. We have already seen that the law of Moses permitted a stranger full access to the worship of God. The law even granted him the doubtful privilege of circumcision. To all intents and purposes, the Gentile could be the equal of the Israelite in every way. The only apparent discrepancy is the restriction against the uncircumcised stranger entering the sanctuary (Ezekiel 44:7). But, then, the uncircumcised Jew was not allowed entry either.

The laws, then, separating Jews and Gentiles in the New Testament times were not the Law of Moses or the Law of God, but the ordinances of men. This is an extremely important distinction.

The Wall of Separation (Ephesians 2)

With this background, we can now understand one of the more important texts often advanced in an effort to prove that the holydays need not be observed. Paul wrote the Ephesians:

For He Himself is our peace, who has made both one, and has broken down the middle wall of separation, having abolished in His flesh the enmity, that is, the law of commandments contained in ordinances, so as to create in Himself one new man from the two, thus making peace (Ephesians 2:14-15).

There are two major questions that arise out of this passage: (1) What is the middle wall of separation, and (2) What exactly is it that is "abolished" in Christ's flesh? The context of Ephesians 2 is that salvation by *grace* is come to the Gentiles. Paul makes it clear that he is writing to a church primarily composed of Gentiles:

> That at that time you were without Christ, being aliens from the commonwealth of Israel and strangers from the covenants of promise, having no hope and without God in the world. But now in Christ Jesus you who once were far off have been brought near by the blood of Christ. For He Himself is our peace, who has made both one, and has broken down the middle wall of separation (Ephesians 2:12-14).

Two theories have been advanced as to what exactly the "middle wall of partition" might be. On the one hand it has been suggested that it is a wall between man and God (Ezekiel 43:8). On the other hand, it is said to be the wall in the Temple area between the Court of the Gentiles and the inner courts (included as a part of the sanctuary) immediately around the Holy Place. Josephus tells us that there was a sign placed in the Court of the Gentiles written in several languages saying that if a Gentile passed beyond this point he would be responsible for his own death, which would immediately ensue.

There is something to say for both ideas. Verse 13, for example, states that the Gentiles, "who sometimes were far off," are now made near by the blood of Christ. One might legitimately ask why it is enough. The latter half of verse 15 states, "For to make in Himself of twain *one new man*, so making peace; And that He might reconcile both [Jew and Gentile] unto God in one body by the cross, having slain the enmity thereby."

What is described is a three cornered reconciliation. For, indeed, how can a Gentile and a Jew both be reconciled to God without being reconciled to one another? If they have both come to the same place – the cross – are they not now together? Then what is it that Jesus "abolished"? In the first place, the word "abolish" is a less than accurate translation. The word is *katargeo* and is found in another passage with rather a different sense:

> He also spoke this parable: "A certain man had a fig tree planted in his vineyard, and he came seeking fruit

on it and found none. Then he said to the keeper of his vineyard, 'Look, for three years I have come seeking fruit on this fig tree and find none. Cut it down; why does it use up *[kartargeo]* the ground?'" (Luke 13:6-7).

The fig tree can hardly be conceived of as "abolishing" the ground. The same word is translated "make void" in Romans 3:31, "Do we then *make void* the law through faith? God forbid: yea, we establish the law."

We are left with an apparent contradiction between these two scriptures. On the one hand we have Paul saying to the Ephesians, "Having abolished in His flesh the enmity, even the law of commandments contained in ordinances," while he says to the Romans, "Do we then abolish the law through faith? God forbid: Yea, we establish the law." If the law, then, is not made void through faith, but rather established, what is it that Jesus "abolished" as described in Ephesians?

What is the "law of commandments contained in ordinances"? One thing is sure – Paul is not talking about the law of Moses, for we have seen that the law of Moses created no enmity between Jew and Gentile. It erected no walls. Under Moses' economy the Gentile was allowed into full fellowship with Israel. He was, indeed, required to be circumcised in order to fully worship God – but, then, so was the Jew. There was no middle wall.

If it wasn't God's law, then, that created the enmity between Jew and Gentile, whose law was it? The answer is plain – it was the commandments, traditions and ordinances of men who *rejected* the commandments of God in order that they might keep their own traditions. (See what Jesus said about this at Matthew 15:1-9, and Mark 7:1-13.)

Speaking of a similar problem, Paul wrote to the Colossians, "Wherefore if ye be dead with Christ from the rudiments of the world, why, as though living in the world, are you subject to ordinances, (Touch not; taste not; handle not; Which all are to perish with the using;) after the commandments and doctrines of men?" (Colossians 2:20-22 KJV).

It is the commandments and ordinances of men which are to

perish, not the law of God. Jesus Christ, then, broke down the middle wall of partition which the Jews, not Moses, had erected between themselves and the Gentiles, having swept aside the enmity with all its purely human prohibitions. Returning to the article's treatment of the law:

> Leviticus dealt with the personal relationship between God and *national* Israel, and was never intended for worldwide obligation, nor to be *binding* on twentieth century disciples. One chapter (23), delineating festivals and holydays, cannot be made holy today, ignoring the other twenty-six chapters as profane and abrogated!

Does this statement imply that it was possible to worship God apart from the relationship between God and national Israel? If, as suggested, there was no "worldwide obligation" to keep the law of Moses, did a different relationship involving a different set of laws exists somewhere else in the world? Or was the only way to worship God being revealed to Israel as God created a relationship (covenant) between Him and them? Was it possible for a stranger to have a relationship with God apart from God's covenant with Abraham, Isaac, Jacob, Moses, etc.?

There is no way to conclude from the law of Moses itself that it was not intended for worldwide obligation. In fact, we learn from the prophets that the law is intended for worldwide application. Give Zechariah 14 a careful read (see chapter 17 of this book). Having read that, what do you conclude? Were these the "national days of Israel," or were they the festivals of God to tell *man* how, when, and where God was to be worshiped?

Only in Jerusalem?

It is fair to say that God was not to be worshiped in a haphazard fashion. He was quite explicit in revealing to man how, when, and where He was to be worshiped. The *where* of that worship is a matter of particular interest. Contrary to assumptions, the law does not specify Jerusalem. The Israelites were told, "Three times in a year shall all your males appear before the Lord your God in the place which He shall choose; in the Feast of Unleavened Bread, and in the Feast of Weeks, and in the Feast of Tabernacles" (Deuteronomy 16:16). Once Israel had entered the land and the tabernacle was placed in Shiloh, the people went up to Shiloh to observe the three "pilgrimage festivals." Later, the Ark was in the City of David, and when the Temple was built it was moved to Jerusalem, and the festivals were held there.

For some unaccountable reason, most of those arguing against the holydays focus heavily on the "place" aspect of the holydays, attempting to show that the holydays could only be kept at Jerusalem. In their zeal, they often overlook the fact that the festivals were kept at *Shiloh* before the Temple was built in Jerusalem.

They argue that Israel was not allowed to sacrifice the Passover in any of their towns (Deuteronomy 16:5, 6), but that it could only be sacrificed at Jerusalem. The article goes on to argue:

> Those keeping it in those days would need roasted lamb and bitter herbs (Passover), sacrifices and wave sheaf offerings (Unleavened Bread), sacrifices (Pentecost), sacrifices and trumpet blowing on new moon (civil new year), sacrifices, expiatory rites and two goats (Atonement), sacrifices, tree boughs and temporary dwellings (Tabernacles), sacrifices (Last Great Day), all taking place at Jerusalem, about the Temple!

If that is true, then how do the Jews manage to keep the festivals today? They have not ceased to observe the Passover since the destruction of the Temple. They, of course, recognize that they cannot sacrifice the Passover, but they can still observe it and they still do. It is quite true that the Jews cannot enter the Holy of Holies on the Day of Atonement (only the High Priest could do that), but they can fast and abstain from labor wherever they are, and they still do.

Some who advance this rather legalistic argument seem to assume that only the males who went up to Jerusalem to keep the Feast of Tabernacles had to abstain from labor, while those who stayed behind were free to work on the holydays. They seem to assume that those who lived in Galilee need not fast on the Day of Atonement. The fact is that devout Jews observed the holydays as far as they could be observed wherever they were. Merely because they lived in Alexandria, they were not relieved of the obligation to fast on Yom Kippur. Any festival could be observed by two or three people getting together for prayer and worship.

If the destruction of the Temple didn't stop the Jews from observing the holydays as far as they were able, why should it stop Christians?

Christ did indeed make the offering of sacrifices obsolete. But the author continues: "Yet, oblations, ablutions, carnal washings and ritualistic sacrifices were part of the Mosaic system, and *could not be omitted* if any part of the system were retained (the days for their observance)."

But why not? They certainly had to be omitted after the destruction of the Temple. There was no choice. But how were the Jewish Christians of Jerusalem able to retain that part of the law of Moses pertaining to vows and purification, then, without retaining the entire system? (See Acts 21:18, explanation to follow.)

The whole argument seems to overlook the fact that relatively few people under the Mosaic system ever offered an animal sacrifice. People could bring sacrifices but only the Levites could "offer" the sacrifice. Many Israelites, even pious Israelites, lived and died without ever seeing a sacrifice offered. But the Levitical system of washing and sacrifices was played out on the stage of the Temple, and represented a very small part of the worship of God for the average man. The article rightly observes:

> There was no justification or spiritual salvation in Moses' law for national Israel! Neither is there any sanctification or spiritual salvation in performing God's law by Christians! Such is attained only by grace through faith (Ephesians 2:8) in the accomplished fulfillment of Christ's sacrifice. Keeping *any* law without accepting Him and all He stands for provides no spiritual benefit.

That statement is absolutely correct. And in emphasizing "any law" I presume the author intends to include the Ten Commandments with the Sabbath as well. But this is a land mine for anyone who believes the weekly Sabbath should be kept while the other Sabbaths need not be kept.

He goes on to say, "The law of Moses contained everything God gave in original form through that servant." In other words, all the laws contained in the first five books of the Old Testament are the law of Moses, but that includes the Ten Commandments.

In writing of the three pilgrimage festivals, the author notes "all three are harvest festivals and undoubtedly originated after Israel entered Palestine." This is revealing and suggests that he accepts the critical theory which considers Leviticus 23 a "legal fiction." That is to say that the book of Leviticus did not originate with Moses, but with the priesthood, much later. But in Leviticus 23 we are told, "And *the Lord spake unto Moses*, saying, Speak unto the children of Israel, and say unto them, Concerning the feasts of the Lord, which ye shall proclaim to be holy convocations, even these are my feasts" (verses 1, 2). Here the holydays are specifically called *Jehovah's* feasts and is stated that they were given *to Moses*. The Graf-Wellhausen school of criticism holds that many of these priestly laws originated much later – some of them in the time of the reconstructed second Temple – and were not written by Moses at all. They are a "legal fiction" in that they are represented as being given by Moses when they weren't.

I prefer to accept the plain statement of both Leviticus and Deuteronomy that the law was given to Moses *before* Israel entered the promised land. The Graf-Wellhausen theory has faded in the light of later discoveries.

The Scriptures don't seem to be concerned so much with where specifically the festivals are to be kept, but that the people come together to keep them. The implication of Deuteronomy 16:16 is that God could choose any place for the festivals. Jesus confirmed this in a rather interesting encounter with the woman in Samaria:

> The woman said to Him, "Sir, I perceive that You are a prophet. Our fathers worshiped on this mountain, and you Jews say that in Jerusalem is the place where one ought to worship." Jesus said to her, "Woman, believe

Me, the hour is coming when you will neither on this mountain, nor in Jerusalem, worship the Father. You worship what you do not know; we know what we worship, for salvation is of the Jews. But the hour is coming, and now is, when the true worshipers will worship the Father in spirit and truth; for the Father is seeking such to worship Him. God is Spirit, and those who worship Him must worship in spirit and truth" (John 4:19-24).

Later, Jesus would tell his Apostles, "For where two or three are gathered together in my name, there I am in the midst of them" (Matthew 18:20). Jesus thus revealed that it was possible to worship God anywhere, not just at Jerusalem.

This is not a new commandment. Israel was prohibited from offering their sacrifices in just any location in order to keep them from falling into idolatry. It was not because God could not be worshiped anywhere except Jerusalem. The superstition that grew up among the Jews that God could only be worshiped in Jerusalem was not the intent of the law of Moses. Nor was it God's intent that the Gentiles would be barred from worshiping Him at His Tabernacle.

The article includes the curious assertion: "When Rome invaded Palestine and Titus' armies decimated Jerusalem (70 A.D.), the Levitical system collapsed, not to revive."

Surely he is aware of Zechariah 14 and Malachi 3, which point to a purified Levitical priesthood offering sacrifices after Christ's return. The Levitical priesthood does not function now solely for the reason that there is no Temple. When the Temple is rebuilt, Levi will once again serve there.

The argument that there was a 40-year vacuum in which the children of Israel did not keep the holydays prior to their entry into the land is tenuous at best. It is true that no circumcision took place in the wilderness (Joshua 5:5-7), and that the Passover could not be observed by the uncircumcised (Exodus 12:48). But it is an assumption to conclude that those who were circumcised did not continue to keep the Passover until the last of them were dead. Joshua and Caleb, of course, provided a permanent link in that they were able to enter the land because they had not participated in the rebellion.

To be sure, certain other ceremonial aspects of the holydays could not be observed in the wilderness – such as the wave sheaf offering. This did not, however, preclude the observance of the days on the calendar (which was revealed much earlier, see Exodus 12:2), and the observance of the days by abstention from labor. We really know little of the details of this time, and it is a gratuitous assumption to argue that Israel did not keep the holydays through this 40-year period.

It may even be irrelevant since Israel's failure to observe the holydays during much of their history is a negative comment on their character and not on the observance of the holydays.

The Temple Veil

Speaking of the sanctuary, the article continues, "The sanctuary was part of the old covenant, a figure to last only until the final sacrifice of Christ. It was then that the great curtain separating the Holy Place from the Most Holy Place ripped asunder, from top to bottom. Temple services ended, as far as God was concerned. (See Hebrews 9:1-12)"

When you are finished studying Hebrews 9:1-12 to see if it says that the Temple services ended when the veil was rent, you might turn back to the 21st chapter of Acts, where a most curious event is recorded. It would certainly seem that Jesus would have taught the Apostles plainly about any matter as important as the abolition of the law or any part of it. The problem is that the only statements he makes during his earthly ministry about the law are supportive (Matthew 5:17-20). Even his reinterpretation of the law is supportive for there is no need to reinterpret what is to be done away (see Matthew 5:27-48).

But if Temple services were to *end* as far as God was concerned, we would certainly expect this to be made clear by Jesus before His departure. Was this the case? How did James and the other leaders of the Jerusalem church see the Temple services "as far as God was concerned"?

Luke records the occasion of Paul's return to Jerusalem after a prolonged absence. He went to see James, and all the elders of the

Jerusalem church. When they had heard Paul's report, they said to him, "You see, brother, how many myriads of Jews there are who have believed, and they are all zealous for the law" (Acts 21:20).

Which law? The Ten Commandments? The ceremonial law? The law of Moses? It must be borne in mind that the New Testament writers do not observe our nice distinctions of law. When they say "the law," they mean "the law of Moses," which to them is the same as "the law of God."

James and the elders continued: "But they have been informed about you that you teach all the Jews who are among the Gentiles to forsake Moses, saying that they ought not to circumcise their children nor to walk according to the customs" (verse 21).

But wait. Didn't the Jerusalem conference (recorded in Acts 15) reject circumcision? Wouldn't it be right for Paul to teach that they ought not to circumcise their children? Look at the verse again. It is not the Gentiles that Paul is accused of teaching to forsake Moses, but the Jews who are among the Gentiles.

Apparently many read this verse and assume that Paul did indeed teach the Jews among the Gentiles to forsake Moses, that they ought not to circumcise their children or walk after their customs. But read on.

> What then? The assembly must certainly meet, for they will hear that you have come. Therefore do what we tell you: We have four men who have taken a vow. Take them and be purified with them, and pay their expenses so that they may shave their heads, and that all may know that those things of which they were informed concerning you are nothing, but that you yourself also walk orderly and keep the law (Acts 21:22-24).

Now is the moment for clarification. Now is the time to tell them that the law of Moses is done away. Now is the time for him to stand firm in the liberty wherewith Christ has made him free and refuse to be under a yoke of bondage. We know that Paul is the kind of man who would have done exactly that. But what did he do?

Then Paul took the men, and the next day, having been purified with them, entered the temple to announce the expiration of the days of purification, at which time an offering should be made for each one of them (v. 26).

What a stunning example. It is one thing for a Christian to keep the holydays, but quite another thing for him to be involved in a Temple ceremony of purification involving holy water, the ashes of a red heifer, and the making of an offering for every one of them. All this was done so that Paul could demonstrate to the Jewish Christians of Jerusalem that these allegations made against him were "nothing."

It seems less than accurate to say that "Temple services ended as far as God was concerned" when the veil was rent in the Temple, for we see Jewish Christians, with the sanction of James and Paul, still availing themselves of the services of the Temple and the Levitical priesthood.

The Early Church Record

But what do we do with all those New Testament Scriptures that refer to the holydays? How do people get around them? Of course, some of these scriptures are simple references to the calendar and can be construed solely as a reference to current events. An example of this is Acts 12:3, where Herod arrested Peter during the days of the Feast of Unleavened Bread. This could be dismissed as a historical reference to the time of year in Jerusalem.

Acts 12:4 (concerning the Passover) falls into the same category, but the article curiously argues as though the Christians were not observing the Passover at all. There can be little doubt that the Christian church in Jerusalem observed the Passover at this time and for a long time thereafter. (See Chapter three of this book.)

Acts 18:21 is of special interest: "But Paul bade them farewell saying, I must by all means keep this feast that cometh in Jerusalem." The article correctly observes that the latter clause in this verse is missing from major manuscripts of the New Testament. That said, it is also present in many manuscripts. It is left to the scholars to discuss whether the verse was present in original manuscripts and later deleted by copyists, or whether it was absent from the original manuscripts and added by copyists.

We may have no difficulty in discerning why some copyists might have deliberately (or accidentally) deleted the phrase, but the question as to why it might have been *added* is another matter entirely. Some have suggested that it was a marginal rendering – an explanation on the part of some copyist as to *why* Paul was going to Jerusalem. The marginal reading may have later found its way into the main text. We then, however, are left with a question as to why a copyist would have given this as a reason unless the holydays still loomed large in their faith. The fact remains that the phrase is present in many manuscripts.

If indeed the phrase was not in Luke's original manuscript of the book of Acts, it must have been a *very early* addition to the text. For how could one make such an addition to the text without a strong oral tradition to that effect, or without a marginal note made by someone who knew what Paul's reason might have been? The fact that the text is disputed may provide just as strong an argument for the observance of the holydays as it would if it were written by the hand of Luke himself.

There is another group of Scriptures which are indeed merely calendar references, but they are calendar references that have nothing to do with a Jewish cultural setting. In Acts 20:6, Luke says, "And we sailed away from Philippi after the Days of Unleavened Bread." The author asserts:

> A time demarcation! Philippi was almost totally Gentile, with not enough Jews to build a synagogue (Acts 16:13). *Nowhere* does the New Testament say, 'We kept the feast,' or 'We observed the Holy Day,' or 'We prepared for the festival.' Legalistic, religious arguments come by *silence, inference* or *analogy*! Nothing is inferred, much less said, about the sanctity of these days or any sacred obligation to perform them. (Emphasis his).

Of course, Luke is not making a doctrinal statement; he is simply giving an account of their voyages. There is no reason to expect him to discuss the sanctity of these days. Indeed if, as we believe, the church was keeping these days, then they were taken for granted. There was no need for Luke to argue the point with his reader.

But unless his reader was acquainted with the Days of Unleavened Bread, why would Luke mention them? And if there was no synagogue in Philippi and the Days of Unleavened Bread were not observed there, what is the significance of Luke's remark? Admittedly, we can only infer that they were observing the Days of Unleavened Bread from this Scripture, but it is of at least passing interest, especially in the light of other Scriptures such as 1 Corinthians 5:7, 8.

Next the author turns his attention to Acts 20:16: "For Paul had determined to sail by Ephesus, in order that he might not have to spend time in Asia; for he was hurrying to be in Jerusalem, if possible, on the day of Pentecost."

What was the point of being in Jerusalem *on Pentecost*? The article suggests, "An additional opportunity to witness for Christ to thronging multitudes of Old Covenant Jews! A time for reunion with fellow ministers in the church!" He doesn't explain why Pentecost would provide a special opportunity for a ministerial reunion, unless the ministers were expected to be there for Pentecost.

But why try to explain away the Feast of Pentecost? The *majority* of professing Christians down through all ages have observed Pentecost gladly as the birthday of the New Testament church! The suggestion that Pentecost should *not* be observed is a relatively late development. The Catholic Church and the Church of England as well as many other Protestants keep the Feast of Pentecost to this day. And, indeed, why not? If Jesus did not intend for the church to continue observing the Feast of Pentecost, it was a grave oversight for Him to give the Holy Spirit on that day. Why argue that the New Testament church didn't keep Pentecost, with all that it meant to them?

In discussing Paul's visit to Jerusalem on this occasion, the author commits a curious error. He cites Acts 21:21, which represents the allegation of the Jews that Paul "taught all the Jews which are among the Gentiles to forsake Moses, saying that they ought not to circumcise their children, neither to walk after the customs."

Arguing from this, the author states flatly, "Paul taught not to keep the rites of Moses' law, including festivals and holydays." What he seems to completely overlook is that this was the *allegation* of the Jews against Paul, and the whole point of the passage is that Paul needs to show the Judean Christians that these things were *not true*. He seems to completely overlook verse 24: "Them take, and purify thyself with them, and be at charges with them, that they may shave their heads: and all may know that those things, whereof they were informed concerning thee, are nothing."

And Paul went along with them! Mind you, this was not done by a meek, subservient, pliable man who was easily intimidated. This was the man who confronted Peter to his face and in public when he dissembled to impress a group of Jews who had come down from Jerusalem to Antioch (Galatians 2:11-14).

There is one other reference in the book of Acts which is also a calendar reference. Acts 27:9 mentions that sailing was now dangerous since the fast (Day of Atonement) was already past. It is quite correct that this simply shows a calendar demarcation, with nothing more intended.

However, it is a calendar demarcation which will be understood by Luke's reader – Theophilus – a Greek Christian. It seems unlikely, if the traditional idea of the abolition of holydays were true, that Luke would have continued to use this type of expression. I think he would have recognized how misleading it could be to his readers.

I Corinthians 5:7, 8

This Scripture is of particular interest, because, after a plain reference to the Days of Unleavened Bread and the symbolism of leavening, Paul says, "Therefore *let us keep the feast*, not with old leaven, neither with the leaven of malice and wickedness; but with the unleavened bread of sincerity and truth."

What do we do with this? The author suggests, "Let us celebrate the feast in the Greek connotes the *continual present tense*, something that is being perpetually accomplished. Christians are in a position of *continual* unleavenedness, a perpetual feast."

Now, that is a neat bit of footwork, but it should be noted at the outset that there is no such thing as a "continual present tense" in the Greek language. The Greek word *heortadzomen* is the first person plural present subjunctive of the verb *heortadzo*, which means "to keep a feast, to celebrate a festival." The verb is derived from the noun *heortee*, which means "a solemn feast, public festival."

The reason for the suggestion of *continuing action* is that Greek tenses convey *kind* of action as well as *time*. The Greek present tense, for example, denotes *linear* action, whereas the *aorist* tense is not only past action, but *punctiliar* action – that is, action that takes place on an occasion or point in the past. Of course, no festival could be kept at a *point in time* for the shortest of them goes on for 24 hours and the Feast of Unleavened Bread continues for seven days.

There is nothing unusual, therefore, about Paul using the present subjunctive for celebrating the Festival of Unleavened Bread. We suggest that had Paul meant something else he would have said something else. The truth is that the Corinthian church was observing the Days of Unleavened Bread. (See the reference to Conybeare and Howson in chapter one.) So the present tense is quite apt.

Conybeare and Howson do not suggest that the festivals were "done away with at the cross." Rather they see that the church continued to keep them long after Christ's ascension. The change, they suggest, took place well after Paul wrote this letter to the Corinthians. The question is whether the church had the *authority* to make that change. Clearly Conybeare and Howson would *not* agree with Prunkard that it was somehow *illegal* to observe these feasts outside Jerusalem. They recognized that many Jews always have done so. One more calendar reference:

> But I will tarry in Ephesus until Pentecost. For a great
> and effective door has opened to me, and there are
> many adversaries (1 Corinthians 16:8-9).

The article argues that this is merely a time demarcation, but it is *quite different* from the time demarcations mentioned earlier in the book of Acts. One can dismiss Luke's references as "after the fact" references simply to denote a time of year. But in this case the Feast of Pentecost is the *limiting factor*. It is a time Paul is looking *ahead* to while making the *demarcation* of his stay at Ephesus. Taken by itself, it cannot be considered final proof, but one still must ask, why Pentecost? Why not "spring," or "summer," or "until my work is finished"?

When we couple this Scripture with an awareness of how important Pentecost was to the early church and what it meant to them, why should we argue that they weren't keeping it? What's wrong with Pentecost? The answer is simple. If we accept Pentecost and Passover, then the holydays were *not* done away. We are "stuck" with the rest of them as well.

The Galatian Problem

It was Peter who observed that Paul wrote of things that were hard to understand and often misunderstood (2 Peter 3:16-17). Quite naturally, Paul becomes the focus of many arguments against holyday observance, especially in Galatians. Here is a common "prooftext" offered by those who oppose holyday observance:

> But now after you have known God, or rather are known by God, how is it that you turn again to the weak and beggarly elements, to which you desire again to be in bondage? You observe days and months and seasons and years (Galatians 4:9-10).

Many commentaries suggest that the "days, and months, and times, and years" were the holydays of Leviticus 23 as well as the new moons and sabbatical years. Dummelow's *One Volume Commentary* puts it this way:

> Days (Jewish feasts or fast day). Months (new moons; compare Colossians 2:16). Times (Revised Version, seasons, such as Passover, Pentecost, etc.). Years (e.g., Sabbatic years). These observances are 'weak and beggarly elements' (verse 9), because they are matters of dry routine, customs which the Gentiles would adopt without understanding their meaning or catching anything of the spirit which lay behind them. They were of no avail for salvation.

But doesn't it seem counterintuitive that Paul would refer to the holydays and other points of the law of God as "weak and beggarly elements"? Actually, the near context of this passage begins in verse 8: "But then, indeed, *when you did not know God*, you served [Greek: were in bondage to] those which by nature are not gods." By this, Paul clearly identifies his audience as non-Jewish. They had previously not known God and had been in bondage, but it was the bondage of idolatry.

Now he asks them how it is possible for them to *turn back again* to the "weak and beggarly elements" unto which they had previously been in bondage. What are the "weak and beggarly elements"? It is those "which by nature are no gods," the idols of verse eight. But how would the observance of the biblical holydays place them in bondage to the weak and beggarly elements of the gods of this world again?

The book of Galatians has been a much misunderstood book. Not understanding the historical situation, we are left to grapple with a seemingly contradictory set of ideas. Nevertheless, there are some things that are abundantly clear in the book. The Galatians had fallen into a system of religion which involved attempts to justify themselves by their own works. And, whether it be the law of God or the laws of men, there is no law given which can make a man righteous (Galatians 3:21). The Galatians were attempting to achieve righteousness by circumcision and the law. It couldn't be done and never could have.

But were they observing the holydays of God in an effort to achieve righteousness? Or were they observing *pagan* days, months, times, and years? The overall context of the book of Galatians implies that the problem was some form of Judaism. The near context of verses 8 through 10 implies *Gentile* observances. How can we resolve this?

First, is Paul saying that it is wrong to "observe" days, and months, times and years? If he is, then not only the holydays of God, but Christmas, Easter, Sunday *and the Sabbath* are all wrong because they are all days which men *"observe."* Not only that, but we are left with a strange contradiction. On the one hand, Paul exhorts the Corinthians, "Let us celebrate the Feast," while he chastises the Galatians for celebrating days.

Fortunately, we are not left with a contradiction, for Paul is not chastising the Galatians for celebrating days. The Greek word here translated "observe" does *not* mean "celebrate." Please bear with me through a technical explanation, for it's important if we are to understand Paul correctly and not fall into the kind of error Peter described. We have already noted the Greek word *heortadzomen* from 1 Corinthians 5:8, which means "to celebrate a festival." In Acts 18:21 the Greek word is *poieo*, which means "to make," or "to do." Paul says that he must "make" or "do" the feast that is coming in Jerusalem.

The word in Galatians 4:10, however, is *paratereo*. The word is a combination of the Greek word *tereo* and the preposition *para*. *Tereo* means "to attend to carefully, take care of." *Para* in composition changes the word it is combined with to denote either a situation of motion from the side of or to the side of, or *violation, neglect, aberration*. It corresponds roughly to our beyond, aside or amiss (*Thayer's Greek-English Lexicon of the New Testament*).

The word *paratereo*, then, seems to imply an *aberration* of observation. It is a rare word, being used only six times in the New Testament, and nowhere does it imply a celebration of a festival. It is important enough for our understanding of this verse to list each of the scriptures in question for you to consider. The rendering of *paratereo* is italicized in each of the verses.

So they *watched* Him *closely*, whether He would heal him on the Sabbath, so that they might accuse Him (Mark 3:2).

So the scribes and Pharisees *watched* Him *closely*, whether He would heal on the Sabbath, that they might find an accusation against Him (Luke 6:7).

Now it happened, as He went into the house of one of the rulers of the Pharisees to eat bread on the Sabbath, that they *watched* Him *closely* (Luke 14:1).

So they *watched* Him, and sent spies who pretended to be righteous, that they might seize on His words, in order to deliver Him to the power and the authority of the governor (Luke 20:20).

But their plot became known to Saul. And they *watched* the gates day and night, to kill him (Acts 9:24).

You *observe* days and months and seasons and years (Galatians 4:10).

When we look at all the references together, it is obvious there is something wrong with the Authorized Version of this last verse. It is clear enough that Paul is not discussing the *celebration* of the holydays. What, then, is he chastising the Galatians for doing? He is chastising them for the aberrant, pharisaical observance of religious customs *as a means of salvation.* Consider the Phillips translation of the passage:

At one time when you had no knowledge of God you were under the authority of gods who had no real existence. But now that you have come to know God, or rather are known by Him, how can you revert to dead and sterile principles and consent to be under their power all over again? Your religion is beginning to be a matter of observing certain days or months or seasons or years. Frankly, you stagger me, you make me wonder if all my efforts over you have been wasted! (vv. 8-11).

Paul is not suggesting that it's wrong to observe days. What he is saying is that it is wrong to observe days *in order to achieve righteousness or justification before God.*

We can argue as long as we wish about which days these were, and never come to a resolution all can accept. But we can agree that the observance of days – any days – does not justify us before God, nor does it achieve salvation. Most Christians will firmly unite around Ephesians 2:8, 9: "For by grace are you saved through faith; and that not of yourselves: it is the gift of God: Not of works, lest any man should boast."

Dummelow was quite correct in saying that the holydays of God were "of no avail for salvation." They were never intended for that. They are, however, of great avail for understanding His plan, for the worship of God at His appointed times, and for growing in grace and knowledge of God's purpose for man.

Merely because the Galatians abused the days does not justify their abrogation, and this is not what Paul suggests. Paul is arguing that the observance of days was not efficacious of salvation. He is *not* saying that the observance of days is wrong. If he were, his statement would include *all* days including Sunday, the Sabbath, Christmas and Easter – all are days, and all observed.

Colossians 2:14-16

Those who argue against the celebration of holydays inevitably find their way to the 2nd chapter of Colossians, and especially to verse 16: "So let no one judge you in food or in drink, or regarding a festival or a new moon or sabbaths."

What is curious about this is that Paul doesn't tell the Colossians that they were not to observe the festivals but simply that they should not let anyone judge them in respect to these matters.

A careful study of the verse, though, reveals some interesting points. First, there are three things in which the Colossians were not to allow themselves to be judged. In the simplest terms they are "meat," "drink" and "respect" (Greek: "part" or "division"). These three words in the Greek are *brosei, posei* and *merei*. All three are in the dative singular and are placed in parallel construction, making a play on words.

The article we are discussing suggests that the meat and drink in this passage are the meat and drink offerings of the law of Moses. The author isn't thinking. How could the Colossians, Gentiles living in Asia Minor, be involved in meat and drink offerings? Weren't these done at the Temple? In Jerusalem?

This interpretation won't stand up on either a lexical or contextual study. The word *brosei*, here translated *meat*, means literally "the act of eating." The word *posei*, translated drink, means literally "drinking." But who would have been sitting in judgment of the Colossians for eating and drinking? Paul gives us the clue beginning in verse 20:

> So if, through your faith in Christ, you are dead to the principles of this world's life, why, as if you were still part and parcel of this worldwide system, do you take the slightest notice of these *purely human prohibitions* – "Don't touch this," "Don't taste that," "And don't handle the other"? "This," "That" and "The other" will all pass away after use! I know that these regulations look wise with their self-inspired efforts at worship, their policy of self-humbling, and their studied neglect of the body. But in actual practice they do honor, not to God, but man's own pride" (Colossians 2:20-23, J.B. Phillips translation).

It was not the *law of Moses* that was causing a problem for the Colossians, but the various ascetic "ordinances of men" after the "rudiments of the world" that were creating the problem. The Colossians were being judged and condemned for eating and drinking, not for offering meat and drink offerings – how could they do that in Colosse?

But what do the holydays have to do with this? Take a look at verse 16 again. The Colossians were told not to allow any man to intimidate them in a handful of issues: eating, drinking, or in a part or aspect of a holyday, or of the new moon, or of the Sabbaths.

The truth is that what Paul is telling the Colossians is that they should not allow men to judge them in the food and drink aspect of their celebrations. Rather than being an abrogation of the holydays, the verse actually implies that the Christians in Colosse were observing them.

Notice also that, if this verse does away with the holydays, the Sabbath goes with them. The article attempts to avoid this conclusion by saying: "Note to what Paul referred: Food or drink (pertained to sacrifices); festival (of which there were seven); new moon (originated the Israelite calendar month, with particular emphasis to the day of Trumpets); Sabbath day (better rendered 'Sabbaths,' or the seven holydays of Leviticus 23)."

He doesn't comment on the fact that he includes the seven annual Sabbaths twice in this listing whereas the verse in its construction is clearly dealing with five distinct sets, and separates each set with the word "or." Read Paul's words very carefully. "Let no man therefore judge you for eating, *or* for drinking, *or* in part of an holyday, *or* of the new moon, *or* of the Sabbaths." "holydays" and "Sabbaths" are not the same in this grammatical construct.

Forgive me for being technical, but, after all, words are intended to convey meaning. Paul's choice of words in this verse is important to *one set of arguments* relative to the observance of the holydays. These arguments are advanced by those who believe that the holydays need *not* be kept, but the Sabbath – the weekly Sabbath – *must* be kept. Protestant commentators, on the other hand, freely include the Sabbath as among those things that are being done away.

We now pass on to Colossians 2:17, which says that the holydays, the new moons, and the Sabbaths "are a shadow of things to come." If we're going to give attention to the tenses of the verbs, we must note at least in passing that this verse says holydays *are* (present tense) a shadow of things to come. If they had been abolished, we would surely have expected Paul to have said they *were* a shadow of things to come. Notice also that, if they are a shadow of things to come, then they have not yet been fulfilled. And, if they have not yet been fulfilled, then they have not passed from the law (Matthew 5:17, 18, assuming one takes that view of Jesus' teaching).

Of course, the Temple was still there and the writer of Hebrews also notes in the present tense that there is still a functioning priesthood.

> There *are* priests that offer gifts according to the law: who serve under the example and *shadow* of heavenly things, as Moses was admonished of God when he was about to make the tabernacle: for see, saith He, that you make all things according to the *pattern* shown to you in the mountain (Hebrews 8:4-5).

What Paul is saying to the Colossians is that the Holy Days and the Sabbaths are shadows, types, images of things to come but that the *real substance* of these things is Christ. By the same analogy, the bread and wine of the Lord's Supper are *shadows* of things that have already taken place. They are not the *substance* of Christ's body and blood, but the images or representations of it.

Merely because something is a "shadow" does not mean Christians should not observe it. It is just another way of saying that some of our observances are *symbolic*. But now let's consider the wider context of Colossians 2:16.

> Beware lest anyone cheat you through philosophy and empty deceit, according to the tradition of men, according to the basic principles of the world, and not according to Christ (Colossians 2:8).

The New Testament church was beset early on by every sort of heresy. They were as many and as varied as fleas on a dog, and doubtless just as irritating. They ranged all the way from the heresies of Simon Magus and Cerinthus to such perverse doctrines as Gnosticism. Every sect of the Jews seems also to have been represented in the early church, and many of them, unfortunately, brought some of their old ideas with them. One thing is abundantly clear from the wording of verse 8. Paul is *not* talking about the law of Moses. He could not *possibly* describe Moses' law as "philosophy," "vain deceit," "the tradition of men," or "the rudiments of the world."

The Greek religions were not without their ascetics, but this heresy was probably Jewish. Paul's allusion to circumcision in verse 11 would lead us to that conclusion.

Nailed to the Cross

> And when you were dead in your transgressions and the uncircumcision of your flesh, He made you alive together with Him, having forgiven us all our transgressions, having canceled out the certificate of debt consisting of decrees against us and which was hostile to us; and He has taken it out of the way, having nailed it to the cross (Colossians 2:13-14 NASB).

The KJV calls this a "handwriting of ordinances" that was nailed to the cross. Was it the law of Moses? Was it the Holy Days? A simple study of the context renders an easy answer. "Having forgiven you of all your trespasses; Blotting out the handwriting of ordinances that was against us." These are appositive statements saying the same thing in different words. How did He forgive us our trespasses? By blotting out the "handwriting of ordinances" that was against us. The NASB has this right when it calls this "the certificate of debt consisting of *decrees against* us."

The law only became "against us" when we broke it. Paul asked, "Is the law sin? God forbid" (Romans 7:7). Elsewhere he said that the law is holy, good, spiritual, that he delighted in the law of God and served it (Romans 7:12, 14, 23, 25). God did not give man a law that was *against* him. How then does the law become "against" us?

> Therefore the law is holy, and the commandment holy and just and good. Has then what is good become death to me? Certainly not! But sin, that it might appear sin, was producing death in me through what is good, so that sin through the commandment might become exceedingly sinful. For we know that the law is spiritual, but I am carnal, sold under sin (Romans 7:12-14).

The law is "against us" when we *break* it. It was not the law that was nailed to the cross, but *our violations* of the *law*, our trespasses, our sins that were against us, that were nailed to the cross.

If Paul had meant to say that the law was nailed to the cross, he would have said so in simple terms.

But what is this "handwriting of ordinances"? The expression is unique, being used nowhere else in the New Testament. The expression in the Greek is *keirographon tois dogmasin*. *Keirographon* is a combination of the word for *hand* and the word for *write*. In Greek writings it means specifically "a note of hand," a "bond of indebtedness," or promissory note. It was a "writing in which one acknowledges that money has either been deposited with him or lent to him by another, to be returned at an appointed time"

(*Thayer's Lexicon*). The only "bond of indebtedness" this could be referring to where Christians are concerned is the law's promise to pay us the *wages of sin* when the note comes due.

Dogmasin, on the other hand, comes from the word *dogma*, which means "an opinion or a judgment as rendered in a court of law, a decree or an ordinance." The phrase "handwriting of ordinances," then, refers to the judgment of indebtedness against us as a result of our trespasses which Jesus nailed to his cross. It was, in a manner of speaking, our *death warrant* that was nailed there, not the law.

Those unfamiliar with the Old Testament will miss something important here. Paul's choice of words is borrowed directly from an obscure Old Testament rite: the trial of jealousy. Paul knew the law so well that the words came naturally to mind.

Jealousy is a familiar emotion, and it is certainly not new. All too often, a man can become jealous of his wife with little or no evidence of wrongdoing. The jealousy can put a cloud over a marriage and even lead to a divorce that is without foundation in fact. In order to head this off, there was a simple trial to be conducted by the priest to put the matter to rest:

> Speak to the children of Israel, and say to them: "If any man's wife goes astray and behaves unfaithfully toward him, and a man lies with her carnally, and it is hidden from the eyes of her husband, and it is concealed that she has defiled herself, and there was no witness against her, nor was she caught (Numbers 5:12-14).

Thus is the predicate established. There is no hard proof of wrongdoing. But a lack of hard proof doesn't establish innocence, nor does it ease the jealousy of the husband. Something had to be done to bring closure. The man was instructed to bring his wife to the priest with the appropriate offerings. The formal ceremony is described in detail.

> And the priest shall bring her near, and set her before the LORD. The priest shall take holy water in an earthen vessel, and take some of the dust that is on the floor of the tabernacle and put it into the water. Then

the priest shall stand the woman before the LORD, uncover the woman's head, and put the offering for remembering in her hands, which is the grain offering of jealousy. And the priest shall have in his hand the bitter water that brings a curse (vv. 16-18).

The poor woman has to stand before God, holding a bowl of grain. The priest is standing before her with a bowl of holy water with a pinch of harmless dust in it. Guilty or innocent, this has to be an intimidating moment. Then, as always at law, an oath is involved and the woman must agree to it:

And the priest shall put her under oath, and say to the woman, "If no man has lain with you, and if you have not gone astray to uncleanness while under your husband's authority, be free from this bitter water that brings a curse. But if you have gone astray while under your husband's authority, and if you have defiled yourself and some man other than your husband has lain with you," then the priest shall put the woman under the oath of the curse, and he shall say to the woman; "the LORD make you a curse and an oath among your people, when the LORD makes your thigh rot and your belly swell; and may this water that causes the curse go into your stomach, and make your belly swell and your thigh rot." Then the woman shall say, "Amen, so be it" (vv. 19-22).

This trial is very different from the trial by ordeal practiced in some societies. In those systems, there is a presumption of guilt. A witch, for example, is thrown into a river. If she drowns, she was innocent. If she floats, she is a witch and burned. There is nothing like that here. If there is no supernatural act, the woman will be just fine. And there is one other presumption of innocence here, and it is the one to which Paul alludes.

> And the priest shall write these curses in a book, and he shall blot them out with the bitter water (v. 23 KJV).

Here is a handwriting of curses that are blotted out. It isn't the law that is blotted out, but the curse upon the guilty sinner. Then the priest has the woman drink the water. If she is guilty, her belly swells and her thigh rots (whatever that may mean). If she is innocent, nothing happens. "But if the woman has not defiled herself, and is clean, then she shall be free and may conceive children" (v. 28).

The words, "handwriting" and "blotted out" come naturally to Paul, a scholar in the law, and the comparison is deliberate.

The Sabbath

In attempting to show that the Sabbath and the Holy Days do *not* "stand or fall together," the author attempts to draw a distinction between the Ten Commandments and the Law of Moses. This is apparently essential to the argument, for nearly every argument on this subject addresses the question. Some also try to draw a distinction between the Law of Moses on the one hand and the Law of God on the other; or a distinction between the Old Covenant and the New Covenant in which they imply that the holydays were a part of the Old Covenant while the Ten Commandments were not.

It is curious that these questions are raised, because all one needs to ascertain the answer is an exhaustive concordance and the patience to look up the relevant Scriptures. Take Nehemiah, for example:

> These joined with their brethren, their nobles, and entered into a curse and an oath to walk in God's Law, which was given by Moses the servant of God, and to observe and do all the commandments of the LORD our Lord, and His ordinances and His statutes" (Nehemiah 10:29).

That the commandments in question include the Sabbath is clear from verse 31, and yet it is "God's Law which was given by

Moses," thus, it was also the Law of Moses. Also, compare carefully Nehemiah 8:1 with verse 8. Here the book of the Law of Moses and the Law of God are equated.

But what about Jesus? Did He observe the distinction between the Law of Moses and the Ten Commandments? In a confrontation with the Pharisees, Jesus asked, "Did not Moses give you the law, and yet none of you keepeth the law? Why go you about to kill me?" (John 7:19). Clearly Jesus saw "thou shalt not kill" as a part of the law Moses gave them.

If someone were to ask you to explain just what is meant by "the law of the Lord thy God," what would you answer? Try the definition given here:

> Only may the LORD give you wisdom and understanding, and give you charge concerning Israel, that you may keep the law of the LORD your God. Then you will prosper, if you take care to fulfill the statutes and judgments with which the LORD charged Moses concerning Israel (I Chronicles 22:12, 13).

The New Testament writers simply don't observe our nice distinctions in the law. When they say "the law," they mean "the law of Moses," and it includes *all* of the law given under Moses' administration, including the Ten Commandments. Notice John's succinct statement, "For the law was given by Moses but grace and truth came by Jesus Christ." (John 1:17). "The law" is the law of Moses. It is also the law of God, for Moses was not the originator of the law.

Also note in passing that Jesus Christ did not come to bring a law. He was not a legislator or lawgiver. The world needed no new law. What was needed was forgiveness for the transgressions of the law and a new administration to interpret the law.

Another point in passing: When Paul was writing to the Corinthians defending the right of the ministry to be supported financially by the flock, what authority did he cite? "Say I these things as a man? Or saith not *the law* the same also? For it is written in *the law of Moses*, Thou shalt not muzzle the mouth of the ox that treadeth out the corn" (I Corinthians 9:8, 9).

If the law of Moses was nailed to the cross, what business does Paul have citing it as an authority to a Gentile church? But why was this law given in the first place? Because God cared about animals? Paul continues: "Is it oxen God is concerned about? Or does He say it altogether for our sakes? For our sakes, no doubt, this is written, that he who plows should plow in hope, and he who threshes in hope should be partaker of his hope" (vv. 9-10).

But what about the argument that the Ten Commandments were not a part of the Old Covenant? First turn to Exodus 34:28, where Moses was back on the mountain with God to get the second set of tablets after the first had been broken: "So he was there with the LORD forty days and forty nights; he neither ate bread nor drank water. And He wrote on the tablets the words of the covenant, the Ten Commandments."

Exodus 24 records the actual ceremony of ratification of the Old Covenant. Prior to this time, God has given the Ten Commandments and a lengthy set of laws regarding slavery, manslaughter, kidnaping, bestiality, oppressing strangers, avoiding mob rule, bribes, the land, the Sabbath, etc. Finally, "Moses came and told the people all the words of the Lord, and all the judgments: and all the people answered with one voice, and said, All the words which the Lord hath said will we do. And Moses *wrote all the words of the Lord* [including the Ten Commandments], and rose up early in the morning, and builded an altar under the hill, and twelve pillars, according to the twelve tribes of Israel" (Exodus 24:3, 4).

Then follows the preparation of burnt offerings and the drawing of blood for sprinkling the blood of the covenant. Moses then stood to read before the people, and what he had written was called "*The Book of the Covenant*." When he had read the book to the people, they all affirmed, "All that the Lord has said will we do, and be obedient" (verse 7). So Moses then "took the blood, and sprinkled it on the people, and said, Behold the blood of the covenant, which the Lord hath made with you concerning all these words" (verse 8).

Note well that it was *all* the words of the Lord up to this point which had been recorded for the people to keep. There's no way it could not have included the Ten Commandments. And it is called "The Book of the Covenant."

What is also worthy of note is that the *tables* of the covenant – the Ten Commandments – had not yet been written. They were engraved in stone by God only *after* the people had agreed to enter into the covenant with Him. Small wonder they are called "the tables of the covenant." They are quite literally the *foundation* of the law of Moses. Notice what is said elsewhere regarding the Ten Commandments:

> And the LORD spoke to you out of the midst of the fire. You heard the sound of the words, but saw no form; you only heard a voice So He declared to you His covenant which He commanded you to perform, the Ten Commandments; and He wrote them on two tablets of stone (Deuteronomy 4:12-13).

> Then the LORD delivered to me two tablets of stone written with the finger of God, and on them were all the words which the LORD had spoken to you on the mountain from the midst of the fire in the day of the assembly. And it came to pass, at the end of forty days and forty nights, that the LORD gave me the two tablets of stone, the tablets of the covenant (Deuteronomy 9:10, 11).

These verses need no comment. Why, then, does *anyone* argue that the passing of the Old Covenant and its laws did away with the holydays while it left the Ten Commandments intact?

Conclusion

The length and breadth of this article are a tribute to the resourcefulness of men who seriously attempt to explain why they don't observe the holydays. And yet one is led to wonder why the opposition is so intense. What is wrong with the festivals? We are not suggesting that they are efficacious for salvation. Only the blood of Christ can do that. The holydays were never intended to forgive sins, make men righteous, achieve entry into God's Kingdom, or any such thing.

But they do play out, as it were, the plan of salvation for all men to see. The holydays are *pregnant* with meaning for the Christian – in fact, they may have more meaning for the Christian than they ever did to the Jew.

The reason for man's resistance must fall in a larger "theology of law," which must be dealt with elsewhere. Which Old Testament laws *should* Christians keep, and which ones should they not keep? What is the relation of the New Covenant to the law? What is the relationship of the law to salvation? All these things belong to another book.

Meanwhile, we are left to consider certain fundamental facts regarding God's Holy Days. They were not merely the "national days of Israel," but the holydays of God revealed to man. They are not efficacious for salvation, except as they portray the plan of salvation. They are a part of God's instructions as to when and how he is to be worshiped. Since the New Testament is not a book of law, relatively little is said about the holydays in the New Testament. But, then, relatively little is said about the Sabbath or any other legislation in the New Testament. They are simply taken for granted.

Any argument against the holydays is going to have to deal with the *established fact* that the early church observed at least some of the holydays. (We have no record one way or the other about the Feast of Trumpets, for example.) Why would the early church observe the Passover, the Days of Unleavened Bread and the Feast of Pentecost if the holydays were abolished?   It may well be that the holydays fell into general neglect in the church in subsequent centuries. Although it is by no means certain that the observance died out, we have no way of knowing. We do know that in later years we have encountered isolated groups of holyday keeping Christians in South America. We traced their origins back to obscure missionaries of the 19th century of whom we have no certain knowledge.

In any case, would the neglect of the holydays mean that a church had apostatized, or simply fallen into error? A careful study of the letters to the seven churches in Revelation 2 and 3 will reveal churches with such appalling errors as the doctrine of Balaam, the doctrine of the Nicolaitanes, fornication, and the eating of meats offered to idols. While the churches at Pergamos and Thyatira

(Revelation 2:19-29) were in danger of having their candlestick removed, they were, for the moment, still considered a part of the Church of God.

Only God can judge how corrupt a church can become – how much error it can absorb – and still be the Church of God. Nevertheless, it is the obligation of all saints in all ages to "earnestly contend for the faith once delivered to the saints" (Jude 3). Those who argue against the holydays seem to overlook one important fact: *The holydays of God are totally centered on Christ and His salvation.* How could the church have ignored them?

One minister suggested that "anyone observing the Atonement day in the seventh month, and the tenth day, is surely not honoring Christ which is our atonement, Romans 5:11, who died for our reconciliation. He died and brought our atonement on the day of Passover. This leaves the old Atonement day void and empty of meaning."

The gentleman making this statement obviously has never observed the Day of Atonement. Christ is the *center* of the Day of Atonement and it is He who is honored on this day just as He is on the day of Passover. It makes just as much sense to say that anyone "observing the Passover on the 14th day of the first month is surely not honoring Christ as our Passover for He is already *fulfilled* the Passover."

When we partake of the symbols of the body and blood of Jesus Christ, we engage in one of the purest of rituals. It is a ceremony pregnant with meaning. Likewise, when we fast in humility on the Day of Atonement we acknowledge Christ as our Savior and look forward to His return, the binding of Satan, and the making of the whole world at one with God.

How could God *possibly* be angry with anyone who fasted and abstained from work on a day which he himself commanded? If we don't believe that the holydays are required of Christians, let's not engage in the absurdity of suggesting that they are *harmful*. To be sure, there are those who make the observance of law (including the holydays and the Sabbath) a substitute for the grace of Christ. But God forbid that we should be guilty of turning the grace of our Lord Jesus Christ into an excuse for ignoring the law.

Not Sure?

If you're still not sure, why not try the holydays? They can't hurt you. Nothing God commanded is going to be harmful to man. It is only man's misuse of God's law that gets him into trouble. If you are not sure, why not give it a try? What do you have to lose? You have more to gain than you could ever imagine!

---

i. Begging the Question: a fallacy in which the proposition to be proved is assumed implicitly or explicitly in one of the premises.

ii. Straw Man: A rhetorical technique based on misrepresentation of an opponent's position. To "set up a straw man" or "set up a straw-man argument" is to create a position that is easy to refute, then attribute that position to the opponent

iii. *International Standard Bible Encyclopedia*, article "*Gentiles*," by H. Porter.

Printed in the United States
151687LV00004BA/1/A

9 781600 470295